COMMANDER'S

KITCHEN

New York

Broadway Books

TI ADELAIDE MARTIN

and JAMIE SHANNON

COMMANDER'S KITCHEN

TAKE HOME *the* TRUE TASTES *of* NEW ORLEANS *with* MORE THAN
150 RECIPES *from* COMMANDER'S PALACE RESTAURANT

BROADWAY

Broadway Books titles may be purchased for business or promotional use or for special sales. For information, please write to: Special Markets Department, Random House, Inc., 1540 Broadway, New York, NY 10036.

BROADWAY BOOKS and its logo, a letter B bisected on the diagonal, are trademarks of Broadway Books, a division of Random House, Inc.

Visit our website at www.broadwaybooks.com

Photography by Eugenia Uhl

Library of Congress Cataloging-in-Publication Data

Martin, Ti Adelaide.
    Commander's kitchen: take home the true tastes of New Orleans with more than 150 recipes from Commander's Palace restaurant / Ti Adelaide Martin and Jamie Shannon.
        p.   cm.
    Includes index.
    1. Cookery, American—Louisiana style.   I. Shannon, Jamie.   II. Commander's Palace (Restaurant)   III. Title.
    TX715.2.L68 M33 2000
    641.59763—dc21   00-026876

FIRST EDITION

ISBN 0-7679-0290-4

10   9   8   7   6   5   4   3   2   1

My mom prefers to think of death as a gathering at the "tavern in the sky" of all her favorite people. Louis Armstrong is there with Ella Fitzgerald, and all around the bar, sipping Sazeracs, are her friends and family. One of the last to arrive is John Brennan, Pernod in hand, with a kind word for everyone. John was a gentleman from an era when the word "gentleman" meant something. I'd like to dedicate this book to John Brennan for all that he taught our whole family about integrity, fun, and grace.

And to my mother, Ella Brennan, and my aunt, Dottie Brennan, who believe in the common good and not just today's popular pursuit of personal agendas. These two hardworking, self-deprecating, boundlessly generous ladies share a love of life and little patience for those who don't. I just keep hoping that when I grow up I'll be like you two.

— TI ADELAIDE MARTIN

I'd like to dedicate this book to Jeanne Antoinette Shannon, who had gone into labor with our first child, Tustin Thomas Shannon, while I was home testing one of our first recipes, Crab and Corn Bisque, which sat on the stove for two days. She is the wife who is still scurrying and running a one-year renovation of our house while keeping a full-time job. Through my career, while I've been at the library or in the kitchen writing recipes or at Commander's, Jeannette has always been strong and supportive. Thank you, because without your support, nothing would have been possible.

I would also like to dedicate this book to my mother, Anne M. Shannon, for her early support and strength—especially her dedication to helping me become what I wanted to be. Deep down, she knew what it would take to make me happy, and she taught me how to work for it.

— JAMIE SHANNON

CONTENTS

ACKNOWLEDGMENTS

*H*anging in several spots around the offices at Commander's is something called "Commander's Palace Common Purpose." It calls Commander's ". . . an organization of many hands but of one mind."

Commander's greatest accomplishment of all is the team of people we've attracted and kept. It is an honor to work day in and day out with this team, but we would especially like to thank some of our long-term employees like George Rico, David Guglielmo, Richard Shakespeare, Stephen Woodruff, Phil Gemus, Ray Brinkman, Eman Loubier, the late Dennis Jeane, and Deserick Davenport.

Commander's Palace "Team Cookbook" was extraordinary: Lally Brennan, who conceived of and pulled the whole darn thing together; Barbara Dietz, who painstakingly tested the better part of the recipes, aiding the whole process with her gentle strength and charm; Stacey Leonhard, who organized and motivated us all; Amy DeBaker and Martha Johansen, who did more testing.

Personally, I want to thank Liz Lennox for allowing our dining room table to be a cookbook catastrophe for over a year, for making my life so darn much fun, and for being my favorite person.

A huge secret of our success is our network of suppliers, who bend over backward to bring us the very best products. We have so much respect for these folks, and we'd simply like to acknowledge a few of them: P&J Oysters, Dan and Ellen Crutchfield, Randy Thibodeaux, Ed Parker, Fred Schwartz, Rick Fernandez, Wayne Hess, Mike Williams, the Muller family, and all the folks at New Orleans Fish House and Becnel brothers.

Now for the people who truly made this book a reality: our agent, Judith Weber, who caringly guided us through the process and nudged and encouraged at every turn; Ken Bookman, who had the patience and innate ability to take what we wrote and make it better; our friend and former Broadway editor, Harriet Bell, who prodded us for years to do this book; and our editor Jennifer Josephy, who added her great style and professionalism.

— TI ADELAIDE MARTIN

*M*y special thanks to the entire Brennan family, especially the ones who helped and supported us on this book—Dottie, Lally, Brad, and Alex, but most of all, Ella Brennan, for all her trust and support. Thank you especially for being such a great mentor.

Special thanks to the Commander's culinary staff, especially the sous chef team, for not missing a beat during the entire cookbook process.

— JAMIE SHANNON

Lagniappe

Lagniappe *is a Creole word you hear everywhere in New Orleans. It means a little bonus, a little something extra and unexpected that you might get, often from a merchant. (At Commander's, we might send out a one-bite treat, such as a smoked-fish hors d'oeuvre.) But lagniappe is so much a part of our language that you'll bump into the word where you might not expect it. For example, it's the title of a features section in our local newspaper,* The Times-Picayune. *We use it in this book, too, to indicate the little extras, whether they be stories or cooking tips, that we've scattered through these pages.*

INTRODUCTION

New Orleans cooking is like jazz. The world is fascinated by the possibilities that can result when good jazz musicians sit together and "make music." So it is with our cooking. When people who care deeply about food use the ingredients and techniques of the entire history of New Orleans cooking, the possibilities are endless.

That could be the credo of Commander's Palace, the restaurant that my family has nurtured for almost three decades, the restaurant that has come to be known as one of the nation's best, the restaurant where the new possibilities are always explored even as the old traditions are revered.

Only recently did I realize that there was nothing normal about the role food has played in my life. My mother is Ella Brennan. With her brother Dick, her sister Dottie, and her late sister Adelaide and brother John, they made a formidable team indeed. Much as the U.S. Army Corps of Engineers occasionally succeeds in changing the course of the mighty Mississippi River, this determined family of restaurateurs, through its involvement with ten restaurants over the last half century, has changed the course of New Orleans cooking. For centuries, New Orleans has been known for its rich gastronomic heritage, but little did I know as a child that my mother and uncles and aunts were busy adding a chapter to that story. That story is about the continuing evolution of America's preeminent native cuisine—New Orleans cuisine.

The key word is *evolution*. The food of New Orleans is a living, breathing thing, a work in progress that is difficult to catch, analyze, describe, or put down on paper. And because it is constantly evolving, Creole cuisine is timeless.

To many knowledgeable food lovers, New Orleans cooking is already the best in the United States, and Commander's Palace offers some of the best food in New Orleans. So why mess with either the cuisine or the restaurant, especially since both are so rich in history and technique? After all, even Mark Twain was said to have once lowered a knife and fork into a plate of steaming pompano from Louisiana's waters, given a long sigh, and remarked that it was "as delicious as the less criminal forms of sin."

⚜

Our cooking at Commander's has been fertile ground for evolution because we are free from trying to control an evolution that cannot be controlled. But historically, radical change is simply not what New Orleanians want in their restaurants. I confess to having felt a certain anxiety myself when, as a child, I would see longtime menu stalwarts disappear. After all, many of our other favorite grand New Orleans restaurants never changed their menus. Locals liked the food, and they expected to see the same things on the menu all the time. (Just a couple of years ago, minor changes at two major New Orleans restaurants warranted breathless stories in our newspaper, *The Times-Picayune.* One had dared to put English on the menu, while the other began accepting credit cards!)

Very slowly, but very surely, New Orleanians began to trust this scrappy Brennan clan. It seemed as if one Brennan or another had always just returned from New York, Paris, or Bayou Têche, having researched and learned more and more about food, wine, cooking, the roots of our native cuisine, and the finer points of service. Somehow, those Brennans always balanced the menu, placing some tried and true classics alongside a reinvention of some other classic dish—or an even bolder new creation. It was certainly harder to run a restaurant this way, but they always delivered quality. Before long, they were hooked on the thrill of perfecting and redefining their beloved New Orleans food. Perhaps it was that love of their native cuisine that guided the Brennans as they seemed to magically know where to tread lightly in changing a dish and where carefree abandon would produce a new classic.

The more the Brennans learned about the foods of the world, the more enchanted they became with their own cooking—and with New Orleans food. I remember, vividly, crabbing all day on the Gulf Coast with my cousins, then watching my Aunt Lynne and Aunt Claire make a marinated crab salad. I can still taste that crab salad (it's an example of what we call "taste memories"), and, when crabmeat is in season, you will find a version of it on the menu at Commander's. Chef Jamie Shannon has probably prepared dozens of versions of that salad during his many years at Commander's. The old ways are fine, and we can always do it one of those old ways, but his newer versions give the old dish a new dimension, present it in a different light. What Commander's tries so hard to do is to stimulate your taste memories with old favorites at the same time as we put you on the edge of your seat with the new stuff.

How does Commander's do it without blurring New Orleans cooking so much that a New Orleans meal could just as easily have come from Los Angeles or New York or Kansas City? My family is obsessed with that dilemma. The answer lies in the very foundation of New Orleans cuisine, which itself began as an adaptation. New Orleans cooking represents the evolution and incorporation of techniques and ingredients from many cuisines, including French, Indian, Spanish, African, and Acadian. If ever there was a cuisine born of a mixture of cultures, it's ours.

Was there a defining moment when we stopped and said, "Okay, this is it; no more changes. This is New Orleans cuisine"? Not really. Maybe we should retain what's most associated with Creole cooking today. But where would we draw the line? For example, Asian cooking would seem to have little influence on the style here, yet for years there has been a large Vietnamese population with a wonderful market of fresh products that its community sells and barters. New Orleans style continues to evolve. Each wave of migration—from the 2,000 slaves imported from the west coast of Africa as early as 1744 to the Vietnamese of today—brings new ingredients and techniques to the mix.

At what point do we halt the evolution? The incorporation of ingredients and cooking techniques of today has been going on since the 1600s. Yet the "fusion" food of today, where often misguided combinations of ingredients and techniques are foisted upon the diner, is not New Orleans cuisine. The fusion that has created Creole cooking has happened organically, and we are proud to nurture it every day.

⚜

I can just see Chef Jamie or my cousin Lally or my mother, Ella, frowning at a dish presented by a young sous chef. Their look says to the cook: "Explain this to me," and behind the look would be other questions and commands: Justify how this dish makes sense. Is the presentation too cute? Does it pander to the latest food photography? Are the ingredients mismatched? Out of context? Why are those ingredients combined? Are most of these products indigenous to our area? There were good reasons why a Creole cook in the past would never use both filé and okra in a gumbo. It's a never-ending process, led by knowledge, experience, and, eventually, instincts. If Commander's Palace has anything to do with it, New Orleans food will always be distinctly New Orleans.

Beyond our love affair with food, another element intertwines itself unmistakably into the Commander's Palace experience. Hospitality, a service mentality, *joie de vivre*, a basic desire to please—call it what you will, but the overriding philosophy is that we are here to create happy memories for you, the diner. However you may define it, it's our reason for being. Professionalism and service skill take a back seat only to warmth, with a sense of fun just below the surface.

We are careful not to intimidate you. From longtime maitre d' George Rico's offbeat humor at the door to parading you through the kitchen to your seat to Main Dining Room Manager Ray Brinkman's greeting of wit and one-liners, we want you to have fun. But it's your definition of fun, not ours. If you want a romantic, quiet table with professional but nearly invisible service—done! If you want to impress out-of-town business guests with lots of hovering service and the fact that everyone in the restaurant seems to know your name—done! And anything in between.

My brother, Alex Brennan-Martin, who runs Brennan's of Houston, calls it "creating restaurant magic." We want you to leave the behind-the-scenes techniques to us and concentrate only on one of life's timeless pleasures—a great meal with good conversation.

✤

You can't understand service or hospitality at Commander's Palace unless you also understand New Orleanians' passion for savoring life's pleasures. I don't know why the *joie de vivre* is so significant a part of New Orleans. Maybe it's because early New Orleans life was so hard that we always knew you can't take it with you. Maybe the sprinkling of above-ground cemeteries was a constant visual reminder to live this life to its fullest. I do know that New Orleanians will not be the ones who rushed through life without stopping to smell the roses (or, in our case, the camellias). Local author Andrei Codrescu calls New Orleans the center of the arts of storytelling, smoking, and flirting.

In a 1993 book, *New Orleans: Elegance and Decadence*, Richard Sexton and Randolph Delehanty describe the persistent dichotomies in our architecture, style, and unique culture. We appreciate decay, for example (not in our school system, but very much in our architecture). I remember being perplexed as a child, not understanding why the brand-new house next door in the city's Garden District already looked old—built to look worn, complete with peeling plaster and crumbling columns. But these very decadent exteriors announce the most elegant of homes.

The same contrasts apply to our citizenry. Our eccentrics are beloved *because* of their eccentricities, not despite them. You can find *all* of New Orleans—black, white, young, old, well dressed, barely dressed—mixing and mingling, singing and feasting, and partying their hearts out at the New Orleans Jazz and Heritage Festival.

This is the long way around to explain that, while systems and training are vital to Commander's style of hospitality, the real key is the warmth and devilish sense of fun that you sense just behind the professional exterior in the restaurant's team members. Most are either natives or folks who came to New Orleans and never left. These pros are folks who themselves admire and have mastered the art of living well. They'll dazzle, refresh, and renew you as much with their unpretentious style and easily surfaced humor as with their technical expertise.

⚜

Finally, make no mistake—this is a family business. And this family is exacting and nurturing, demanding and fun-loving. While the names of now-famous chefs and well-known restaurateurs who were groomed and mentored at Commander's Palace roll off the tongues of natives, no one has been mentored more than my generation of cousins and siblings who stood at the knees of our parents. The University of Commander's Palace was run by the hardest-working and greatest team of mentors a young restaurateur wannabe could dream of. Ella, Dottie, Dick, and the late John and Adelaide Brennan—a family of siblings—schooled us in the "hands-on know-how" and inspired us with grace and dignity in the hard times, uproarious fun in the good times, and a driving ambition to never stop improving: to be, simply, The Best. They taught us that the biggest enemy of the best is the good.

Ella and Dick led the team, but always felt the goals could not have been reached without Dottie, John, and Adelaide. Though Dick can now most often be found greeting old friends and new at his son Dickie's smashing Dickie Brennan's Steakhouse or at nearby Palace Café, his day-in, day-out contribution to Commander's Palace was immeasurable. Uncle Dick's focus on the ABCs—or, as we say, "fanatical commitment to the consistent execution of the fundamentals"—will never be forgotten.

Cousins Lauren and Dickie Brennan; Ralph, Cindy, and Lally Brennan; Brad Brennan; my brother, Alex Brennan-Martin, and I have all spent time behind the stoves, in the dining room, and in the dish room. Each has contributed to the success of Commander's Palace. Lally is the younger-generation member who has been at Commander's the longest, and her style and influence are everywhere.

Many a night I have watched Lally move through a dining room outfitted in stunning, simple elegance, deferentially greeting a table of dignitaries, sharing a soulful laugh and a devilish story with some locals, and giving direction to the staff, who adore her, just with her eyes. She is always unaware of the uplifting effect she has just had on the entire room. When you have been the recipient of Lally Brennan's brand of grace and hospitality, you will not soon forget it. Brad Brennan has worked in every position from cook to dining room manager and has worked in restaurants from Chicago to San Francisco. Brad's love of wine has been infectious, making oenophiles out of many of us, but his gentle manner, dedication to being the best, and ready smile with customers and team members have made him a beloved fixture of Commander's Palace. The group at the helm of Commander's Palace since 1997 are Lally Brennan, Brad Brennan, and me, under the watchful eye of Ella and Dottie Brennan, who live next door—literally.

That team would not be complete without the talent and friendship of our acclaimed chef, Jamie Shannon, who pushes, nurtures, and derives more life, passion, and fun out of this wonderful restaurant business than anyone who has gone before. It is simply a pleasure and an honor to work alongside Jamie each day.

⚜

If some of the next generation shows interest in this crazy, wonderful business (and by the look of them wandering in and out of the kitchen as comfortably as if it were their backyard, they do), then Commander's Palace will grow and evolve with a new generation.

The continuity of one family ensures that Commander's Palace always pays homage to its culinary roots. But it also dares us to fuel a spirited evolution of today's Creole cuisine. For this, Commander's Palace has been rewarded with the ultimate compliment—being considered a New Orleanians' New Orleans restaurant.

It is our hope that Commander's will be New Orleans' restaurant for the ages.

The history of New Orleans and Creole cuisine is glorious, the possibilities are endless, and the daily challenge is a happy one. Join us in creating new taste memories as we continue to redefine our native cuisine.

CREOLE OR CAJUN?

Creole and Cajun cuisines are like high school sweethearts who part ways and go on to live full but separate lives, only to meet again when life's triumphs, failures, and influences have made them even more complex and intriguing.

To understand Creole cooking and its old friend, Cajun (or Acadian) cuisine, you've got to know something about these two cultures. They're distinct, but they're also similar—equally tragic and storied.

Both groups came from France and settled in Louisiana, but they did so from very different paths. When the French began colonizing Louisiana in 1698, the area was already inhabited by Native Americans. They taught the French colonists, who had no wheat or flour for years at a time, how they could live, and live well, off the land. The Native Americans cultivated corn, mirliton (a type of squash), and dried beans, and showed the French how to thicken stews with the powdered sassafras now known as filé powder. So the original French settlers began adapting their cuisine—in all its sophistication—to the heretofore unfamiliar but abundant and hearty indigenous seafood, fowl, aromatic vegetables, and, of course, rice.

By 1721, as the French attempted to colonize the area to keep it from Britain, hundreds of Germans were lured to "the Paris of the New World."

The Germans farmed, adding fresh produce and fine bakeries. In 1727, at Bienville's request, the Ursuline nuns arrived to help with schooling and medical care. The nuns taught that parsley was good to lessen garlic's odor, sage could lower a fever, and bay leaf would keep soup from spoiling—among other things, like reading and writing.

As society grew, the French aristocrats prided themselves on the talents of their cooks—most often black cooks who had learned the French techniques but had added their rich African history of foods and cooking. Their ancestors had traded for centuries with the Arabs and they had learned to farm corn, garlic, yams, eggplant, onions, okra, rice, and kidney beans. These cooks were the first to use the peasant French thickener known as roux.

In 1762, as the cuisine began to flourish and New Orleans became known for elaborate feasts in elegant homes, King Louis XIV of France was playing cards with his cousin, King Charles III of Spain. King Louis stumbled and New Orleans was lost to Spain. (Others say this was again an effort to keep Louisiana from Britain.) Culinarily at least, it was a turn of good luck for Louisiana, as the Spanish arrived and put their indelible stamp on Creole cuisine, which was becoming a vigorously original cooking style. The Spaniards loved their pepper and knew that it would slow the growth of bacteria in a stew as well. But perhaps their greatest contribution was the tomato, which the French had thought was poisonous. The tomato is the foundation of Creole sauce, court bouillon, and lots of other foods.

In 1755, the seeds of Cajun cooking were planted. A group of French expatriates living in one of the first major French colonies in the New World were banished from their home, Acadie. Acadie was a colony that encompassed parts of what are now Nova Scotia, New Brunswick, and Maine. Fifteen hundred of the French Acadiens (bastardized into the term "Cajuns") were expelled for refusing to pledge allegiance to the flag and the King of England. The Acadiens, following the Mississippi River all the way down to an area where French was spoken, the land was fertile, and they could practice their religion, settled west and south of New Orleans. In 1785, another influx of the destitute Acadiens who had resettled in France were offered free homes in French-speaking Louisiana by a Spanish government eager to colonize its stronghold in Louisiana.

Louisiana was ceded back to France in 1801 and to the United States in

1803 in the Louisiana Purchase. And in 1815, at the Battle of New Orleans, Andrew Jackson was again fending off those pesky British. But by then the roots of these two distinct cuisines were in place. The Cajuns became aggressively independent from the outside world and necessarily protective of and loyal to one another. They had endured much and they came to love the rich, soupy land and the vast web of waterways in which they toiled. Their desire for independence, aided by the impassability of much of the swampy terrain they inhabited, kept their culture and cooking distinct and vibrant. They developed a come-one-come-all, celebrate-for-any-reason-or-no-reason *joie de vivre*. A rowdy bunch, they liked fiery food to match. They used lots of peppers, okra, onions, paprika, garlic, and a soothing bed of rice. They favored one-pot cooking, such as jambalaya and sauce piquante, and festive parties called boucheries, where different families slaughtered a hog and made hog's-head cheese, sausage, roasts, and crackling.

Only a few hundred miles and a few dozen marshes and bayous away, New Orleans' Creole cooks were already entrenched in an altogether separate and original style of cooking. Mimicking the lavish banquets of the court of the French and Spanish royalty, the Creoles liked to entertain grandly. They developed societies with endless balls and occasions for formal socializing. The food was always center stage. Entertaining at home, a hostess might serve shrimp rémoulade with crisp greens, crabmeat crêpes with a cream sauce, followed by redfish court bouillon and/or quail in a potato nest, and ending with *petits gateaux* or petits fours, all served on her French Quarter balcony or in her courtyard.

So if Creole is the more elegant city cooking, using a sauce on a piece of fish or game and making delicate desserts, Cajun is the more robust country farmhouse cooking—an often bolder one-pot cooking style. The differences lie not in the ingredients, where proximity alone led the two cuisines to overlap, but instead in the intensity of the seasoning and the dishes one chooses to prepare. Both often use roux as the foundation of sauces, and both season food with herbs, vegetables, and spices more heavily than other American cuisines, though Cajuns will do so more liberally than Creoles. It's something like comparing the food in Paris to the food in Provence. Similar, but distinctly different.

The courtship between Cajun and Creole cuisine began in the 1960s, with the opening of one of New Orleans' first "Cajun restaurants," the Bon Ton Café, founded by Alzina Pierce from Bayou Lafourche. A New Orleans Cajun restaurant still sounds like an oxymoron to New Orleanians and Cajuns alike, but I think the two cuisines were fated to intersect beginning one day in the 1970s. It happened during Paul Prudhomme's reign in the kitchen at Commander's Palace, with the invention of Blackened Redfish, a dish that had long been called Seared Redfish. Before then, New Orleans' Creole cuisine would never have included the lowly redfish, which was previously considered "trash fish," in a restaurant setting, nor the lowly crawfish. Paul's rustic Cajun cooking and Commander's more sophisticated Creole cuisine careened down a collision course. The boundaries have been deliciously blurring ever since.

For whatever reasons, many folks don't understand the distinctions between the two cuisines and cultures. "Creole" simply denotes French or Spanish colonists and their descendents, particularly those who maintain some of the customs and language of their mother country. In fact, the word *Creole* comes from around 1780, when the Spaniards governing New Orleans named all residents of European heritage "Criollo." The term eventually applied to their descendants as well.

To complicate matters, however, a French-speaking slave of a Frenchman was labeled a Creole Negro (distinct from the American Negro, who spoke English, and the African Negro, who spoke neither French nor English). Further, some French-speaking "Free People of Color" were considered Creoles. So the word *Creole* has come to include African Americans as well.

As I write this, my friend Artina Fontenot discusses Cajun versus Creole with me. She is from Ville Platte, Louisiana, is of Indian and African American descent, but speaks only French—Cajun French—at home. And what she cooks is the delicious result of three hundred years of New Orleans' past. Need I say more?

—TI ADELAIDE MARTIN

A HISTORY OF COMMANDER'S PALACE

Commander's Palace takes its name from the restaurant's first owner, Emile Commander, who opened for business in the early 1880s. The restaurant has operated continuously, owned since 1969 by New Orleans' Brennan family, whose members have been active in civic affairs as well as in the city's restaurant industry.

Commander's Palace operates in an old Victorian mansion at the corner of Washington Avenue and Coliseum Street in New Orleans' fashionable Garden District. Its previous chefs, notably Paul Prudhomme and Emeril Lagasse, have achieved top recognition in their field, and its current chef, Jamie Shannon, has continued that tradition. Chef Jamie has continually tweaked and developed the Commander's Palace menu to achieve what the Brennans call "haute Creole" cuisine, and he has been recognized with numerous awards, most notably the James Beard Foundation's 1999 designation as the best chef in America's Southeast and the Robb Report's June 1999 Best of the Best list of the world's five best chefs.

The restaurant itself has also been generously recognized for its achievements, winning two James Beard awards—in 1993 for the restaurant that gives the best service in America, and as America's most outstanding restaurant in 1996. Commander's consistently has been voted #1 overall in New Orleans by the *Zagat Survey.*

CHEF JAMIE'S TIPS

*I*t's almost a cliché of cooking, but it's so true: Get the best ingredients money can buy and don't ruin them. But it's what the Commander's Palace kitchen is all about. We enhance our food, we don't ruin it. We use the right cookware, the right techniques, and the right seasonings to make every dish the best that a Creole kitchen can turn out.

New Orleans almost can't help being a great food city. Surrounded by so much water—saltwater, freshwater, brackish water—and blessed with a long growing season, the abundance of seafood, great seasonal produce, and many varieties of game are great influences on the cuisine. And because New Orleans is a port city, it has a large immigrant population, so numerous cooking techniques and culinary traditions have reached into one of the world's greatest cuisines to create a true American-born cuisine.

The most important activity in Commander's Kitchen involves a favorite word of Ella Brennan, the matriarch of New Orleans cuisine. The word is *Creolize.* We want every new cook who sets foot in Commander's Kitchen to have a sense of our seasoning and techniques.

More than anything else, Creolizing a cook means to teach the cook about seasoning. Every new Commander's cook starts by viewing our seasoning film, in which we stress the importance of seasoning both sides of a piece of fish or all sides of a piece of meat, the importance of seasoning any flour used for dredging, the importance of seasoning garnishes. Whether it's pepper, spice, and salt, onion or garlic, or just a touch more cream or butter, I'll often jokingly say that when something tastes right, that's the time to add a little more. It's often a joke, but it conveys the Creole idea.

But our Creole idea isn't just more, it's also better. Many a night, we'll serve scarce but highly sought-after blue-fin tuna or fresh figs, and we know we're the only ones in town serving it—sometimes because we buy all that the small farmer has.

Commander's is always looking for new and improved products, chiefly by working with local growers and markets. Sometimes we even invest in small farmers to grow the foods we want. We want to be cutting-edge while honoring our traditions, utilizing local products to update grand Creole dishes.

Creole cuisine is not loaded with subtleties. We like to push things right to the edge. I might taste a dish with basil in it, and if I like the taste of the basil in the dish, my first instinct will be to use a little more basil. The same thing goes for olive oil or garlic. And it applies to cooking techniques, too. We do a lot of braising, for example. So if you're braising some poultry, looking for tender meat, well, we'll braise it until it's falling off the bone. We'll push it to the edge, to its limit.

Here are a few of the equipment and technique choices that I've developed over the years—always with the food in mind:

Seasoning. We like to make our own seasoning blends, especially our Creole Meat Seasoning and Creole Seafood Seasoning (pages 293 and 294). Even for ordinary salting, I prefer to use kosher salt—not for the seasoning mixes, where a finer salt blends better, but for everything else, which I think benefits from a cleaner taste. It's also easier to work with in our humid climate, and, because we use our fingers, it gives a better feel. Sometimes I'll use sea salt, especially on tomatoes and oysters. And anytime I season with spices, especially pepper, I definitely prefer a freshly ground version. We mainly use black pepper in Commander's Palace kitchen, even in some white sauces, but we grind many of our spices fresh, when the natural oils in the seed are much more potent.

Cookware. I'm real big on the cast-iron skillet and other heavy-gauge cookware, which is why these recipes use a lot of those heavy pots and pans. Maybe it's because there's something traditional and romantic about a piece of equipment that has probably been handed down over the generations, but I like cooking with it. I think food benefits from the higher cooking temperatures that you just couldn't get away with in a lighter skillet. It's the perfect skillet, for example, for sautéing omelet fillings as well as preparing the eggs. Or to use in preparing the Sesame Pepper-Crusted Tuna Salad (page 82), where the right skillet helps me give the tuna the right treatment.

The stovetop roasting pan. The roasting pan is how I make a restaurant recipe more home-friendly, and Creole cooks have always used roasting pans a lot. Flip through the recipes in this book, and you'll see one technique used over and over: placing a large, heavy-gauge roasting pan over two burners of the stovetop. Braised Lamb Shanks with Merlot Mushroom Sauce (page 164) are a perfect example, but in all those recipes, either you've just roasted something in the oven, or you're about to. But I'll cook vegetables or deglaze the pan or do something else in the same pan because I want to use the liquid in that pan to capture the true flavors of whatever I've got roasting. (A side benefit is that you're not dirtying another pan.)

The oil temperature. Invest a few dollars in a little clip-on thermometer. It'll be worth it. Frying is an art, and it's a high-calorie disaster only when you do it wrong. The whole idea is for the oil to be hot enough to cook the food but not so hot as to burn it. The name of the game is temperature control, but you can't control temperature if you don't know what the temperature is. A little thermometer that's always monitoring your oil temperature is the way to do it. It's much more accurate than trying to figure out how quickly a bread cube turns brown or looking for water droplets dancing on the surface. And your oysters, for example, as in our Corn-Fried Oysters with Horseradish Cream (page 40), will taste like the sea instead of like oil.

⚜

Once a cook has become Creolized, he or she can progress through the stations of the kitchen. This is where the passion takes hold. Before we know it, our cook wants to go to the docks and see the fish, or hear Dottie talk about the dish he heard she ate in New York, or come in at 4 A.M. to watch the baker feed the yeast.

It happens at home, too. As good as the recipes in this book are, each time you use your own homemade mayonnaise or bread crumbs or roasted peppers, you'll be making your food a little better.

Two of my favorite kitchen activities are preparing dishes for the Chef's Table and for Krewe meal. The Chef's Table is a premium spot for just a few diners a night, diners who will get to taste the fanciest and most elegant dishes we can put together. And Krewe meal is our fun term for the meal we prepare for our staff, the stick-to-your ribs fare that you'll probably think of as the ultimate in home cooking.

Chef's Table and Krewe meal represent the extremes of what we do in Commander's Kitchen. But both are where we experiment and let our passion for cooking burst forth. The recipes in this book strive to hit both ends of that spectrum—and a lot of spots in between. Go through enough of these recipes and you'll be Creolized, too.

—JAMIE SHANNON

Lagniappe

MARDI GRAS

Pete Fountain's Half Fast Marching Club. Say that real fast. This is not an organization that takes itself too seriously. Its members have one purpose: to engage in as much silliness and fun as one human can take.

Each year, Pete's club of 50 or so marchers meets on Mardi Gras morning at 6:30 to begin the zaniest, most disorganized, most beloved march from the Garden District through dozens of neighborhoods and bars to the French Quarter. All along the way, television and radio crews interview the costumed, imbibing, and self-deprecating marchers for progress reports.

Since Pete Fountain and all the Brennans share a lot of French Quarter history, Dick Brennan invited Pete and his gang to start their festivities each year at the Commander's bar. We have continued the tradition, even though Mardi Gras is one of just three days during the entire year that Commander's Palace is closed. So each Mardi Gras morning we serve Pete and the Half Fast Marching Club a hearty breakfast and allow them to act as their own bartenders. They love getting behind the bar and whipping up their own concoctions. It's a sight to behold. Businessmen, doctors, lawyers, musicians—all in their satin marching club costumes and masks, weighed down with beads, always with someone pulling a little red wagon of "refreshments" for the road.

*L*ike so many other things at Commander's Palace, our entire wine philosophy and presentation have evolved over many years. As with every other part of your dining experience at Commander's, we've worked very hard to make wine a relaxing, unintimidating, and pleasurable part of your visit.

A few decades ago, before, say, 1960, most Americans were not drinking wine with their dinner. My family did, though. Wine was served with meals, period. It was a natural part of everyday life. I remember as a child being allowed the occasional single sip of wine. To me, it was obvious that wine could give the flavor of food a whole new dimension. To this day, I enjoy wine most with a meal, though a great glass of Pinot Noir or Beaujolais is what I'll choose most often at cocktail hour as well. We were more like Europeans in that sense, so it was even more exciting to watch how wine would become part of life in America, too.

But in the 1950s and 1960s, fine-dining establishments in New Orleans were serving a great deal of French cuisine, and so the French wine industry spent a good deal of time courting New Orleans restaurateurs. Our family got the "wine bug" from those charming Frenchmen. They knew that people's interest in (and consumption of) wine grew proportionately with their knowledge of wine and wine making. We would host the French wine people on their visits to New Orleans, and my parents even stayed in one of their beautiful châteaux (the Cruse family's château, Le Dame Blanc) on a trip to Bordeaux. The picture of that magnificent château hung on the wall in our home, and the grandeur and mystique of these French wine makers were forever imprinted in my imagination. I have been drawn to wine people ever since.

We were always so impressed with French wine and, like everyone else, assumed that wine with that much depth and character could not be matched in America. It was simply the *terroir*—all the factors that collide magnificently in certain spots on earth to produce the world's finest wine grapes.

Then along came those daring gents from California—the Davis family of Schramsberg Vineyards and a fellow named Robert Mondavi among them—who seemed to be on a personal mission to convince not only restaurateurs but the rest of the world, too, that California's wines could match and, dare they say it, exceed those of France.

So many people did not believe it could be done, but my mother, Ella Brennan, was an early and ardent believer and booster. I remember meeting Robert Mondavi at parties in our home—grand parties that our family threw to honor the Mondavis and to spread the word to New Orleans that this California wine maker would play second fiddle to none.

It's hard to imagine now, but in 1979 when our family opened Mr. B's Bistro in the French Quarter with an American-only wine list, it garnered industry headlines as a daring thing to do.

We are wine lovers, oenophiles, "grape nuts," and the thousands of bottles of wine that we stock come not just from California and France but from Chile, New Zealand, Italy, and anywhere else that produces wines that we like. It seems as if our love of wine has been infectious in our restaurants. There are not only regular tastings and wine seminars but even in-house wine clubs. One outgrowth of all this has been an idea minted and implemented by one of our senior oenophiles—my brother, Alex Brennan-Martin. He invented, at the restaurant he runs today, Brennan's of Houston, the Wine Table. You've heard of a Chef's Table? Well, the Wine Table works the same way, only it's centered around wine instead of food. Alex's idea fit so well with our philosophy of the importance of wine that we did what all good restaurants do—we stole the idea for Commander's Palace. At a special table in the main dining room, with its own cabinet of the finest wineglasses and all manner of wine paraphernalia, you are served a selection of wine along with a tasting menu paired to match the wine. Our wine director, Richard Shakespeare, known around Commander's as the Wine Guy, will spend as much or as little time with you as you desire. He is a fountain of knowledge and has an exceptional palate. Some groups are so serious that they taught us more than we taught them. Other groups just want to learn a little something interesting. But most of the people at the Wine Table just want to enjoy some extraordinary wines with a great meal and conversation.

Our unabashed enthusiasm for wine and a sincere desire to share information about wine in an unpretentious way led us to an important change in how we present wines to our guests. Instead of a wine list organized by country or grape variety, we group our wines by their taste profile. This allows you to see a Chianti Classico next to an Australian Rosemount Cabernet–Merlot–Petit Verdot blend. Why? Because they have similar taste profiles, and we want that similarity to help you feel safer ordering a wine that you've never tasted before. The wines are also listed in each section from lightest to heaviest, not by price. We assume you don't need help figuring out what price range you're interested in, but you may not know whether a certain New Zealand Sauvignon Blanc is lighter or heavier than a Joseph Drouhin Rully. We've done that work for you. Examples of the section headings are "Elegant and Light Wines" and—under "Red Full-Bodied"—either "Softer Luscious" or "Big and Bold."

In pairing wine and food, think of natural affinities. Ask yourself what the food and wine have in common. Flavor? Weight? Texture? For example, do the buttery notes in a rich Chardonnay have affinity with butter sauce or crabmeat? How about a fresh-tasting, herbal Sauvignon Blanc with just-shucked fresh oysters.

In making these pairings, remember an old adage: "Follow the sauce." But be open to breaking the rules. As much as we like to talk about the merits of how well this wine pairs with that food, we recommend ignoring any rule that may interfere with your personal enjoyment of wine. So although you might hear that seafood must be paired with white wine, we often recommend a red wine with grilled tuna or with other fish topped with a pungent or complex sauce.

In other words, if you like it, drink it. Sure, once you get the wine bug and become a bit of an oenophile, it's fun to learn and to discuss the intricacies of wine making. But never let that interfere with the simple, basic pleasure of enjoying wine. That is our philosophy and that is why we call Richard Shakespeare the Wine Guy and not the sommelier or the cellar master.

Yes, there was a single moment when I drank some wine and was transported. It was a 1991 Sanford Pinot Noir. Maybe it was everything else about the evening—on a Caribbean beachfront with someone I love so very much—that was perfect as well. But until that moment, I always took wine for granted. On this night, this wine was perfection—for me. It's that magical aura wine can add to your meal that we're always looking for.

We like to say that we're in the business of making memories. But one of the first things we teach our team at Commander's Palace is to relax. A favorite quote of mine is by renowned wine writer Jancis Robinson, from *Tasting Pleasure: Confessions of a Wine Lover*: "I have found that it is perfectly possible to drink pretty much anything while eating pretty much anything else . . . I think that for every dish there probably is one perfect wine, but for most of us life is too short to work out what it is."

But she also says, "It takes just one sniff and sip . . . to make you realize that wine is capable of reaching not just your throat and nose, but your brain, your heart, and occasionally your soul."

OMMANDER'S KITCHEN

COCKTAILS,
EYE-OPENERS,
AND OTHER
DRINKS

t has been said that New Orleans, surrounded on all sides by

rivers, lakes, and marshes, owes its very existence to liquid. And left to the

whims of Mother Nature, New Orleans would have vanished long ago, over-

taken by the powerful Mississippi River, were it not for the Army Corps of

Engineers, which changed the river's course.

Yet to many New Orleanians, there is another liquid history. You think

New Orleans' greatest contribution to the world was jazz? How about the

cocktail? It goes back to the French Quarter apothecaries of the 1790s, when, legend has it, A. A. Peychaud began adding his family's secret formula for bitters to brandy and dispensing it at his family's pharmacy.

"Join me in the bar for a cocktail," says my mother, Ella Brennan, to friends or friends of friends she greets at the door at Commander's Palace. The offer lies somewhere between a spontaneous suggestion and a command; but, nevertheless it's an offer that almost no one has ever refused and none has ever regretted. Mother has been on a lifelong mission to make sure as many people as possible experience the real New Orleans—*her* New Orleans. And that means your meal begins with a cocktail. And if you hesitate for even a moment when she asks what you'd like to drink, she'll probably say, "How about a Sazerac? You have to try a Sazerac." (If it's brunch, she'll probably say, "How about a Milk Punch?")

And so it begins—telling stories of old times and making new memories. She begins to weave the spell. People happily fall victim to her take on how life should be lived in her New Orleans.

The bar at Commander's Palace is small, squeezed between the kitchen and the patio with windows onto both. And like so many things at Commander's Palace, it just works, even though it's often crowded. In the 1970s, many American bars became automated, with machines dispensing the liquor to control costs. I remember our parents frowning on that, telling how a good restaurant gives a good solid freehand pour. And real bartenders flip, stir, and shake to get their froth. After all, it's all part of the show. We like to see a French 75 poured through a fancy strainer and a Ramos Gin Fizz shaken in a cocktail shaker with drama and flair before it gets strained into a cocktail glass. Now, if you add to that recipe a couple of tall tales and true tales, well, as we like to say, "That's what living in New Orleans is all about."

Cocktails are back—again. The fun of ordering a martini, a French 75, a stinger, a Cosmopolitan, or a Sazerac is back. For most of New Orleans, it never really left. This chapter is filled with our favorites—old and new. Cheers.

*B*randy Milk Punch is a smooth drink that helps soothe that morning-after feeling but is just as popular for brunches and Christmas gatherings. I also learned how nice and rejuvenating it is on my Mardi Gras float, where a gallon of Commander's Palace Brandy Milk Punch was the perfect boost during five hours of throwing beads to the crowd. Before long, various float-mates had joined in, and my punch consumption was up to 4 gallons. Years ago, one of them, a Mrs. Slatten, asked for a refill. When I apologetically told her there was no more, she got out her cell phone and sent her car and driver to Commander's Palace for a fresh supply. The driver met our float on the parade route and restocked us. A tradition lived on.

1½ cups milk	½ cup sugar
½ cup heavy cream	½ cup very cold water
12 ounces bourbon	1 tablespoon vanilla extract
1 egg white (optional)	Nutmeg to taste

COMBINE the milk, cream, bourbon, egg white, sugar, water, and vanilla in a large pitcher. Stir well, or, if you have a lid, shake. Serve in rocks glasses and sprinkle each cocktail with some nutmeg.

Bloody Mary

To quote Chef Jamie, "Our Bloody Mary is kick-ass." We use home-made horseradish, homemade Worcestershire, fresh vegetable juice, and pickled peppers (marinating in a huge wine barrel in the middle of the kitchen). We dip the rim of the glass into Creole seasonings, and we top off the drink with a splash of vodka from a bottle frozen into a block of ice that's carried to your table—with all eyes in the dining room following it. Now *that's* a Bloody Mary!

1½ ounces vodka

1 teaspoon prepared horseradish, any color

1 teaspoon or 2 splashes Worcestershire sauce (homemade, if possible, page 305)

2 dashes Garden Hot Sauce (page 302) or hot sauce of your choice

½ cup vegetable juice or tomato juice

Garnish:

Creole Seafood Seasoning (ours, page 294, or store-bought), to taste

1 medium-sized pickled pepper, skewered with sugar cane or toothpick (see Note)

1 medium-sized piece pickled okra, skewered with sugarcane or toothpick (see Note)

PLACE ice cubes in an Old Fashioned glass until it's two-thirds full. Add the vodka, horseradish, Worcestershire, hot sauce, and vegetable juice. Cover the glass with a shaker, shake well, then let rest in the shaker. Wet the rim of the glass and coat the entire rim with Creole seasoning. Pour the drink back into the glass and garnish with the pepper and okra.

NOTE: Although at Commander's we use sugarcane for our skewers, out-side of our region you may not be able to buy it very readily, so skewer with toothpicks instead.

CHEF JAMIE'S TIPS

I use canned vegetable juice when I don't have access to freshly squeezed juice. If you like extra seasoning, as I do, season the top of the drink with a few grindings of freshly milled pepper and a sprinkling of kosher salt. (An Old Fashioned glass is another name for a rocks glass. Any 12-ounce cocktail glass will do the job.)

Jamie and Emeril's Florida Margarita

MAKES 6 COCKTAILS
OR 3 LARGE DRINKS

I can just picture these two characters, longtime friends, sitting on the beach behind "groovy shades," sipping margaritas. They have a thing about their shades. Of course, this isn't just any old margarita. Not with these two. Jamie says Emeril Lagasse gave him this recipe years ago and he still loves it.

6 ounces (1 can) frozen lime juice
    concentrate

6 ounces tequila

3 ounces Triple Sec (or another orange-
    flavored liqueur)

2 ounces kosher salt for rims of glasses
    (optional)

PLACE the lime juice concentrate in a blender. Add the tequila and Triple Sec, fill the blender to the top with ice cubes, and run the blender until the mixture has a slushy consistency. Pour the salt onto a small plate, wet the rim of each glass, and place the wet rim onto the salt so that it coats the rim. Pour the margarita mix into the glasses.

Place the glasses in the freezer for 15 minutes so the drink stays cold longer.

Watch out; these go down effortlessly on a hot day, and they pack a good punch!

 CHEF JAMIE'S TIPS

Sazerac

*L*egend has it that the Sazerac is the original cocktail. It surely is the most New Orleans drink you can order. When you sidle up to a bar and nonchalantly order a Sazerac, you've arrived, you "get it." (Have just one, though; you won't be nearly as attractive as you think after two.) Some sources say it was first served at the Sazerac Coffee House in New Orleans. Others say the name came from the French brandy originally used in it called Sazerac-du-Forge. (Although the original recipe used rye, Commander's uses bourbon.) Others, including my family, believe it came from the Sazerac Bar in the Vieux Carré. That now-closed institution was an all-male bar where men did business—and drank Sazeracs.

1½ ounces bourbon	2 dashes angostura bitters
1½ teaspoons sugar	1 tablespoon Herbsaint or Pernod
4 to 5 dashes Peychaud's bitters	1 lemon twist

HALF-FILL a shaker with ice cubes. Add bourbon, sugar, and bitters. Shake well. Pour the Herbsaint into an Old Fashioned glass, then spin the glass to coat the sides of the glass with the liqueur. Discard the remaining liqueur after coating the glass. Strain the shaker contents into the glass. Rub the rim with the lemon twist and drop the twist into the drink.

*P*icture a tray of silver goblets sweating with cold on the outside with a mint sprig straddling the rim. You've used a muddle, or small baton, to pull all the flavor from the mint, and you're feeling like a true bon vivant, a plantation owner of years gone by welcoming his guests onto the veranda.

12 large or 20 small mint leaves

1½ teaspoons sugar

2 ounces bourbon

¼ ounce brandy, or to taste

1 mint sprig, for garnish

PLACE the mint leaves and sugar in a 10-ounce water glass or a traditional silver julep glass. Muddle, or crush, the ingredients against the side of the container to turn the mixture into a mint syrup. Half-fill the glass with crushed ice, and muddle the ingredients a few more times. Fill the glass completely with crushed ice. Add bourbon and stir well.

TOP off with the brandy and garnish with the mint sprig.

CHEF JAMIE'S TIPS

If you don't have a special baton to muddle the ingredients, use the back of a wooden spoon.

A great way to crush ice is by placing it in the center of a clean towel, folding up the towel, and smashing it against the counter.

You might want to add a splash of water before adding the brandy.

Absinthe Frappé

MAKES 1 COCKTAIL

*I*f you can get your hands on any absinthe, please let us know. It was banned in the United States early in the twentieth century, and with its legendary reputation as an aphrodisiac, this cocktail has an appropriate air of mystery to it. In the absence of absinthe, substitute Pernod or Herbsaint. Only shaved or cracked ice will do, and be sure to use well-iced glasses. If you have a cocktail shaker, this is the time to use it. Otherwise use a long spoon to agitate the mix and to put frost on the glass.

1½ ounces Herbsaint or Pernod   ½ ounce simple syrup (see Note)

CHILL a tall, thin glass in the freezer. Fill the glass with ice chips, add the Herbsaint and the simple syrup, and, with an iced-tea spoon or cocktail spoon, stir vigorously until the glass starts to freeze up, about 1 minute.

NOTE: Make a simple syrup by combining equal parts sugar and hot tap water, stirring until the sugar is dissolved, then chilling.

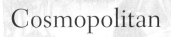

*T*his drink has made a big comeback in New Orleans, especially in the summer. Drinking this classic cocktail served in an oversized martini glass, you definitely feel very cosmopolitan. My Aunt Adelaide sometimes wore a gold swizzle stick that retracted into a gold pendant as a necklace, and I can still see her swizzling her cocktail with her necklace to the amazement of everyone watching.

1½ ounces vodka

½ ounce Triple Sec or another orange-flavored liqueur

¼ ounce lime juice

1 ounce cranberry juice

1 lime slice, for garnish

POUR vodka, Triple Sec, lime juice, and cranberry juice over ice in a large mixing glass. Stir and strain into a chilled martini glass. Squeeze the juice from the lime slice into the glass, and garnish with the slice.

French 75

MAKES 1 COCKTAIL

*W*hen I was a young girl, I thought my aunts were as glamorous as anyone I'd seen in a movie. Traveling with them and waiting for dinner or after a play in a hotel bar, I'd see the men order a Scotch, perhaps, but the women would pose with cigarettes and long, long holders and order martinis, Sazeracs, or, sometimes, a French 75. I couldn't wait to grow up! The French 75 is made with gin or brandy and is topped with Champagne. It was named after a powerful French 75-millimeter weapon. It may look elegant in that sleek Champagne glass, but there's power in them bubbles.

1¼ ounces gin or brandy

1 teaspoon sugar

1½ teaspoons lemon juice (save a twist for garnish)

4 ounces Champagne

PLACE 4 ice cubes, the gin or brandy, sugar, and lemon juice in a shaker. Stir and strain into a Champagne glass with ice and top off with Champagne. Garnish with a lemon twist.

CHEF JAMIE'S TIPS I've tried this with both brandy and gin, and to my taste, the gin is more refreshing—especially over ice.

Cocktails, Eye-Openers, and Other Drinks

10

"SPORTING GENTLEMEN"

"Commander's was not *a brothel," says my mother protectively. It was, however, known as a place where "sporting gentlemen" (don't you love terms you've never heard but can instantly glean their meaning?) could use a private entrance on Coliseum Street to escort their lady friends (not their wives) to an intimate dinner in a small private dining room upstairs or a private booth with curtains downstairs. Discretion was the staff and management's forte.*

Commander's did develop a bit of a risqué reputation for a time. During this era, Adelaide, Ella, and Dottie, who lived nearby, were directed by their mother to walk on the other side of the street, not in front of Commander's Palace, on their way to school or to the streetcar. That was a funny memory they recalled on the day they bought the restaurant.

New Orleans Weather Forecast

MAKES 1 COCKTAIL

There is a spicy rum made in New Orleans called N.O. Rum. The vibrant and surreal label is done by a part owner of N.O. Rum and one of our favorite artists, James Michalopoulas. Chef Jamie combines it with ginger beer for a super-refreshing summer rum beverage. Drinking these, especially in the stormy late summer and early fall months, has become as much a ritual as watching the weather forecast and keeping track of the unpredictable hurricanes meandering toward the Gulf of Mexico.

1½ ounces dark rum (we use N.O. Rum)   1 lemon or lime slice

4 ounces ginger beer (see Note)   1 sugarcane skewer (optional)

FILL a tall, narrow glass with ice. Add the rum and the ginger beer. Stir, and garnish with the citrus slice and the sugarcane.

NOTE: Ginger beer isn't really a beer. It's a spicy, distilled soda.

CHEF JAMIE'S TIPS  This drink originated in Bermuda with a brand called Black Seal Rum.

*I*nvented in Louisville but adopted by New Orleanians, the Old Fashioned has been a mainstay in New Orleans for a long time. You feel like a pharmacist or a voodoo priestess making this cocktail. A dash of this, a squeeze of that, and a lump of sugar crushed on the bottom. Some rules: No shaking allowed (only stirring), and prepare it in the same glass you serve it in (preferably a rocks glass). Above all, when ordering an Old Fashioned, strike a pose that says, "Been there, done that, and let's do it all again."

1 medium orange slice

1 maraschino cherry

1 tablespoon sugar

1½ ounces bourbon

1 dash angostura bitters

4 dashes Peychaud's bitters

PLACE the orange slice and cherry in a rocks or Old Fashioned glass, add the sugar, and crush against the side of the glass until the fruit is well broken up and the sugar is dissolved. Add 4 ice cubes, the bourbon, and the bitters, and stir with a cocktail spoon until well blended. Add 4 more ice cubes and serve.

Plantation Porch Punch

MAKES 4 SERVINGS

o need for a big party to kick back with one of these. This is one smooth drink at the end of a long day at the beach or the Jazz Fest. The best garnish is a wide balcony, a cool breeze, and a rocking chair.

1 orange, halved and cut into thin slices

1 lemon, halved and cut into thin slices

1 grapefruit, quartered and cut into thin slices

4 ounces light rum

1 ½ cups orange juice

1 ½ cups grapefruit juice

2 tablespoons Peychaud's bitters or grenadine

4 ounces dark rum

PUT one-quarter of the fruit in a large glass pitcher, fill the pitcher halfway with ice, put another one-quarter of the fruit atop the ice, then fill the pitcher the rest of the way with ice. Place in the freezer until the pitcher is well chilled and frosted, about 45 minutes.

DIVIDE half the remaining fruit among 4 tall glasses. Add ice three-quarters of the way up each glass, then add the remaining fruit. Place the glasses in the freezer for a few minutes.

TO SERVE, remove the pitcher from the freezer. Slowly pour equal amounts of light rum, then orange juice, over the ice in the pitcher, add a portion of grapefruit juice, add the bitters, and then the dark rum. Do not stir, but put the pitcher on the serving table and let the layers slowly blend together. Pour into the chilled glasses.

CHEF JAMIE'S TIPS This is a very visual drink, with each ingredient making its own color layer. Any grapefruit juice works, but I prefer ruby red.

Ramos Gin Fizz

MAKES 1 COCKTAIL

Cocktails are back. Of course, in New Orleans, the home of the original cocktail, they never really went away. Henry Ramos invented this one at his restaurant, Meyer's, in about 1880. This cocktail must be shaken until very frothy or you'll lose the whole point, which is the fizz.

1 1/2 ounces gin
1 tablespoon simple syrup (see Note) or 1 1/2 teaspoons sugar
1/2 medium egg white
1 tablespoon lemon juice
2 ounces heavy cream or half-and-half
4 drops orange flower water

HALF-FILL a cocktail shaker with crushed ice. Add gin, simple syrup, egg white, lemon juice, cream, and flower water. Shake well and strain into a cocktail glass.

ALTERNATIVELY, place ice in a blender jar until it's one-quarter full, add all the ingredients, blend thoroughly, and serve in a large glass.

NOTE: Make a simple syrup by combining equal parts sugar and hot tap water and stirring until the sugar is dissolved.

Lagniappe

SOLO DINERS

We've had a longstanding policy of offering all solo diners a drink on the house. It's our way of letting them know that they'll get no short shrift from us. We appreciate their coming and, frankly, we all dine alone on occasion ourselves. We go out of our way to make you feel pampered, not neglected.

*E*ven New Orleanians sometimes want a flavorful, nonalcoholic drink, so we like to keep this on hand at the bar during the summer. When we get big fresh Meyer lemons from Plaquemines Parish, this beverage is especially rewarding. Dottie Brennan is the force behind all things lemon at Commander's. First, she wanted a great lemon dessert, and after almost four years of bad lemon experiments, we got the Lemon Flan (page 284). Next, she begged for a great lemonade. We're all glad she did.

12 large lemons

2¹/₂ cups sugar

5 cups cold water

1 tablespoon grenadine

CUT the lemons in half, top to bottom. Remove and discard the tips from the ends of each lemon half, to the point where the pulp begins. Cut the lemon halves into thin slices, each about ¹/₈ to ¹/₁₆ inch thick. Set aside 20 slices. Place the others in a large bowl, add the sugar, and mash for about 5 minutes with a heavy wire whip or spoon until the sugar is syruplike. Stir in the cold water, and, using a sieve, strain a quarter of the mixture at a time into a serving pitcher. Squeeze the lemon pieces to extract all the juice, leaving only the rind and seeds to discard. Repeat until all the lemons have been strained.

ADD grenadine and stir. Add the remaining lemon slices and serve in a tall glass with lots of ice.

CHEF JAMIE'S TIPS

This lemonade is strong and sweet, and you might want to keep in mind where you're serving it. Here in New Orleans, it's so hot that the ice will melt pretty quickly and dilute the intensity of the lemonade. But if it's cooler, and the ice lasts longer, the mix won't be diluted.

Instead of grenadine, which usually contains no alcohol, I like to substitute a few dashes of Peychaud's bitters, which have a high alcohol content.

Irish Coffee

We are a big Irish family, and we sell a lot of Irish coffee. Every St. Patrick's Day sees Commander's packed with Irish and Irish wannabes. For many years, Dick and John Brennan invited 75 of their best buddies in for a grand, all-male, completely irreverent St. Patrick's Day luncheon—complete with Irish coffees at the end, which was sometime around 5 or 6 P.M. You've never seen more handsome smiling Irishmen in uglier green jackets. We love these guys. As for the drink, use a glass with a handle, not a cup, and top it with a big dollop of nonsweetened whipped cream. The brown sugar sweetens it enough.

2 ounces Irish whiskey

4 ounces hot coffee

1½ teaspoons brown sugar, or to taste

1 large dollop (about 2 ounces) whipped heavy cream, unsweetened (see Chef Jamie's Tips)

POUR the whiskey into a large, warmed glass, add the coffee, and stir in the sugar. Gently spoon in the whipped cream so it floats on top.

CHEF JAMIE'S TIPS

As simple a recipe as this is, I have preferences for some of the ingredients. For coffee, my favorite is a strong brew, such as the chicory coffee we drink in New Orleans. I like using brown sugar because I think it goes especially well with the whiskey, but you can use regular granulated sugar, too. Irish coffee mugs are great for serving this drink because they are made of glass with the handle at the bottom, so the hot coffee won't burn your hands. But be sure the mug is warmed so that you don't chill the coffee.

Lagniappe

COFFEE AND CHICORY

New Orleanians have always taken their coffee very seriously. Long ago, chicory was added to New Orleans coffee as an extender that lent a distinctive strong flavor to the more expensive coffee bean. The chicory roots (not the leaves) are kiln-dried and roasted. The coffee trade has always been big business in New Orleans, with a high local demand and lots of coffee beans traveling through the Port of New Orleans.

Commander's Palace serves French Market brand coffee and chicory, and many visitors find it too strong. But our theory is, "When in Rome . . ."

We can't understand the idea of pouring cold milk into hot coffee. So we heat our milk. That way you can pour hot milk into hot coffee. Enjoy.

Iced Coffee

The rest of the world is finally catching up to New Orleans in appreciating the nuances of coffee—like understanding the range of possible flavors and styles and knowing what dissipates coffee flavor. Coffee roasting, much like wine making, is an art form. I drink iced coffee every day. Because it steeps for 12 hours, the oil from the bean is steeped into the cold-drip coffee, lending it smoothness. Never, never drink iced coffee made from hot coffee. It's terrible and defeats the purpose.

1 pound ground coffee and chicory, or dark
    roast (if you buy beans, grind on
    "coarse" or "percolator" setting)

3½ quarts cold water
1 tablespoon good-quality vanilla extract

POUR the ground coffee into a one-gallon pitcher. Add water, make sure that all the grounds are wet, and stir if necessary. Let stand at room temperature for 12 hours. Drain through a large fine strainer, such as a chinois or fine sieve. Discard the grounds and strain a second time, using a coffee filter or double layer of cheesecloth, to remove excess grounds and sludge. Add vanilla and refrigerate. This mixture will keep for up to a month. It produces a sludgelike concentrate.

TO SERVE, place one-quarter cup of coffee concentrate and one-quarter cup of cold water over ice, adding milk and sugar if desired.

IF YOU'RE using a coffee toddy, which has a hole in the bottom with a filter and cork, follow the directions above, but pull the cork and drain into a carafe. There's no need to strain through a filter or cheesecloth.

CHEF JAMIE'S TIPS I like my coffee half milk and half concentrate with a lot of ice. Be sure to use a quality vanilla. Decaffeinated coffee is fine. To make great hot coffee by the cup, just pour a quarter cup of this mixture in a mug, add water, then microwave. Dottie Brennan taught me this.

*W*e're serious about iced tea and serve endless pitchers of the brew, especially during the hot summer months. Pouring out of a glass pitcher into a tall glass, the glass sweating beads of water, well, your eyes can almost taste the fresh mint floating on top. To our taste, cold-brewed tea is less bitter. We like this version best, but mango mint is popular, too.

1 large bunch fresh mint (about 2¹/₂ ounces)

3 oranges, halved top to bottom, end slices discarded, sliced ¹/₈ inch thick

²/₃ cup honey, or to taste

2 quarts cold water

6 Earl Grey tea bags

WASH the mint, and place it in a large glass pitcher. Add the orange pieces, then the honey. Use a wooden spoon to crush the ingredients until they're lightly broken up and the bottom of the pitcher contains orange juice mixed with mint and honey. Add the cold water and stir. Place the tea bags on top and cover the pitcher with plastic wrap. Place on a counter for up to 12 hours, or until the mixture reaches the desired strength.

Remove the tea bags and squeeze any remaining liquid from them back into the pitcher.

STIR gently to avoid disturbing the bottom of the pitcher too much. Serve in tall glasses over ice.

CHEF JAMIE'S TIPS

If you are using bulk packed tea, 1¹/₂ teaspoons equals 1 bag. Don't stir or break up the mint and orange too much. That will keep the tea clearer and put fewer particles into each glass. Strain if you wish.

Drinking iced tea on a hot day is a Southern state of mind. To me, just the sight of the glass pitcher sweating, with its fresh mint and fruit, is cooling, even before I've taken a single sip.

2

FINGER FOODS AND APPETIZERS

ver notice that appetizers are usually the most daring dishes on a restaurant menu?

Restaurateurs instinctively know a couple of things about human nature. One is that customers are more likely to try new things—Frogs' Legs with Crystal Hot Sauce Beurre Blanc, for example—when they are committing to a smaller appetizer portion instead of an entire entrée portion. Another theory is that some foods are just too *some*thing—too rich, too spicy, too weird—to eat as an entrée. Restaurateurs know this not only by instinct but by menu score—the list of how many orders of each item they serve.

So it's not us, it's you. We love that side of you—the adventurous side that's sometimes not the side you feel like showing. We know ourselves that sometimes nothing is more soul-stirring than the anticipation and arrival of a familiar tart. Some nights, you want us to keep our truffled this and our gastrique that and just let you revel once again in Shrimp Rémoulade. Or how about an entire dinner of hors d'oeuvres? Bite-sized crab canapés, shrimp mousse on endive, and as much garlic bread as you want? I did it once. Gorgeously unrespectable. Spent an entire weekend at the Windsor Court having massages, cocktails, and trays of hors d'oeuvres for dinner. I highly recommend this as a cure for whatever ails you.

So from the exotic to the familiar, for food that can dazzle as well as comfort, these are the appetizers and finger foods that we (and you) have come to love.

Whether you want to impress your guests with Crab and Corn Johnny Cakes with Caviar, you need a Tangy Shrimp Dip to put out for your buddies, or you just want to go into a corner and commune with a big overstuffed artichoke by yourself, you will find some home runs here.

And if you decide you want multiple appetizers as your meal, we won't look at you funny. We'll smile a conspiratorial smile and tell you our favorites.

Tangy Shrimp Dip

MAKES APPROXIMATELY 3 CUPS

*T*he Creole seasoning gives this shrimp dip its signature tang, making it perfect party food.

1 pound shrimp, any size, boiled and peeled
    (see Boiled Shrimp, page 132)
8 ounces cream cheese, cut in large dice
8 tablespoons (1 stick) butter, at room
    temperature, cut in thirds
1/2 teaspoon hot sauce, or to taste
1 tablespoon Worcestershire sauce

1 teaspoon Creole Seafood Seasoning
    (page 294) or any Creole seasoning
    mix, or to taste
1 teaspoon lemon juice
1/4 cup chopped parsley
Toast points or crackers

PLACE a third of the shrimp, a few at a time, in the workbowl of a running food processor. When well blended, add a third of the cream cheese and one hunk of the butter. Add the hot sauce, Worcestershire, Creole seasoning, and lemon juice, and purée until well blended. Turn the machine off, remove the lid, scrape the bottom and sides of the bowl with a rubber spatula, then return the cover.

TURN the machine on and add half the remaining shrimp, a few at a time, and the remaining cream cheese and butter, half at a time. Blend until well incorporated, about 20 to 30 seconds, then remove the cover and again scrape the bottom and sides of the bowl. Adjust the seasoning, and purée for about 10 seconds. Remove the mixture, place in a mixing bowl, and fold in the parsley. Place in a decorative bowl. Slice the remaining shrimp in half, top to bottom, and use them to decorate the top of the spread. Serve with toast points or crackers.

About the same weight (or a bit less) of smoked salmon can be substituted for shrimp. Be careful not to oversalt when seasoning, since the shrimp are somewhat salty.

CHEF JAMIE'S TIPS

Finger Foods and Appetizers

Crab and Cream Cheese Dip

MAKES APPROXIMATELY 3 CUPS OR ABOUT 50 BITE-SIZE CANAPÉS

*L*iving next to Commander's Palace is perfect for my mother, Ella, and my Aunt Dottie Brennan. It's a lively household, and these two love to entertain. When they do, a call to the restaurant might go like this: "Jamie, Dottie and I are having some special friends over to the house for cocktails before we come next door to dinner. Could you send over some Crab and Cheese hors d'oeuvres?" Garnish the crab dip with lump crabmeat to give it a finished look, or fold in some claw meat for a less expensive but equally elegant version.

1 pound crabmeat, any kind, picked free of shell

8 ounces cream cheese, in large dice

1 teaspoon hot sauce, or to taste

2 teaspoons Worcestershire sauce

1 teaspoon prepared horseradish, or to taste

2 tablespoons Creole mustard or other coarse mustard

1 bunch green onions, thinly sliced

Kosher salt and freshly ground pepper to taste

Toast points

PLACE half the crabmeat in the workbowl of a food processor. Add a third of the cream cheese, the hot sauce, Worcestershire, horseradish, mustard, two-thirds of the green onions, the salt, and pepper. Purée, running the processor for about 15 seconds. Scrape the sides and bottom of the bowl with a rubber spatula, add half the remaining cream cheese, and purée until well blended, about 15 seconds. Stop and scrape the bowl again, add the remaining cream cheese, and process until well incorporated. Adjust seasoning. Fold in the remaining onions and crabmeat and serve as a dip. Or, to make canapés, reserve the remaining crabmeat, place the purée in a pastry bag, and pipe it onto crackers or toast points. Season the reserved crabmeat, and garnish the canapés with the crabmeat and the remaining green onions.

CHEF JAMIE'S TIPS

Blue crabs are my favorite, but any grade of crabmeat can be used. This crab dip need not be limited to canapés. Place the mixture in a bowl, fold in the remaining crabmeat and green onions, and serve as a spread for crackers, homemade breads, or toast points. But if you are making canapés, don't fold in the crabmeat and green onions until the mixture is piped out or they'll get stuck in the tip. The mixture is easier to work with if it's at room temperature.

TOAST POINTS

We prefer toast points to crackers. They have more flavor, more texture, and more elegance. At Commander's, brioche toast points are often served with a seafood mousse. Make them from our quick Crispy Bread (page 312), or use a good-quality white bread with the crusts removed. After slicing into the shape of your choice, place the slices on a cookie sheet, brush the surface with melted butter, and toast them carefully under the broiler, without turning them over. Arrange them on a serving tray or plate topped with shrimp or salmon mousse, smoked fish mousse, or crabmeat ravigote. Serve at room temperature.

Spicy Pecans

*B*eing gracious when unexpected guests drop by has always been important to us. To avoid being caught off-guard by surprise visitors: (1) Keep a bottle of white wine and a bottle of Champagne in the refrigerator; (2) hide a piece of good, long-keeping cheese in the fridge and some crackers in the pantry; and (3) have some of these Spicy Pecans at the ready. Warning: Keep this up, and people will stop by a lot.

4 tablespoons (½ stick) butter

¼ cup honey

1½ tablespoons kosher salt

2 teaspoons cayenne pepper

½ pound pecan halves

PREHEAT the oven to 325°F.

MELT the butter in a medium saucepan over medium heat. Add the honey, salt, and cayenne pepper, bring the mixture to a boil, and cook for 1 minute, stirring. Remove from the heat, and add the pecans to the honey mixture. Stir to mix well. Spread the coated pecans on a sheet pan, and bake in the preheated oven for 15 to 20 minutes, stirring every 5 minutes, possibly more often toward the end. Serve when cooled, first separating any pecans that stick together. Store in an airtight container.

CHEF JAMIE'S TIPS The moisture content of the pecans could leave behind some excess liquid in the pan. If that's the case, cook the nuts a bit longer, being careful not to let them burn, or simply drain the liquid after you've finished cooking the nuts.

MAKES APPROXIMATELY 3 CUPS,
ENOUGH FOR ABOUT
50 HORS D'OEUVRES

*C*all this poor man's foie gras. With a touch of cognac and toast points, you could fool a lot of people. But in New Orleans, there's no need— we love chicken liver. Great flavor and versatility make this chicken liver spread a popular staple for us.

1½ pounds chicken livers

½ pound (2 sticks) plus 1 tablespoon butter

1 small head garlic, cloves peeled and coarsely chopped

1 large onion, coarsely chopped

Kosher salt and freshly ground pepper to taste

1 teaspoon freshly grated nutmeg

¼ cup brandy

1 tablespoon Worcestershire sauce

1 teaspoon hot sauce, or to taste

RINSE the livers under cold water, removing any veins, and pat dry with paper towels.

MELT the 1 tablespoon of butter over high heat in a large sauté pan, add the garlic and onion, and stir, letting the mixture brown for about 4 minutes. Add the livers, season with salt and pepper, and cook, stirring, for about 2 minutes. Reduce the heat and continue cooking until the livers are almost done, stirring occasionally, for about 8 minutes.

ADD the nutmeg and deglaze the pan with the brandy, scraping any glaze from the bottom of the pan. Add the Worcestershire and hot sauce, remove from the heat, and place the livers in a bowl. Refrigerate for about 20 minutes, or until mostly chilled, stirring after 10 minutes.

PLACE the livers in the workbowl of a food processor and purée. Scrape the sides and bottom of the workbowl with a rubber spatula. Continue to purée, and add the remaining butter about 3 tablespoons at a time. Adjust seasoning. The final consistency should be like that of whipped butter. Transfer to a serving dish, and refrigerate for about 1 hour, covered with plastic, to allow the mixture to set up, but serve at room temperature to make it more spreadable.

SERVE with toast points or crackers as an hors d'oeuvre, either by itself or with chopped onions, capers, chopped hard-cooked egg, olives, chopped shallots, or mustard. If covered with plastic, the spread will keep up to 2 weeks in the refrigerator.

This is an economical way to make hors d'oeuvres for a crowd. Pass this spread through a sieve before chilling to make it extra smooth, or you can pipe the spread onto toast points.

 CHEF JAMIE'S TIPS

Finger Foods and Appetizers

A FANATICAL COMMITMENT TO THE CONSISTENT
EXECUTION OF THE FUNDAMENTALS

My uncle, Dick Brennan, always called it the ABCs. We all knew what he meant. If you don't faithfully execute the basic elements of the restaurant business, day in and day out, your history in the business will be short and financially painful. In other words, serve hot food hot and cold food cold, make your stocks the long, laborious, correct way, and keep the bathrooms clean.

Of course, there's a lot more to it than that. But neglecting all the little things, the ones that aren't glamorous or fun, is what trips up most people in most businesses. They are the things that will never be noticed if you do them well. We call it the absence of negatives. First, you must get those fundamentals right. You must have, as Uncle Dick said, "a fanatical commitment to the consistent execution of the fundamentals."

*W*e can never seem to make enough of these for a party. Ours have a hint of cayenne and go down well with a cold beer. Put these in a tin and give them as gifts for Christmas—or for any special occasion.

10 ounces (2½ cups) grated sharp Cheddar cheese

1½ cups all-purpose flour

8 tablespoons (1 stick) butter, at room temperature, cut into ½-inch dice

2 medium egg yolks, well beaten

1 teaspoon cayenne pepper, or to taste

Kosher salt and freshly ground black pepper to taste

PREHEAT the oven to 400°F.

PLACE the cheese and the flour in a large bowl, mix well with your hands, and combine as if you were forming a ball. Add the butter, and work with your hands to incorporate it for about 30 seconds. Add the egg yolks and mix with your hands for about 30 seconds. Add the cayenne, salt, and pepper, and knead the dough for 3 minutes, until it forms a shiny ball.

IF YOU have a strong, heavy-duty pastry bag with a large star tip, or a cookie press, fill it with a quarter of the dough. Squeeze out the dough into strips about ⅓ inch wide, ⅓ inch thick, and 1½ inches long onto an ungreased cookie sheet. (You'll need a little muscle if you use a pastry bag.) Leave a little room for the straws to expand, so you'll probably need two pans. If you don't have a pastry bag or cookie press, roll out the dough on a lightly floured surface, and cut the dough as described with a knife or a pizza cutter. Repeat with remaining dough.

PLACE in the oven and bake for about 15 minutes, or until the straws are a golden orange and are cooked all the way through.

Let cool on the pans. Remove and serve, or store as you would cookies, in an airtight container at room temperature.

Use a good-quality Cheddar; the straws will vary depending on the cheese you use. And be careful with the seasoning. The cheese you use may be salty, so taste it and adjust the additional seasoning accordingly.

CHEF JAMIE'S TIPS

Finger Foods and Appetizers

Pickled Shrimp

*T*his is a wonderful picnic dish in a jar (and a great gift for a foodie, too). We call them Pickled Shrimp, even though they're actually cooked and marinated, not really pickled. Serve as an hors d'oeuvre, a first course, or tossed with mixed greens as a salad.

1 medium red onion, in small dice

1 bunch green onions, thinly sliced

1 cup chopped fresh parsley

1/2 teaspoon crushed red pepper flakes, or to taste

6 cloves garlic, peeled and minced

1/4 cup Creole mustard or other coarse mustard

2 tablespoons sugar

Kosher salt and freshly ground pepper to taste

3/4 cup cane vinegar, malt vinegar, or cider vinegar

11/4 cups extra-virgin olive oil

2 bay leaves

3 pounds medium to large shrimp, cooked as for Boiled Shrimp (page 132), peeled and deveined, tails on

COMBINE the red onion, green onion, parsley, crushed red pepper, garlic, mustard, and sugar in a large bowl, and season with salt and pepper. Add the vinegar, and whisk in the oil in a slow, steady stream until the marinade is emulsified. Add the bay leaves and adjust the salt and pepper. Add the shrimp and stir. Refrigerate for 12 to 24 hours, stirring occasionally. This will keep for up to 5 days in the refrigerator.

Stuffed Artichokes

MAKES 6 SERVINGS

This is my idea of comfort food. When I was a kid, I ordered a stuffed artichoke whenever I was taken to a restaurant, and I begged for them at home. Maybe it was so satisfying because it was so primitive–something you're forced to eat with your hands, scrape against your teeth, dip in a pungent vinaigrette. These artichokes are gently cooked, drained, and filled with a stuffing of cheese, olive oil, bread crumbs, and minced garlic. The stuffing may sound Italian, but the stuffed artichoke is a Louisiana cooking treasure.

6 large artichokes

2 bay leaves

Juice of 3 medium lemons

7 cups freshly made fine bread crumbs

1/2 cup chopped fresh basil

1/2 cup chopped fresh oregano

1/2 cup chopped fresh parsley

1 large head garlic, cloves peeled and minced

1 1/2 cups freshly grated Parmesan cheese

1 cup extra-virgin olive oil

Kosher salt and freshly ground pepper to taste

WITH a paring knife, cut the stems off the artichokes so they stand up, and slice about 1/2 inch from their tops. Use scissors to snip off the thorny leaf tips. Place the artichokes in a pan with enough cold salted water to cover, and add the bay leaves and the juice of 1 lemon. As soon as the water boils, cook for 10 minutes or until the artichoke leaves begin to open. Remove from the water, place in a roasting pan, and let drain.

PREHEAT the oven to 350° F.

COMBINE the bread crumbs, juice from the remaining lemons, basil, oregano, parsley, garlic, Parmesan cheese, olive oil, salt, and pepper in a large bowl and mix well with your hands until all the crumbs are well coated.

Holding the artichokes over the crumbs, gently stuff some of the mixture between each layer of leaves. Be fairly generous with the stuffing. Place the artichokes back in the pan, cover with foil, and place the pan in the preheated oven. Bake for 40 minutes or until the artichokes are almost done and the stuffing is hot all the way through. Uncover and cook for 15 minutes more or until the leaves are easily pulled away.

Serve hot, cold, or at room temperature.

CHEF JAMIE'S TIPS This recipe cooks the artichokes in two phases—first by boiling, then by roasting. They should not be fully cooked after the boiling, but if they seem undercooked when roasting, add a little water to the pan.

Lagniappe

AQUA PAINT

When Ella, Dottie, Adelaide, John, and Dick Brennan took over the day-to-

day operation of Commander's Palace in 1974, they wanted to let the world

know that things had changed, that they intended to return Commander's to

the top ranks of New Orleans restaurants. Adelaide and the restaurant deco-

rator decided that they should paint the dreary, brown Victorian mansion

aqua blue, even though everything else in the neighborhood was a tasteful

white, beige, or brown. I was so embarrassed that I pretended to be sick and

refused to go to school. Aunt Adelaide tried to assure us all that "it would fade

beautifully."

Some neighbors were appalled, and it took us all some getting used to.

Of course, now we all love it. It has become something of a trademark. You

can even go to a paint store in New Orleans and ask for Commander's Blue.

New Orleans–Style Barbecue Shrimp

MAKES 4 APPETIZER SERVINGS
OR 2 ENTRÉES

*W*hen you want a quick dish full of lusty New Orleans flavor, barbecue shrimp is worth every messy drip. Three tips: Don't overcook the shrimp; cook the shrimp with their heads on because that's where all the flavor is (check Mail-Order Information on pages 319–320 so you can buy them that way); and have lots of crisp French bread on hand to dip into the sauce. And you've just got to eat these shrimp with your hands—the better to peel them and soak the bread in the sauce.

2 pounds large shrimp, heads on

2 tablespoons Creole Seafood Seasoning (page 294) or any Creole seasoning mix, or to taste

1 tablespoon olive oil

1 large head garlic, cloves peeled and minced

2 tablespoons chopped fresh rosemary

3 tablespoons Worcestershire sauce

3 tablespoons hot sauce or to taste

1 large lemon, juice removed, quartered (reserve the juice)

⅓ cup beer

Kosher salt and freshly ground pepper to taste

8 tablespoons (1 stick) butter, at room temperature

LIGHTLY toss the shrimp with half the seasoning. Preheat a large skillet over high heat, put the oil in the pan, and heat until the oil begins to smoke. Place the garlic and rosemary in the pan, and stir to lightly brown the garlic, being very careful not to burn it. Add the shrimp and stir carefully. Add the Worcestershire, hot sauce, lemon juice, and lemon quarters.

DEGLAZE the pan with the beer, stirring to release any bits clinging to the bottom, and boil the mixture to reduce while shaking the pan. Allow the shrimp to cook for 2 to 2½ minutes (timing will depend on size) and add the remaining seafood seasoning, salt, and pepper. When the shrimp have finished cooking, the liquid should have a saucy consistency. Reduce the heat to medium-high and add the butter a bit at a time, stirring, until the sauce is thick. Adjust seasoning. Remove lemon pieces.

SERVE with French bread, lots of paper napkins, and finger bowls. Garnish each serving with a lemon piece.

CHEF JAMIE'S TIPS Make sure the shrimp are fresh or else skip this recipe. Check the color, smell, and attachment of the head and legs. Because of the weight of the head and shells, one pound yields only about 8 ounces of edible meat. This dish is cooked very fast, so advance preparation of ingredients is important. It is critical that you keep an eye on the garlic so that it doesn't burn while you cook the shrimp.

Lagniappe

FRYING

Frying well is an art. My mother, Ella Brennan, believed restaurants had it all wrong, that frying could be done delicately and with finesse to produce a beautiful product, not a greasy, heavy blob. The key rules: The oil must be brand new, don't overfry, fry right before serving, and make your food as thin and flat as possible. Fry oysters just until the edges curl. Pat down and flatten catfish so that it fries more evenly for a shorter time—again, just until it's crispy and the edges curl. Fry rabbit in a skillet, not a fryer. It's a longer, slower, lower-heat process, but it keeps the rabbit from becoming too dark and greasy. Mom remembers sitting at the kitchen table with her brother John while their mother, Nellie Valentine Brennan, made them oyster Po' Boys, one at a time. Her sandwich was right out of the pan and so lightly breaded and fried that all the flavor of the oyster came through. It was Mom recounting that story that set Chef Jamie on the course to develop the methods we now use at Commander's—to return frying to the art form it once was.

Crab and Corn Johnny Cakes with Caviar

MAKES 6 TO 8 APPETIZERS
OR 25 TO 30 HORS D'OEUVRES

*H*ere's a beautiful example of how elegant Creole food can be. We do a crab-and-corn version of a johnny cake instead of blini, and they're tiny. A johnny cake is a savory pancake that is fluffy. The cake marries the crab and corn flavors to perfection. We add a dollop of crème fraîche and some Louisiana caviar. I always feel like I'm in high cotton when I get to have a few of these. We offer them on our Christmas holiday menu and on our hors d'oeuvre menu.

Cakes:

½ cup sifted all-purpose flour

½ cup cornmeal, any color

1 teaspoon baking powder

1 tablespoon sugar

1 teaspoon kosher salt

½ cup whole milk

1 medium egg, separated

2 tablespoons melted butter

¼ pound crabmeat, any kind, picked free of shell

About 3 ounces corn kernels, removed from 1 freshly shucked cob

Garnishes and caviar:

¼ cup Crème Fraîche (page 308) or sour cream

2 large shallots, cut in small dice

3 hard-cooked egg yolks, minced (use whites in another recipe)

¼ cup chopped fresh parsley, or as needed

2 to 3 ounces caviar, any kind

PLACE the flour, cornmeal, baking powder, sugar, and salt in a large bowl and mix until well blended. Make a small well in the center of the mixture, stir the milk, egg yolk, and half the melted butter into the well, and mix until well incorporated.

IN A SEPARATE BOWL, whisk the egg white to a medium to stiff peak, and gently fold it into the batter. Fold in the crabmeat and corn. Do not overwork the mixture.

PLACE a nonstick skillet or griddle over medium to low heat for about 30 seconds, and lightly brush the surface with some of the remaining melted butter. Spoon heaping teaspoons of the batter to form separate pancakes on the skillet surface. Make as many as possible but leave yourself enough room to flip the cakes. The finished cakes should be bite-size, about the size of a quarter. Don't let them bubble around the edges. Reduce the heat to low, and cook for about 5 minutes, or until the cakes are lightly browned. Flip the cakes and cook 2 minutes more, or until done. Remove and set on a serving tray or appetizer plate. Repeat, lightly brushing the pan with melted butter and cooking additional cakes until all the batter has been used.

FOR THE GARNISH: Spoon about $1/2$ teaspoon of crème fraîche on each cake. Then sprinkle shallots, egg yolks, and parsley over the cakes and additional parsley over the entire surface of the serving platters. Spoon caviar on top of each dollop of crème fraîche.

CHEF JAMIE'S TIPS

Whipped egg whites make for lighter cakes, so carefully fold in the whites to keep air bubbles intact. And keep the crabmeat pieces as intact as possible.

Cook the cakes over very low temperature; don't fry them. A perfectly cooked cake should be smooth and tan, moist, and completely cooked. You don't want a dark, crisp ring around the edge.

Make sure the caviar is the last garnish, so it's not covered up by the others. And to keep the crème fraîche from melting too fast, the cakes should be warm but not too hot.

Corn-Fried Oysters with Horseradish Cream

MAKES 8 APPETIZER OR 4 ENTRÉE
SERVINGS

*S*o there I was on a panel with other restaurateurs and we were asked what we'd like for our last meal. One said, "Foie gras." Another said, "Caviar." Yet another said, "Truffles." Then it was my turn: "Oyster Po' Boy, dressed." That's how much I love fried oysters. The ultimate Po' Boy is made with corn-fried oysters, just like the ones in this dish. And the keys to the ultimate corn-fried oysters are these: *Don't over-fry the oysters, and serve them immediately after frying.* This dish cries out for a good amber beer. (A Po' Boy is simple. See page 298, the introduction to Creole Tartar Sauce.) By the way, New Orleanians love shoestring potatoes, so if you think you can fry both the potatoes and the oysters, we've got the potatoes as an optional addition.

Horseradish cream:

1/4 cup white vinegar
1 cup heavy cream
1 cup prepared horseradish

Kosher salt and freshly ground pepper to
    taste

Oysters:

8 cups vegetable oil, for frying
1 cup all-purpose flour
1 cup masa flour or fine-ground cornmeal
1 cup cornmeal

1/2 cup Creole Seafood Seasoning
    (page 294), or to taste
40 raw oysters, shucked, in their own
    liquor
Kosher salt
Chopped fresh parsley (optional garnish)

Shoestring potatoes (optional):

4 medium russet potatoes, peeled and cut
    into 1/8-inch matchsticks (see Note)

Kosher salt

MAKE the horseradish cream first. (In fact, you can make it in advance and reheat it.) In a small saucepan over high heat, bring the vinegar and cream to a boil. Add the horseradish, and season with salt and pepper. Simmer for 1 minute, or until sauce is hot. Remove from heat.

THEN cook the oysters. In a 6-quart or larger pot, heat the oil to 325°F to 350°F on a deep-fry thermometer. While the oil heats, thoroughly combine the flour, masa, cornmeal, and Creole seasoning in a large bowl and dredge each oyster in the mixture, letting the oyster liquor act as an adhesive. Shake off excess coating, and set the oysters aside until all are coated.

FRY the oysters in small batches to avoid crowding and prevent a drop in the oil temperature. Cook the oysters for about 45 to 60 seconds, until their edges curl and turn crisp and brown. Pull the oysters from the oil and drain on a cloth towel. Season immediately with salt.

SERVE immediately atop a pool of warm horseradish sauce, and garnish with chopped parsley, if desired.

IF YOU'RE MAKING THE POTATOES, fry them first in oil that has reached 325°F to 350°F while you prepare the oyster coating. After you fry the potatoes, use the same oil to fry the oysters. The potatoes are fried in small batches for 2½ to 4 minutes per batch, depending on their cut size, or until golden brown. Stir to prevent sticking and to encourage even cooking. After cooking, drain on a cloth towel, and season immediately with salt so that the salt sticks. Set aside in a warm area.

NOTE: Use as much of the potatoes as possible when you cut them. Cut into strips ⅛ by ⅛ by 4 inches long. Rinse the cut potatoes in cold water until the water runs clear, tossing occasionally and stirring with your hands. Drain the potatoes well before frying, being sure to shake off all excess water, so they don't burn; be careful when you drop the potatoes into the oil, because any excess water will cause the oil to boil up violently. Potatoes can be cut with a mandoline. See Chef Jamie's Tips (page 201) accompanying Shoestring Potato–Crusted Lyonnaise Fish.

 CHEF JAMIE'S TIPS

The key to successful deep-frying—crisp food that's not soggy—is making sure the oil is hot enough so the food cooks without absorbing oil yet not so hot that the food burns.

Some tips for this dish:

• Use clean oil, and never overcrowd the fryer.

• Frying time and crispness of the potatoes will depend on cut, size, age, and starch content.

• Use a deep-fry thermometer to help you keep the oil at a constant temperature.

• Don't overcook the sauce or you risk losing the pungent horseradish flavor. Taste the horseradish before using it, because the flavor can vary from batch to batch.

• Serve fried oysters immediately.

Roasted Gulf Oysters with Artichokes

MAKES 8 APPETIZER SERVINGS OR AN
HORS D'OEUVRES PLATTER

*I*f you own oyster plates, this is the time to bring them out. If not, you'll quickly understand why dishes using oyster shells have traditionally been served on a bed of rock salt—it keeps the oysters from sliding around on the plate. Jamie seasons the salt garnish with aromatic cloves, peppercorns, cinnamon, and garlic to make the arrival of this dish at the table a celebration of aromas. So enjoy this Creole-Italian favorite combination of bread crumbs, olive oil, herbs, Parmesan cheese, oysters, and artichokes. But don't eat the garnish.

6 large artichokes, stems trimmed

Salt to taste

2 tablespoons olive oil, plus more for
    drizzling

12 medium cloves garlic, peeled and minced

Kosher salt andfreshly ground black pepper
    to taste

Juice of 2 large lemons

1 tablespoon minced fresh oregano

4 cups fresh coarse bread crumbs (from
    about two slightly dried 12-inch
    baguettes)

1/4 cup freshly grated Parmesan cheese

1/4 cup minced fresh flat-leaf parsley

4 dozen freshly shucked large oysters

Garnish:

Rock salt

2 tablespoons whole peppercorns

2 tablespoons whole cloves

1/2 cup whole peeled garlic cloves

8 whole cinnamon sticks

1 lemon, cut in 1/8-inch-thick slices

8 bay leaves

ARRANGE the artichokes upside down in a large steaming basket set in a large pot over 2 inches of water and 1 tablespoon of salt. Cover and bring to a boil over high heat. Reduce the heat to moderate, and steam the artichokes until they're tender when pierced with a knife, or until the large leaves pull off easily, about 25 minutes. Drain, run under cold water to stop the cooking, and transfer to a platter. When cool enough to handle, remove the artichoke leaves (you can eat them as a snack, if you'd like). Using a small spoon, scrape out and discard the hairy chokes. Cut each artichoke bottom into eighths, like a pie, which will yield one artichoke slice per oyster.

ADJUST your oven racks so the top rack is one-third of the way down. Preheat the oven to 450°F.

HEAT 1 tablespoon of olive oil in a skillet over high heat. When the oil begins to smoke, add the artichoke pieces, garlic, and salt and pepper to taste. Cook and stir about 2 minutes, letting the garlic brown but not burn. Remove from the heat, add the lemon juice, remaining tablespoon of olive oil, and oregano, and stir gently.

IN A LARGE BOWL, combine the bread crumbs, Parmesan, parsley, and additional salt and pepper to taste, and drizzle lightly with additional olive oil.

SET the oysters in their shells, on ovenproof oyster plates, or on large baking sheets, fitting them snugly to prevent tilting. Place 1 artichoke slice plus a portion of the garlic mixture on each oyster, drizzle with additional olive oil, and mound 2 tablespoons of the bread-crumb mixture on top.

ROAST the oysters on the top shelf of the oven for 8 to 10 minutes, until the liquid in the shell starts to boil and the bread crumbs brown. Meanwhile, mix the garnish ingredients on a sheet pan and place it in the lower part of the oven. Roast both together.

TO SERVE, layer the garnish on individual plates or a large serving platter, and arrange the oysters on top. Warn your guests that the salt and garnish are not meant to be eaten. Serve immediately.

NOTE: The artichokes and the seasoned bread crumbs can be prepared ahead and refrigerated separately for up to a day.

Lagniappe

THE VIEW FROM NEW YORK

One year when Commander's was nominated for the James Beard Outstanding Restaurant award, the New York gala was broadcast live, with live remote shots through the night from the five restaurants nominated. A bunch of us were in New York. There haven't been any live remotes since, and this may be why.

Three times they cut to live shots of Lally at Commander's. During the third shot, we could see that it was raining pretty hard, but we had no idea that only minutes after that shot, water started coming into the restaurant. The storm was causing one of the biggest floods ever in New Orleans. Water was rising, the electricity was going off and on, ceilings were leaking, and a small fire started in the kitchen.

As the water receded and the last guest finally went home at 4 A.M., Lally almost collapsed. We had no idea. Jamie, Ella, Dottie, Stephen Woodruff, and I were sitting happily in the Monkey Bar in New York, talking about how great Lally had looked on television. The storm was bad enough to close the New Orleans airport, and we were stuck in New York. Not a bad thing, unless you're worried about your business back home floating away.

3

GUMBOS, SOUPS, AND STEWS

New Orleans is a soup town," says Ella Brennan, my mother. As far back as anyone can remember, soup was the traditional first course at all dinners, and gumbo was often the main course at suppers or lunches.

From Oyster Chowder to Red Bean Soup, these soups are the heart of Creole cuisine. No wonder eating soup as a main course is as common as catching beads at a Mardi Gras parade. These are serious soups. Just add a small green salad and a glass of wine to any one of them, and you have a jazzy New Orleans meal.

People love our soups so much and have such a difficult time choosing among the many offerings at Commander's Palace that a zillion years ago, our family added what we call "one-one-one" to the menu—demitasse cups of the turtle soup, our gumbo du jour, and our soup du jour. People find it a perfect way to get a quick New Orleans soup fix, usually as a first course.

❧

Gumbo might well be the greatest food that Louisiana kitchens offer to the world. We claim it as an original New Orleans and Louisiana creation.

Where did it come from? My answer is bouillabaisse. Both use the foods at hand, and that's an important similarity, but the most glaring difference between bouillabaisse and gumbo is roux. And it's the most important. Most gumbos begin with a roux, and because being able to stretch a dish was probably essential for the early Louisiana settlers, adding roux to a bouillabaisse and using the local fish and shellfish would seem natural.

Early Creole and Cajun cooks used everything that found its way into their kitchens, kind of like good restaurant kitchens today. Throwing out good bones that could be used for stocks or stale bread that had a future life as bread pudding, stuffing, or croutons? Wouldn't happen. So it's no mystery that all sorts of ingredients found their way into gumbo. Some say there are as many gumbos as there are cooks.

In 1803, a society banquet in New Orleans featured 24 gumbos. Each of them was different, but they all fell into one of two distinct categories—okra gumbos and filé gumbos. Most home cooks fall into one camp early on and stay there for life. At Commander's, we do both. But we *never*—and here is the main catch—use okra and filé at the same time. No savvy cook would.

Okra came from Africa with the slaves, and it was prized for its earthy flavor and its ability to thicken a stew. With long simmering, the pods inside the vegetable turn gummy and thicken the gumbo. The African word for okra is *gombo*, its derivative being the word "gumbo" that is now used generically to describe the entire category of rich stews.

At one time, fresh okra was available only in the summer, so there was a vital need for a year-round thickener. Filé powder, introduced by the Louisiana Choctaw Indians, was made from the dried leaves of Gulf Coast sassafras trees and was sold at the French Market. A spoonful of filé when it's added at the end of the gumbo's preparation turns a stock into a hearty gravy. An inexperienced cook can overcook or boil filé, and that creates a stringy mess.

Using both filé and okra will cause a gumbo to become too thick, and the two flavors will cancel each other out. So a cook must choose between okra and filé when making gumbo.

At Commander's, we tend to use okra in our seafood gumbos and filé in gumbos with game. Hindsight suggests that the abundance of both okra and seafood in the summer months must have played a part in this culinary thinking.

Until the mid-'70s, my family ate mostly seafood gumbo. The Creole chef then at Commander's, Jimmy Smith, showed us a spicy dark-roux gumbo with andouille from his home in the bayou called Gumbo YaYa. Gumbo YaYa got its name from all the cooks in the kitchen "yaya-ing" while they cooked. Ella, Dick, Dottie, and John all went crazy for it.

Gumbo YaYa led to a rediscovery of all the different gumbos we enjoy again today: Speckled-Belly Goose Gumbo, Seafood Gumbo with Okra, or Gumbo Z'Herbes, a gumbo of just herbs and greens created by the superstitious Creoles for Good Friday, when, it was believed, you would have good luck for the coming year if you ate seven greens and met seven people during the day.

Many gumbos served in restaurants today are often disappointing. Either they're taken for granted by old cooks using shortcuts or they're poorly prepared by young cooks who seem uninterested in the laborious process and the necessary long, slow cooking times.

We have returned gumbo to the pedestal it deserves by serving it as an entrée at the restaurant as well as at our family gatherings. After a Mardi Gras parade or a football game, we would return home with a group of 40 or more and see our mother and aunts set out beautiful antique terrines holding intense-smelling seafood gumbo next to porcelain bowls of white steaming rice next to wine glasses already filled with glimmering, crisp Chardonnay next to platters of garlic bread. That was dinner!

Whether it's Crab and Corn Bisque or Turtle Soup, these dishes aren't second-class citizens; they deserve center stage.

Red Bean Soup

This soup is to New Orleans what black bean soup is to the Southwest. We love red beans, and if you have any of Monday's Red Beans and Rice (page 219) left on Tuesday, you can put them to good use in this hearty, stick-to-your-ribs, flavorful meal.

1 pound dried red beans

1 pound smoked ham or andouille sausage
   (see Chef Jamie's Tips)

1 tablespoon butter

2 medium onions, cut in medium dice

1 medium head garlic, cloves peeled and
   minced

2 bell peppers, cut in medium dice

3 stalks celery, cut in medium dice

1 tablespoon Creole Meat Seasoning (page
   293), or to taste

5 quarts cold water

2 bay leaves

1 tablespoon hot sauce, or to taste

Kosher salt and freshly ground pepper to
   taste

1 bunch green onions, thinly sliced

PICK through the beans to remove any debris, and rinse them thoroughly. If you use ham, cut it into medium dice; andouille sausage should be sliced.

MELT the butter over high heat in a large soup pot or Dutch oven until it starts to smoke, about $2\frac{1}{2}$ to 3 minutes. Add the onion, garlic, bell pepper, celery, and Creole seasoning, and sauté for 8 to 10 minutes, or until the mixture starts to turn brown and tender. Stir occasionally.

ADD the meat and cook for about 5 more minutes, to the point where the vegetables become very cooked and brown. Add the beans and cook until the liquid from the vegetables has evaporated. Stir frequently for about 2 minutes.

ADD 3 quarts of the cold water and the bay leaves, bring to a boil, and cook for about 10 minutes, skimming away any foam that might rise to the top. Cover, reduce the heat to medium-high, and let simmer, stirring occasionally, for 1 hour. Reduce the heat to medium low. Remove the bay leaves from the pot and set them aside.

PURÉE half the soup in a food processor or blender. Return the puréed soup to the pot, add the remaining 2 quarts of water, and stir until well incorporated. Boil for about 5 minutes, then reduce to a very low simmer. Return the bay leaves to the pot, and let cook uncovered, stirring occasionally, for about 1 hour, or until the soup reaches the desired consistency. Add hot sauce and adjust the salt and pepper. Be careful not to let soup stick and burn.

THE FINAL consistency can be adjusted by adding water to thin it or by cooking the entire mixture a little longer to thicken it.

SERVE the soup with a sprinkling of green onions.

CHEF JAMIE'S TIPS

Any of several pork products could be used in this soup. My favorite is pickled pork, generally found only in certain parts of the Deep South. These are small cuts of pork that have been pickled in a salt brine. It takes a long time to cook, and, because it is so salty, you probably won't add any more seasoning to the soup.

You could also use ham hocks, my second favorite, but you'll need to use more because ham hocks, though very flavorful, are largely bones. So cook them until the meat is falling away, then dice the meat. I also dice the skin, which I think is great.

If you use pork on the bone, remove the meat from the bone and return it to the soup pot before you purée the soup.

You can make lots of adjustments to this soup. In fact, you should. The meat you use will determine how much seasoning you add; the consistency you prefer will determine how much water you use; how tender you like your beans will determine how long you cook them; and the consistency and bean cooking time will determine the yield. This soup can burn easily, so be careful not to let anything stick.

Creole Tomato and Fennel Soup

MAKES 4 QUARTS, ENOUGH FOR 16 APPETIZER OR 8 ENTRÉE SERVINGS

*O*ur thinking on tomatoes is pretty simple: When tomatoes are out of season, don't use them. For months at a time, we skip tomato soup and omit tomatoes from salads, but when Creole or beefsteak tomatoes (or whatever your local treasure might be) are in season, eat them any way you can—even just sliced with a touch of salt. This soup has no fat but plenty of flavor.

8 large Creole or vine-ripened tomatoes, 6 cored and roughly chopped, 2 cored, peeled, seeded, and diced
1 large head of fennel, leaves removed and discarded, stems roughly chopped, bulb cut in medium dice
2 small onions, 1 roughly chopped, 1 cut in medium dice
1 medium head garlic, cloves peeled, half the cloves minced, half sliced
Kosher salt and freshly ground pepper to taste
2 quarts Chicken Stock (page 71)
1 cup fresh basil leaves, cleaned

COMBINE the roughly chopped tomatoes, fennel stems, roughly chopped onion, and minced garlic in a large pot over high heat, season with salt and pepper, and cover. The liquid released from the vegetables as they are heated makes oil unnecessary. Keep an eye on them as they cook for 25 to 30 minutes, or until the vegetables are tender, stirring occasionally.

ADD the chicken stock and simmer for about 15 minutes. Purée with a handheld blender or in a blender or food processor for about 30 seconds. Add the basil, and process until the mixture is smooth but still a bit thick. Strain through a medium sieve, pushing through excess pulp but discarding large pieces of tomato skin.

PLACE the diced tomato, fennel bulb, diced onion, and sliced garlic in a large soup pot and cook over medium-high heat, stirring occasionally, for about 10 to 12 minutes, or until vegetables are tender. Add the strained liquid, bring to a simmer, and adjust the salt and pepper.

CHEF JAMIE'S TIPS

Use only the ripest tomatoes, and avoid overcooking the soup or the light, fresh flavor will be lost.

Because this is a light soup with no fat added, make sure the ingredients go in the pot before the heat goes on to prevent scorching.

Add the basil halfway through the puréeing, so the basil will cook some but won't lose its flavor.

Thinly sliced basil and Cheese Straws (page 31) make a great garnish for this soup.

I love the day after traditional meals. In New Orleans, many people cook a ham for New Year's. The best part is saving the bone and making this great split pea soup the next day, but ham hocks can be used as well. After all the celebrating and overindulging, this soup is simple and satisfying. All you need is some hot French bread and the ever-present glass of wine.

MAKES ABOUT 4 QUARTS, ENOUGH
FOR 16 APPETIZER
OR 8 ENTRÉE SERVINGS

2 pounds dried split peas

2 tablespoons butter

3 large leeks, tops discarded, washed
    thoroughly, white parts sliced
    ¼ inch thick

8 cloves garlic, peeled and sliced

4 stalks celery, cut in large dice

6 medium carrots, cut in large dice

2½ pounds lean ham hocks, cut ½ inch
    thick, or leftover ham bone

3 quarts Chicken Stock (page 71)

2 bay leaves

Kosher salt and freshly ground pepper to
    taste

WASH the peas in cold water, keeping an eye out for debris, and set them aside.

MELT but do not brown the butter in a large soup pot over high heat. Add the leeks, garlic, celery, and carrots, and cook for 5 minutes, stirring occasionally. Add the hocks and cook about 3 minutes, or until the leeks are tender and the aroma of ham becomes evident. Add the peas, stirring constantly, and cook for about 3 more minutes, or until the peas turn a bright green.

ADD the chicken stock, bay leaves, salt, and pepper. Bring to the boil and cook uncovered for 30 minutes, stirring often. Reduce the heat and simmer for 30 more minutes or until the liquid is creamy and the peas are just starting to break down, stirring often. If the soup becomes too thick, add a little water. Adjust the salt and pepper. Remove the hocks from the soup pot, set them aside, and let them cool. Remove the meat from hocks, dice it, and add it to the soup. Serve garnished, if you wish, with large croutons and a sprinkle of hot sauce.

Other smoked pork products, such as a ham bone with ham on it, can be used instead of ham hocks. I like to use chicken stock for a rich flavor, but water can be substituted.

 CHEF JAMIE'S TIPS

Gumbos, Soups, and Stews

Cauliflower and Brie Soup

MAKES 4 QUARTS, ENOUGH FOR 16 APPETIZER OR 8 ENTRÉE SERVINGS

*E*ver see a cauliflower the size of a volleyball? The committed farmers from Becnel's in nearby Plaquemines Parish have been dazzling us with cauliflowers that are as impressive in taste as they are in size. The beauty of this satisfying rich winter soup is how the Brie and the fresh cauliflower blend into one another. Don't overcook the cauliflower or it will lose much of its flavor. To add a little panache, garnish the soup with well-seasoned croutons or with a floating dollop of caviar and a dot of hard-cooked egg yolk and chive.

2 heads cauliflower, about 3½ pounds total, cleaned and trimmed	Kosher salt and white pepper to taste
10 tablespoons (1 stick plus 2 tablespoons) butter	1½ quarts Chicken Stock (page 71)
	2 tablespoons all-purpose flour
2 medium onions, peeled and diced	8 ounces Brie cheese, with rind, cut in medium dice
1 head garlic, cloves peeled	¼ cup heavy cream (optional)
1 medium bunch celery, diced	

CLEAN the cauliflower by removing the leaves, coring, and cutting into large florets. Set aside.

MELT 8 tablespoons of the butter in a large soup pot. Do not let the butter brown. Add the onion, garlic, and celery, cover the vegetables, and cook over medium heat to "sweat" them, stirring occasionally, until they are tender, about 5 minutes. Season lightly with salt and pepper. Stir in the cauliflower, cover, and cook for 5 to 7 minutes.

COMBINE the cauliflower and stock, and purée with a hand mixer, a blender, or a food processor. Mix until creamy white and smooth. Return to the pot and bring to a boil.

NOW make a small amount of light roux to add to the soup: Melt the remaining 2 tablespoons of butter in a small saucepan over medium heat, stirring constantly, and add the flour. Cook until the roux smells nutty and is the consistency of wet sand. Do not brown it. Whisk into the soup and bring to a simmer.

Add the Brie, a few pieces at a time, and blend until the cheese has melted into the soup. Add cream, if desired, and adjust seasoning to taste.

Roasted Eggplant and Garlic Soup

MAKES 4 QUARTS, ENOUGH FOR 15 APPETIZER OR 8 ENTRÉE SERVINGS

*T*his dish has Commander's written all over it," says Chef Jamie. He grew up in a very Sicilian neighborhood in New Jersey where the predominant language and cuisine were Italian. Eggplant was grown in the backyards and appeared in many dishes in place of costly meat. But eggplant is a Creole favorite, too, as evidenced by this simple soup.

3 large eggplants, peeled and cut into
    1-inch cubes
2 medium heads garlic, cloves peeled
1 large white onion, diced
1/2 cup olive oil
Kosher salt and freshly ground pepper to
    taste

2 quarts Chicken Stock (page 71)
1/4 cup chopped fresh basil
1 tablespoon hot sauce
2 teaspoons curry powder

SOAK the diced eggplant in a bowl of cold, salted water for 45 minutes, and drain in a colander. Preheat the oven to 450°F.

PLACE the drained eggplant, garlic, and onion in a single layer in a large roasting pan, toss with the olive oil, and season lightly with salt and pepper. Roast for 1 hour or until the vegetables are golden brown, stirring occasionally. Place the roasted vegetables in a large stockpot, add the chicken stock (which should cover the vegetables), bring to a boil, reduce the heat, and simmer for 30 minutes.

ADD the basil, hot sauce, and curry powder. Purée the mixture in a blender or food processor until smooth. Add some stock if the soup is too thick or bring gradually to a boil and reduce if it is too thin. Adjust salt and pepper.

I like using a hand-held immersion blender to purée a mixture like this right in the pot. It's a very friendly tool. It's inexpensive, easy to clean, and eliminates the need to transfer a large mixture from one vessel to another.

 CHEF JAMIE'S TIPS

Gumbos, Soups, and Stews

Turtle Soup

*I*f you asked New Orleanians the single dish they most closely associate with Commander's Palace, I'm sure it would be our Turtle Soup. As popular as turtle soup is in New Orleans, some people often substitute beef or veal for the turtle meat, sometimes referring to it as "Mock Turtle Soup." Our version has always been hearty with the real thing—like a stew that can be a meal on its own. We serve it at Mardi Gras parties in coffee cups, to warm up after all that winter-night parade-watching.

12 tablespoons (1½ sticks) butter

2½ pounds turtle meat (see Note), cut in medium dice (beef, or a combination of lean beef and veal stew meat may be substituted)

Kosher salt and freshly ground pepper to taste

2 medium onions, in medium dice

6 stalks celery, in medium dice

1 large head garlic, cloves peeled and minced

3 bell peppers, any color, in medium dice

1 tablespoon ground dried thyme

1 tablespoon ground dried oregano

4 bay leaves

2 quarts Veal Stock (page 73)

1 cup all-purpose flour

1 bottle (750 ml) dry sherry

1 tablespoon hot sauce or to taste

¼ cup Worcestershire sauce

2 large lemons, juiced

3 cups tomatoes, peeled, seeded, and coarsely chopped

10 ounces fresh spinach, washed thoroughly, stems removed, coarsely chopped

6 medium eggs, hard-boiled and chopped into large pieces

MELT 4 tablespoons of the butter in a large soup pot over medium to high heat. Brown the meat in the hot butter, season with salt and pepper, and cook for about 18 to 20 minutes, or until liquid is almost evaporated. Add the onions, celery, garlic, and peppers, stirring constantly, then add the thyme, oregano, and bay leaves, and sauté for 20 to 25 minutes, until the vegetables have caramelized. Add the stock, bring to a boil, lower the heat, and simmer uncovered for 30 minutes, periodically skimming away any fat that comes to the top.

WHILE the stock is simmering, make a roux in a separate pot: Melt the remaining 8 tablespoons of butter over medium heat in a small saucepan and add the flour a little at a time, stirring constantly with a wooden spoon. Be careful not to burn the roux. After all the flour has been added, cook for about 3 minutes until the roux smells nutty, is pale in color, and has the consistency of wet sand. Set aside until the soup is ready.

USING a whisk, vigorously stir the roux into the soup a little at a time to prevent lumping. Simmer for about 25 minutes. Stir to prevent sticking on the bottom.

ADD the sherry, bring to a boil, add the hot sauce and the Worcestershire, and simmer, skimming any fat or foam that comes to the top. Add the lemon juice and tomatoes, and return to a simmer. Add the spinach and the chopped egg, bring to simmer, and adjust salt and pepper as needed. This soup freezes well.

NOTE: We use alligator snapping turtles, a farm-raised, fresh-water species available all year. Turtle meat usually comes in $2\frac{1}{2}$-pound portions, so this recipe is written to use that quantity. Although it's illegal to use sea-raised turtle, farm-raised is fine. It freezes well and can be ordered by mail (see pages 319–320).

 CHEF JAMIE'S TIPS

Caramelize the vegetables and meats thoroughly, by cooking until the natural sugars form a thick dark liquid, to get a nice dark color.

Remember, this soup is like a stew and could be eaten as a main dish. Because of its thickness, prepare it in a heavy pot, and stir frequently to avoid burning.

Crab and Corn Bisque

MAKES 4 QUARTS, ENOUGH FOR 16
APPETIZER OR 8 ENTRÉE SERVINGS

*S*weet blue crabs and sweet corn are both plentiful in the summer, which is when we serve this long-time favorite, much to the delight of my cousin Tommy Brennan, who comes by often to pick up a gallon or so of this bisque.

6 ears fresh corn

2½ pounds gumbo crabs (see Chef Jamie's Tips), tops, aprons, and gills removed

1 tablespoon dried thyme

2 medium onions, 1 coarsely chopped, 1 in small dice

6 stalks celery, 3 coarsely chopped, 3 in small dice

1 small head garlic, cloves peeled and minced

1 bell pepper, coarsely chopped

Juice of 1 lemon

2 teaspoons Creole Seafood Seasoning (page 294), or to taste, or your favorite Creole seasoning

¼ cup pickling spice or Crab Boil (not liquid; see recipe on page 296)

12 tablespoons (1½ sticks) butter

¾ cup all-purpose flour

Kosher salt and freshly ground black pepper to taste

1 cup heavy cream

1 tablespoon chopped fresh thyme (optional)

1 pound crabmeat, any variety, picked clean of shell

⅛ teaspoon hot sauce, or to taste

1 bunch green onions, thinly sliced

REMOVE the husks from the corn, and, with a paring knife, cut off the kernels over a large bowl. With the back of the knife, scrape the cob to remove any remaining bits of corn into the bowl. Set the corn kernels aside. Break the cobs in half and put the pieces in a large pot.

RINSE the crabs in cold water, chop each into 4 pieces, and add them to the pot. Add the dried thyme, the coarsely chopped onion and celery, half the garlic, the bell pepper, lemon juice, seafood seasoning, and pickling spice. Cover with about 3 quarts of cold water, and bring to a boil. When the liquid boils, reduce the heat to a simmer and skim away any foam and impurities that rise to top. Continue simmering uncovered for 1 hour. Strain this crab stock through a fine sieve and set aside.

MELT the butter in a large, heavy pot over medium heat, but do not brown it. Add the remaining onion, celery, and garlic, stir with a wooden spoon, and cook until the onion is translucent, about 3 minutes. Do not brown. Add the flour ¼ cup at a time, stirring constantly with a wooden spoon. Cook about 2 minutes, or until all the flour is well incorporated. It will have a nutty smell and a pale color.

WHISK the crab stock into the pot, 1 quart at a time, until well incorporated. Bring to a boil, then simmer for 5 minutes. Add the corn kernels and season to taste with salt and pepper. Add the cream and fresh thyme, stirring constantly. Gently stir in the crabmeat. Season with hot sauce and adjust the seasoning. Serve with the green onions sprinkled on top.

 CHEF JAMIE'S TIPS

Gumbo crabs are blue crabs that are found on the Atlantic Coast and Gulf of Mexico. The tops are taken off and the apron and gills have been removed. Other types of crab, including Dungeness, can be substituted.

Before adding cream, be sure that the soup is of the desired consistency. Adjust it if necessary by adding more stock or water to thin it, or by heating and reducing to thicken.

Gulf Coast Summer Bouillabaisse

MAKES 8 ENTRÉES

This seafood bouillabaisse, thick with vegetables and seafood, is one of our light summer entrées. With vine-ripened tomatoes and the abundance of seafood that's at its peak in the summer, this one-dish meal is a seasonal treat that we all look forward to.

3 stalks celery, in medium dice
1 medium onion, in medium dice
2 medium green bell peppers, in medium dice
16 cloves garlic, peeled and thinly sliced
1 tablespoon olive oil (you may not need it)
Kosher salt and freshly ground black pepper to taste
1 medium head fennel, in medium dice
2 bay leaves
2 quarts Seafood Stock (page 72) or Chicken Stock (page 71)
1/2 pound new potatoes, sliced 1/8 inch thick

2 large tomatoes, cored, peeled, seeded, and cut in medium dice (use canned chopped tomatoes if fresh ones are out of season)
1/2 pound fish fillets, in large dice (use any saltwater fish, such as flounder, sea trout, redfish, or snapper)
1/2 pound medium shrimp, peeled
1 pint shucked oysters
1 tablespoon chopped fresh tarragon or basil
1/2 pound crabmeat, any variety, picked clean of shell
1 bunch green onions, thinly sliced

PLACE the celery, diced onion, peppers, and garlic in a large stockpot. Turn the heat to high, stir, and cook until the vegetables give up their liquid and are tender, about 8 to 9 minutes. If the vegetables start to stick, add the olive oil. Season with salt and pepper.

ADD the fennel and bay leaves, sauté for 1 minute, add the stock and potatoes, and bring to a boil. Skim and simmer, stirring occasionally, for 5 minutes or until the potatoes are about half-cooked (test by removing a slice and cutting it). Add the tomatoes, stir, and simmer for about 7 minutes.

ADD fish fillets and shrimp, stir, and simmer for about 1½ minutes, or until the seafood looks halfway cooked. Stir in the oysters and herbs. Cook for about 1 minute, until the edges of the oysters curl. Add the crabmeat, stir, simmer, and adjust seasoning. Turn off heat.

SERVE in large bowls, and sprinkle with green onions.

Because this summertime stew is so light, you need to serve enough. At Commander's Palace, we serve it as a 15-ounce entrée in a large pasta bowl. Even though it has a broth, this is a stew, not a soup, which is why it contains so many ingredients.

I think fennel is great with seafood, especially seafood stews, but some people don't like its licorice flavor, so consider it optional. When cooking with fennel, I trim the stems off, split the bulb in half, and dice it like an onion. Depending on how woody the stems are, I will pick off the feathery leaves and dice them. A small amount of leaves makes a nice garnish, but in large quantities, they can be bitter or overpowering.

Do not adjust seasoning until the very end because the seafood, especially the oysters and their liquor, might make the stew salty.

Oyster Chowder

MAKES 4 QUARTS, ENOUGH FOR 16 APPETIZER OR 8 ENTRÉE SERVINGS

*W*hile clams in chowder can sometimes become a bit tough, fresh oysters stay plump and salty-sweet, and rendered salt pork adds a depth of flavor. Use oyster liquor for flavor and potatoes for thickening.

8 ounces salt pork or bacon, cut in small strips

2 medium onions, in small dice

3 stalks celery, in small dice

10 cloves garlic, peeled and minced

2 medium bell peppers, in small dice

¼ cup flour

1 quart clear chicken stock, clear seafood stock, or oyster liquor

3 bay leaves

1½ pounds potatoes, half of them cooked and put through a ricer, milled, or mashed, half uncooked but cut in small dice

1 cup heavy cream

3 pints shucked oysters in their liquor

Kosher salt and freshly ground pepper to taste

Hot sauce

1 bunch green onions, thinly sliced

2 tablespoons butter (optional)

PLACE a soup pot on high heat for 1 minute. Add the salt pork and cook to render for about 5 minutes, or until fat is clear and colorless, stirring occasionally. Add the onions, celery, garlic, and peppers, and cook for about 15 minutes or until vegetables are tender and onions are clear. Stir occasionally.

ADD the flour, stirring constantly so that nothing sticks to the bottom during cooking. Cook for about 2 minutes or until the flour is well distributed and the mixture thickens. Add the stock and bay leaves and simmer uncovered over medium heat for 25 minutes. Add mashed potatoes, stir, and simmer for about 3 minutes. Add diced potatoes, simmer, and stir occasionally, cooking for about 25 minutes or until potatoes are tender.

STIR in the cream, bring to a boil, cook for 2 minutes, and add the oysters. Cook until the edges of the oysters curl, then season with salt and pepper. Spoon into serving bowls, add a dash of hot sauce and a sprinkling of green onions to each serving, and serve with a bit of the butter, if desired, floating on top.

CHEF JAMIE'S TIPS It is much easier to cut salt pork when it is frozen.

Oyster liquor, also called oyster liquid, is the juice from the oyster that runs off during shucking. Chicken or seafood stock, or canned clam juice, are all great substitutes.

Don't season to taste until you have added the oysters, because they and the pork can be salty.

You can adjust the consistency by adding a few tablespoons of blond roux to make a thicker soup or adding more stock or cream for a thinner soup.

Lagniappe

CAPTAINS' DINNER

Each service team at Commander's Palace is led by a captain—the one who pulls together your whole service experience and is responsible for your servers magically appearing and disappearing at all the right times. Believe me, it's not magic. They're pros working hard to make it look like magic. We depend on and respect them so much that once a year we salute them with an event that we've come to anticipate eagerly.

The captains sit at one long table in a private room and we—the family and management team—serve them a five-course feast accompanied by fine wines. It's a blast. They don't miss a chance to point out our service faux pas, and we laugh at ourselves all night long. There are lots of practical jokes, but it ends with toasts and a room full of people who are proud to work and laugh together.

Gumbo YaYa

MAKES ABOUT 4 QUARTS, ENOUGH
FOR 12 ENTRÉE SERVINGS

*G*umbo YaYa led to the reemergence of many classic non-seafood gumbos that had long been overlooked in fine dining establishments. All of a sudden, gumbos once eaten only at home began appearing in restaurants all over town—duck and wild mushroom gumbo, rabbit gumbo, quail gumbo, turkey and andouille gumbo, and so on.

1 small chicken, quartered	Pinch of dried oregano
Kosher salt and freshly ground pepper to taste	Pinch of dried basil
	Pinch of dried thyme
3/4 cup all-purpose flour, sifted, plus extra for dusting	4 bay leaves
	2 1/2 quarts cold water
3/4 cup vegetable oil (or any oil with a high smoking point)	1 1/2 pounds andouille or other smoked sausage, sliced 1/4 inch thick
3 large onions, in medium dice	1 tablespoon filé powder
7 stalks celery, in medium dice	1 tablespoon hot sauce, or to taste
4 bell peppers, in medium dice	Boiled Rice (page 252)
12 cloves garlic, peeled and minced	3 green onions, thinly sliced
1 teaspoon cayenne pepper, or to taste	

SEASON the chicken with salt and pepper, and dust it with flour. Shake off excess flour.

HEAT the oil in a large, heavy, dry pot over high heat until it reaches its smoking point, about 3 minutes. Sear the chicken in the hot oil until it is golden brown, about 5 minutes on the first side and 4 minutes on the second. Remove the chicken from the pot.

WHEN the oil has returned to the smoking point, make a roux by slowly adding the flour to the oil, stirring constantly over high heat with a wooden spoon until the roux is the color of milk chocolate, about 3 to 5 minutes. Scrape the sides and bottom of the pot as you stir. Be careful not to burn the roux; if black spots appear, you will need to start over.

WHEN the roux has reached the desired color, add the onions and cook for 1 minute. Add the celery and cook for 30 seconds. Add the bell peppers, scrape the bottom of the pot, and cook for 1 minute. Add the garlic, cayenne, oregano, basil, thyme, and bay leaves, and season with more salt and pepper. Slowly add the water, stirring constantly to avoid lumps of roux.

ADD the chicken and the sausage, stir, bring to a boil, then simmer for about 2½ hours, skimming away any excess fat from the surface of the gumbo. When the meat falls off the bones, remove the skin and bones from the pot. If necessary to get the liquid to the desired consistency, add water or simmer to reduce.

RETURN to a boil and stir in filé. Stir vigorously to avoid clumping until the filé is dissolved. Adjust the salt and pepper, and finish with hot sauce to taste.

SERVE over boiled rice and garnish with green onions.

 CHEF JAMIE'S TIPS

Read more about making a roux on page 300.

Oil is released from the roux and the sausage, so skimming excess fat from the gumbo is important.

Some people like a thick gumbo, while others prefer it thin, so adjust it to the desired consistency. For me, it depends on the weather. I like it thick in the colder weather and thinner in the warmer months.

Seafood Gumbo with Okra

MAKES 5 QUARTS, ENOUGH FOR
ABOUT 16 ENTRÉE SERVINGS

*L*et me tell you how I make my gumbo." That's how many conversations begin in these parts. Although no dish better defines New Orleans cooking than seafood gumbo, there are probably as many gumbos as there are cooks. Here's ours. At the beginning, we add gumbo crabs to impart a great flavor of the sea. Add shrimp and oysters at the end so they don't become overcooked and rubbery.

3/4 cup vegetable oil

3/4 cup all-purpose flour

3 onions, in medium dice

1 medium bunch celery, in medium dice

4 green bell peppers, in medium dice

6 medium cloves garlic, peeled and minced

1 teaspoon cayenne pepper, or to taste

Pinch of dried oregano

Pinch of dried basil

Pinch of dried thyme

4 bay leaves, preferably fresh

Kosher salt and freshly ground pepper to taste

2 quarts cold water

1 1/2 pounds gumbo crabs or blue crabs (hard-shell tops off, gills removed, cut in half, with claws cracked with back of knife)

1 pound andouille sausage, sliced in 1/4-inch rounds (sausage should be smoked and firm; other smoked sausage can be substituted)

1/4 pound okra, tops removed, in 1/8-inch-thick rings

1 pound medium shrimp, peeled and deveined, tails on

1 quart shucked oysters, in their liquor

Hot sauce to taste

Boiled Rice (page 252)

3 green onions, thinly sliced

POUR the oil into a heavy, dry stockpot with a capacity of at least 8 quarts, and heat the oil until it is very hot. Make a roux by slowly adding the flour and stirring constantly with a wooden spoon for about 3 to 5 minutes, until the mixture is the color of milk chocolate. Scraping the sides of the pot and stirring constantly are the key to a good roux. Be careful not to burn the roux; if black spots appear, it will be unusable and you will need to start over.

ONCE the roux is the proper color, add the onions, cook for 1 minute, add the celery, and cook for 30 seconds. Add the bell pepper, and scrape the bottom of the pot. The aroma should be slightly burned and very appealing. Add the garlic, cayenne, oregano, basil, thyme, bay leaves, salt, and pepper.

ADD the cold water to the mixture, stirring constantly to prevent lumps. Add the crabs and sausage, bring to a boil, then simmer, uncovered, for 45 minutes, skimming constantly and stirring occasionally to avoid sticking.

ADD the okra and cook for 15 minutes more, skimming off any fat. Stir gently so as not to break up the okra. Add the shrimp, the oysters, and the oyster liquor, and bring to a boil. Reduce the heat and simmer for 10 minutes.

FINISH the soup with your favorite Louisiana hot sauce, then adjust the salt and pepper to taste. Serve over the rice, and garnish with the green onions.

Skimming gumbos is essential to a good, clean shine. You may want to adjust consistency by adding more water to thin it or simmering to thicken it. **CHEF JAMIE'S TIPS**

Gumbo Z'Herbes

I wonder what visitors think as they stroll though the French market and hear the vegetable man chanting, "Get your gumbo greens here for good luck, fresh lucky greens here"? Being a city with a large Catholic population, New Orleans has many superstitions based on religious practices. During Holy Week, Catholics are not supposed to eat meat, and so long ago, Gumbo Z'Herbes—"of greens"—was developed to replace meat and seafood gumbos. Along the way, the superstition developed that if you made a gumbo of 7 greens and met 7 people that day, you would have good luck for the year.

1 bunch mustard greens	1 large onion, in medium dice
1 bunch collard greens	2 green bell peppers, in medium dice
1 bunch turnip greens	1 head garlic, cloves peeled and minced
1 bunch beet greens	½ teaspoon ground cloves
1 bunch fresh spinach	1 teaspoon ground allspice
1 bunch fresh parsley	¼ teaspoon cayenne pepper
3 bunches green onions, thinly sliced	3 pounds ham hocks, split, or ham, diced
¼ cup salt, for washing greens	Kosher salt and freshly ground pepper to taste
4 quarts water	
½ cup vegetable, corn, or safflower oil	1 tablespoon hot sauce or to taste
½ cup all-purpose flour	Boiled Rice (page 252)

REMOVE all stems, midribs, and brown spots from the mustard greens, collard greens, turnip greens, beet greens, spinach, and parsley. Coarsely chop the greens, and, with the green onions, wash in a basin of cold water with the ¼ cup salt added. Drain and wash twice more in plain cold water to be certain that all dirt has been removed.

PLACE the greens in a large stockpot with the 4 quarts of water, place over high heat, cover, and bring to a boil. Then reduce the heat to medium high and cook for 1 hour. The greens should be nearly tender. Drain, but save the cooking liquid, and set aside.

PLACE the oil in a large dry soup pot over high heat for about 3 to 4 minutes, and bring to the smoking point. Slowly add a third of the flour, and stir with a wooden spoon or a whisk to incorporate with the oil. After about 15 seconds, add half the remaining flour, and stir again until well incorporated, taking care not to burn the mixture. After another 15 seconds, add remaining flour, continue stirring, and cook until the mixture—your roux—is dark brown. Work quickly, scraping the sides and bottom of the pot constantly for another 10 to 15 seconds. Add the onion, bell peppers, and garlic, and stir. Then add the cloves, allspice, and cayenne, and stir again. Add the greens, stirring frequently, and cook for 10 to 15 minutes, or until the greens are very tender and start to turn very dark. Add all the cooking liquid and the meat, and season lightly, keeping in mind that the ham may be salty.

BRING to a boil, cover, and reduce heat to a simmer, skimming constantly. Cook for about 1 hour or until the meat is tender. Remove the ham hocks, remove the meat from any bone, and dice. Return the diced meat to the gumbo, and adjust seasoning. Add hot sauce. Serve with the rice.

CHEF JAMIE'S TIPS

While I was researching this recipe, I found one reference that said, "Precision measuring is never done in this gumbo." That's because what you use is flexible, and how much of it you use is flexible too. Any combination of greens you can find—and it should be a combination—such as cabbage, celery leaf, arugula, or watercress, would work fine, as would any number of herbs, such as basil, thyme, marjoram, and bay leaves.

These choices will change your recipe. But whatever you use, clean the greens well. Salt helps. When you cook the greens, if they don't all fit in the pot at first, place as much as you can in the pot, let them cook down, then add the rest.

When you add the liquid from cooking the greens into the gumbo, be sure there is no grit at the bottom of the pot.

I like to use whole cloves and allspice, even whole dried cayenne, and grind them myself.

Different meats can be used. I like hocks best. Some recipes use veal brisket, tasso, and/or bacon. This gumbo was invented for Holy Week, when many Catholics don't eat meat and when oysters would be a great addition to the soup.

More details on making a roux can be found with the Dark Roux recipe on page 300.

Speckled-Belly Goose Gumbo

MAKES 3 TO 3½ QUARTS, ENOUGH
FOR ABOUT
10 ENTRÉE SERVINGS

*W*hen the Louisiana legislative session once overlapped with the opening of duck-hunting season, it didn't take long to see what a mistake that was. The governor vowed he would never let *that* happen again. Men in Louisiana hunt. A lot. That includes Chef Jamie. So when Jamie heads to Gueydan, Louisiana, and returns to camp with speckled-belly geese, he knows what to do. Don't have a speckled-belly goose handy? Substitute a domestic goose.

1 speckled-belly goose, about 4½ pounds	½ teaspoon dried oregano
Kosher salt and freshly ground pepper to taste	½ teaspoon dried basil
	½ teaspoon dried thyme
¾ cup all-purpose flour, plus additional for dusting	4 bay leaves
	2½ quarts cold water
¾ cup vegetable oil	1½ pounds andouille or other smoked sausage, cut in ¼-inch slices
3 medium onions, diced	
7 stalks celery, diced	1 tablespoon filé
4 bell peppers, any color, diced	1 tablespoon hot sauce, or to taste
12 medium cloves garlic, peeled and minced	Boiled Rice (page 252)
Cayenne pepper to taste	3 green onions, in thin slices

CUT the goose into quarters, season liberally with salt and pepper, and dust with flour. Shake off excess flour.

HEAT the oil in a large, heavy, dry pot until it begins to smoke, about 3 minutes. Add the goose and sear the meat about 1 minute on the first side, 2 minutes on the second, until it is golden brown. Remove the goose and set aside.

RETURN the oil to its smoking point. Make a roux by slowly adding the flour, stirring constantly over high heat with a wooden spoon or a whisk until the mixture is the color of milk chocolate, about 3 to 5 minutes. Be careful not to burn it; if black spots appear, you will need to start over.

ADD the onions to the roux, and cook for 1 minute, stirring. Add the celery, and cook for 30 seconds. Add the bell peppers, scraping the bottom of pot, and cook for 1 minute. Add the garlic, cayenne, oregano, basil, thyme, bay leaves, and additional salt and pepper. Slowly add the water, stirring constantly to avoid lumps of roux.

ADD the goose and the sausage, stir, and bring to a boil. Reduce heat, and maintain on a slow simmer, uncovered, for 3½ to 4 hours, skimming frequently to remove any excess fat from the top of the gumbo. When the meat falls off the bones, remove the skin and bones from the pot. Adjust the gumbo to the desired consistency, reducing liquid a bit to thicken it or adding a little water to thin it, if necessary. Return to a boil, and stir in the filé. Stir vigorously to avoid clumping until filé is dissolved. Adjust the salt and pepper, and finish to taste with the hot sauce of your choice. Serve with the rice, and garnish with the green onions.

Duck, rabbit, quail, or pheasant can be substituted for goose. Roux is one of those cooking things that are perfected by feel more than by a recipe. But scraping the side and bottom of the pot while stirring constantly is essential to a good roux.

 CHEF JAMIE'S TIPS

Lagniappe

WINDOW OR AISLE?

Since we've come to love our Speckled-Belly Goose Gumbo so much, we made a batch to serve one night when we were cooking at the James Beard House in New York. When a sous chef, who will go nameless, forgot to pack the gumbo with the rest of the food at Commander's Palace, we had to buy the gumbo a coach airplane ticket to get it there on time.

Chicken Stock

*T*he true test of a serious cook—professional or home—is a crystal-clear, intensely flavorful consommé. You can't get one without a good clear stock, which is at the heart of much of our cooking—from bouillabaisse to Veal Daube Creole. It's easy to make and store, and it can be eaten by the bowlful as is or used as part of another dish.

3 pounds cut-up chicken or chicken bones	3 bay leaves
2 medium onions, diced	1 small bunch parsley stems
4 stalks celery, diced	Pinch of kosher salt
3 medium carrots, diced	½ teaspoon dried thyme
1 head garlic, cloves peeled and left whole	½ teaspoon dried basil
4 quarts cold water	½ teaspoon dried oregano
1 tablespoon whole black peppercorns	

WASH the chicken thoroughly with cold water, place in an 8-quart or larger stockpot, and add the onion, celery, carrots, garlic, and cold water. Bring to a boil, immediately reduce the heat to a slow simmer, and skim away any foam, excess matter that rises to the top, or fat that floats to the top.

ADD the peppercorns, bay leaves, parsley stems, salt, thyme, basil, and oregano. Cook at a slow simmer for 4 to 6 hours, uncovered, periodically skimming away fat and proteins that rise to the top. Do not stir the stock at all. After cooking, strain through a fine-mesh strainer, taking care not to disrupt the stock by mixing or by moving the chicken around. A second straining through cheesecloth will result in an even clearer stock, and chilling will cause any remaining fat to congeal at the top, making it easy to remove.

Keep the liquid from becoming cloudy. Cook the stock at a simmer (not a boil), frequently skim away matter that floats to the top, don't stir while the stock cooks, and do not disturb the mixture while you strain the cooked liquid.

 CHEF JAMIE'S TIPS

Fish or Seafood Stock

MAKES ABOUT 2 QUARTS

"Good stock in the box is like money in the bank," Chef Jamie likes to say. Forget the shortcuts. Stock is a strained liquid that has had meat, fish, or vegetables cooked in it, and good, clear stocks are the foundation of most of our cooking. A good stock gives you flavor without making a soup or sauce unnecessarily heavy. Our Oyster Chowder is a good example of how we use this stock. For home cooking, freeze stock so it's available whenever you need it.

2 pounds fish bones, cut up (they should
    be from non-oily fish; you can also
    use crabs, shrimp heads, or a
    combination)
2 tablespoons olive oil
8 cloves garlic, peeled
1 small onion, diced
1 bunch green onions, sliced
2 stalks celery, diced

2 teaspoons salt
1½ cups white wine
Juice of 1 small lemon
2 quarts cold water
2 teaspoons whole black peppercorns
2 bay leaves
6 parsley stems
2 large sprigs fresh thyme or 1 teaspoon
    dried thyme

RINSE the bones thoroughly, until the water runs clear. Drain and set aside.

COMBINE the olive oil, garlic, diced onion, green onions, celery, and salt in a stockpot over medium heat, and stir. Simmer until the vegetables are softened, about 5 minutes. Add the fish bones and stir, simmering, for 5 minutes. Add the wine and lemon juice, cook for 1 minute, and add the cold water, peppercorns, bay leaves, parsley stems, and thyme.

BRING the mixture almost to a boil, and skim off any impurities. Simmer for about 20 minutes, turn off the heat, and let sit for 10 more minutes.

STRAIN the stock through a cheesecloth-lined sieve set over a container that fits well. Ladle the stock from the pot. Do not pour it and do not disturb the solid ingredients or you risk allowing impurities into the finished stock that can cloud the liquid.

CHEF JAMIE'S TIPS This stock is a great way to utilize leftover fish trimmings, or almost any other seafood.

    Use fresh seafood that has a sweet smell to it. Don't use frozen shrimp shells that have been boxed, as they tend to have a lot of preservatives on them.

    Once the water is added, do not stir the stock. By letting the stock rest, all the impurities will sink to the bottom. Stock should be chilled immediately. It can be refrigerated for a few days or frozen for a few months.

*G*ood cooks make good stocks. There are no shortcuts and there is no good substitute. As with all stocks, you can make this one in large quantities and freeze the extra for a few months until you need it. We use our veal stock in many veal dishes, such as our Veal Chop Tchoupitoulas, and elsewhere, such as in our famous Turtle Soup.

5 pounds veal bones, in 3-inch pieces	6 quarts cold water
2 medium onions, peeled and diced	2 teaspoons dried rosemary
4 stalks celery, diced	2 teaspoons dried thyme
3 medium carrots, diced	2 teaspoons dried oregano
2 large tomatoes, diced	4 bay leaves
2 heads garlic, cloves separated and peeled	1 tablespoon whole black peppercorns

PREHEAT the oven to 425°F.

RINSE the bones in cold water, place them in a large roasting pan, and roast them until they're golden brown, approximately 40 minutes, stirring occasionally. Using tongs, remove the bones from the pan and transfer them to an 8-quart or larger stockpot.

LEAVE any rendered fat in the roasting pan, and add the onions, celery, carrots, tomatoes, and garlic. Return the pan to the oven, and roast, stirring occasionally, until the vegetables are caramelized, approximately 55 minutes.

MEANWHILE, cover the bones in the stockpot with the water and bring to a boil. Skim any excess foam from the top, reduce the heat to a simmer, and cook for 3 hours, being careful not to let the mixture boil. Continue to periodically skim fat and foam.

ADD the roasted vegetables to the stockpot. Discard any fat from the roasting pan and deglaze with about 1 cup of cold water by bringing it to a boil while scraping all the browned bits from the bottom of the pan. Add this to the stockpot along with the rosemary, thyme, oregano, bay leaves, and peppercorns, and simmer for 3 more hours.

USING a ladle, strain the stock through cheesecloth or a fine sieve, being careful not to stir the stock. Cool and refrigerate. Excess fat can be removed from the top after it has congealed.

Gumbos, Soups, and Stews

Lagniappe

BREAKING BREAD

A friend of the family, a Northern lady who has been around the track a few times, recalls the first time she sat down to a meal with my mother, Ella Brennan: "She gripped the bread at one end and extended it to me, asking, 'Will you break bread with me?' It was the first time I had literally been invited to 'break bread,' and I was utterly charmed." Just a little touch of the hospitality that's in our bones.

4

SALADS

 remember riding home from high school one day and, much to my surprise, hearing a popular local radio commentator interviewing my mother. I don't recall the original purpose of the interview, but somehow they had wandered into a conversation about Commander's Onion-Crusted Fried Chicken Salad. This commentator could not fathom fried chicken in a salad. To him, it was an oxymoron. To him, salads were what ladies on diets ate.

He was pushy in trying to make his point, and Mom graciously but steadfastly tried to educate him about the beauty of salad for salad's sake—

that although people certainly ate salads for health reasons, salads should have their own distinction and not be thought of as second-class citizens.

Explaining to him the drama and goodness of onion-crusted fried chicken pieces with Bibb lettuce, homemade blue cheese dressing, and roasted peppers seemed a tremendous waste of time. But Mom was relentless and won him over in the end.

We'll just let him miss out on the crispy Soft-Shell Crab Salad and my family's favorite, Miss Claire's Marinated Crab Salad.

What we serve as a tuna salad today has no resemblance to what I took to school for lunch. Seared rare tuna salad—our version here is called Sesame Pepper-Crusted Tuna Salad (page 82)—explodes with freshness and flavor. The hearty tuna stands up well to the pepper, crunchy greens, and anchovy dressing. When we occasionally get blue-fin tuna, we fight for the day-after scraps for one of these salads. This is a salad serious enough that you can drink a red wine with it.

Or try Pulled Chicken and Ginger Pasta Salad (page 96). Even something as simple as chicken salad—we try to improve it. Chef Jamie has done it. The chicken is rubbed with minced garlic and spices, wrapped in plastic wrap, then wrapped again in aluminum foil to keep all the flavor in. Then we boil the chicken and pull the meat from the bones. People say, "I've never tasted chicken like this. It's so moist, so much flavor." When Jamie first did this one, Lally and I ate it every day for about a month. No kidding. As we do with everything else at Commander's, we examined something as basic as chicken with a microscope and asked ourselves how we could make it better.

Both these salads represent what we're trying to do with Commander's Haute Creole today: intensifying flavors, locking them in, magnifying them. We want your eyes to roll back in your head reeling with the pleasure of that first bite.

Show off your salads best by serving them on chilled plates, with hand-torn lettuce, the freshest greens, and the appropriate dressing—and toss it just before serving.

*O*ften, simple is best. Foods like Creole tomatoes and Vidalia onions have real short seasons, so when they're at their peak (June, July, and August in Louisiana), go for it. We love our Creole tomatoes so much that when they finally arrive we often just slice them, add a touch of salt and pepper, and drizzle a balsamic vinaigrette over them.

³/₄ cup balsamic vinegar

1 cup fresh basil leaves, cleaned

³/₄ cup extra-virgin olive oil

Kosher salt and freshly ground pepper to taste

4 large Creole or vine-ripened tomatoes

1 medium bunch watercress or arugula

1 large sweet onion, such as Vidalia, peeled and thinly sliced

2 ounces hard cheese, such as aged goat cheese or Parmesan

IN A SMALL saucepan over medium to low heat, bring the balsamic vinegar to a simmer and cook until it is reduced to one-third its original volume, the bubbles seem smaller, and it is thick enough to coat the back of a spoon. Let cool.

PLACE the basil and oil in a food processor and purée. After about 1 minute, scrape the sides of the workbowl with a rubber spatula and run the machine again. Season the purée with salt and pepper, remove, strain through a fine sieve if desired, and set aside.

SLICE the tomatoes about 1 inch thick. Season the greens, onion, and tomatoes with salt and pepper, and divide among 4 plates. Grate some cheese over each salad. Drizzle a portion of the vinegar, then the basil oil on each salad.

CHEF JAMIE'S TIPS

Tomatoes should be only vine-ripened and always at room temperature. Sea salt goes best with tomatoes because its fine grain penetrates fast and reacts with the acids, making the tomato taste sweeter.

A balsamic vinegar reduction depends on the quality and age of the vinegar. Experiment with different brands. A longer-aged vinegar results in more residual sugar and thus will not need to be reduced as much as others.

Restaurant trick: I like using squeeze bottles for this dish. It's so much easier to drizzle using squeeze bottles individually filled with the reduced vinegar and basil oil.

Apple, Watercress, and Stilton Salad

MAKES 8 SERVINGS

*T*his elegant winter salad makes a wonderfully light first course before a heartier winter entrée such as lamb or osso buco or as Ella and Dottie Brennan usually serve it, as part of a holiday meal. The dressing is lightened with roasted and puréed apple and onion, and it's finished with a reduction of balsamic vinegar, which should be prepared in advance.

2 cups balsamic vinegar

3 flawless apples, any variety

5 cloves garlic, peeled and coarsely chopped

1 medium red onion, cut in half top to bottom and thinly sliced

1/2 cup olive oil

Kosher salt and freshly ground pepper to taste

1/4 cup apple brandy

1 cup large walnut pieces

3 bunches watercress, stems removed at base, cleaned, and spun dry

1 cup crumbled Stilton cheese

REDUCE the vinegar ahead of time, if desired: Bring it to a boil in a small saucepan and cook over medium-high heat until it is reduced in volume to about 1/3 cup, the bubbles seem smaller, and the liquid thickens. Be careful not to burn it. Pour the reduction into a small container and refrigerate until needed.

PREHEAT the oven to 400°F.

CORE, seed, and thinly slice one of the apples and place in a small roasting pan. Add the garlic, half the onion, 2 tablespoons of the olive oil, and the salt and pepper and toss to coat with the oil. Bake for 25 to 30 minutes, or until the mixture is brown and tender. Remove from the oven and pour the brandy into the pan, scraping up any glaze that might be clinging to the bottom. Purée the mixture in a blender or food processor, slowly drizzle in the remaining oil, scrape the bowl, and blend the dressing for a few more seconds.

REDUCE the oven heat to 350°F. Spread the walnut pieces out on a small baking pan and roast for about 15 minutes, taking care not to burn them.

CORE, seed, and thinly slice the remaining 2 apples. Toss the watercress, the remaining onion, and the apples with the dressing in a large bowl. Adjust the salt and pepper if necessary. Divide the salad among 8 plates and sprinkle an equal amount of cheese and walnuts over each. Drizzle some of the chilled vinegar around the edge of each plate and on top of the salad.

Balsamic vinegar varies greatly from brand to brand. A good balsamic vinegar has a dark brown color and is made from 100 percent trebbiano grapes that have been aged a minimum of 12 years in 5 barrels, each of a different wood. The better (and more expensive) the vinegar, the thicker it will be to begin with and the less you will need to reduce it. As the vinegar cools, it will become a lot thicker. When it's at its reduced stage, it's very easy to burn because the sugars are condensed.

When buying watercress, look for dark green leaves. Watercress will turn yellow in just one day if it's not stored properly, so keep ice on it if necessary. When cleaning watercress, cut off the stems below the point where they are tied. And clean it thoroughly because insects love watercress.

Fried Oyster Salad

At Commander's, the salads that our customers order the most have something fried on them. Fried oysters, fried chicken, fried crawfish. Go figure. The message is pretty clear to me: People here eat salads because they like them and they taste great, not because they think they're low-cal or "good for you." This one is Chef Jamie's favorite. The Anchovy-Garlic Dressing is salty and tangy, and romaine lettuce is sturdy enough to hold the dressing well. But the best part is the hot, plump, lightly fried oysters on the cold crisp lettuce.

1 large head romaine lettuce

8 cups vegetable oil, for frying

1 cup all-purpose flour

1 cup cornmeal, any color

1 cup masa flour

1/4 cup Creole Seafood Seasoning (page 294) or other Creole seasoning, plus extra for the oysters

2 pints shucked oysters in their liquor

1 1/2 cups croutons

1 red onion, cored and thinly sliced top to bottom (or julienned)

1 recipe Anchovy-Garlic Dressing (page 95)

Kosher salt and freshly ground pepper to taste

1 cup grated Parmesan cheese

3 roasted peppers (store-bought or see page 306) or pimientos, sliced

TEAR the lettuce leaves into bite-size pieces, discarding any large stems and the core. Wash thoroughly and spin dry or let drain in a cool area.

HEAT the oil in a 6-quart or larger pot until it reads 325°F to 350°F on a deep-fry thermometer.

IN A LARGE BOWL, thoroughly mix the flour, cornmeal, masa, and seasoning. Dredge each oyster in this mixture, letting the oyster liquor act as an adhesive. Shake off excess coating. Fry the oysters in small batches to keep them from sticking together and to prevent the oil temperature from falling too much. Cook the oysters for about 45 to 60 seconds, until the edges curl and they are crisp and brown. Remove the oysters from the oil, drain them on a cloth towel, and season immediately with additional seafood seasoning.

PLACE the lettuce, croutons, onions, and anchovy-garlic dressing in a large bowl, and adjust salt and pepper if necessary. Toss to blend all ingredients, then divide among 6 plates. Sprinkle each serving with Parmesan cheese, place slices of roasted pepper on top, and arrange the oysters around the greens. Serve immediately.

Although romaine is my lettuce of choice here, other crisp lettuces can be substituted, but I recommend a crisp head.

Oysters are usually sold by the pint. You will need 5 to 6 ounces per serving. Be sure the oil is hot enough so the oysters cook without absorbing oil, yet not so hot that the oysters burn. Work fast so you can serve the oysters quickly after they're cooked.

 CHEF JAMIE'S TIPS

Sesame Pepper-Crusted Tuna Salad

MAKES 6 ENTRÉE SALADS

This is a refreshing seafood salad. The ingredients are common enough—romaine lettuce, anchovy dressing, olives, a slice of focaccia, and fresh tuna—but the tuna, seared in a honey pepper sesame crust, shows off best when it's rare, while the searing gives an added texture contrast that makes this salad as addictive as sushi. Dottie Brennan is nuts for this salad. My brother, Alex Brennan-Martin, and Chef Carl Walker serve a glorious version of this dish at Brennan's of Houston. But since they were both weaned at Commander's Palace, we figured we could steal it. Thanks, guys!

2½ to 3 pounds tuna loin, in one piece
¼ cup honey
¼ cup sesame seeds
Kosher salt and fresh pepper, coarsely ground, to taste
¼ cup olive oil
6 slices dense whole-grain bread
24 anchovy fillets (about ¼ cup)
8 cloves garlic, peeled and minced

2 tablespoons red wine vinegar
3 medium heads romaine lettuce, cleaned, with large stems removed and leaves cut bite-size
1 large red onion, cut in half, thinly sliced
1 cup olives, cut in half and pitted
2 roasted peppers, thinly sliced (store-bought or page 306)
1 cup crumbled feta cheese

PLACE the tuna on a sheet pan, brush all over with the honey, sprinkle evenly on all sides with the sesame seeds, and season all sides with salt and pepper. Be sparing with the salt, because the other ingredients in this dish are naturally salty, and be generous with the pepper, which is the main ingredient in the crust.

PREHEAT a large cast-iron skillet over high heat for about 4 minutes. Put half the olive oil into the pan, and sear the tuna for about 1½ minutes, or until crisp and dark on one side. Turn the tuna with a spatula, and sear remaining sides for 1 to 1½ minutes each. Remove the fish, taking care not to tear the crust. It's okay if some tuna sticks to the pan. Refrigerate.

GRILL the bread in the same hot pan for 1½ to 2 minutes per side, or until it is crisp and well toasted. Set the bread aside.

TO MAKE the dressing, place the anchovies in a mixing bowl, add the garlic, and mash with a fork until a light paste has formed. Whisk the remaining olive oil and the vinegar into the paste until all ingredients are well incorporated.

REMOVE the tuna from the refrigerator and, with a very sharp knife, slice it as thin as possible. Combine the lettuce, onion, olives, peppers, and cheese in a large bowl and toss with the anchovy dressing.

PORTION an even amount of salad on each of 6 plates, and arrange an even amount of tuna on each salad. Serve with the grilled bread.

When selecting tuna, pick a loin with a deep red color. This dish works best if you **CHEF JAMIE'S TIPS**
use a piece about 6 inches off the tail, or a smaller loin. It will be easier to slice and
will cook evenly. Serve the meat rare, unless that's not to the liking of you or your
guests. If so, cook to desired temperature.

Be careful when you adjust the seasoning, because the feta, olives, and anchovies are
all salty. Use coarse pepper for the outside crust of the tuna.

Lagniappe

SEASONING COOKWARE

Believe it or not, we buy our cast-iron cookware in hardware stores. These skillets and pots need to be "seasoned" before they can be used for cooking. First, rub the skillet or pot (and any lid) inside and out with canola or vegetable oil. Then heat the oiled skillet or pot in the oven to get it very hot, remove from the oven and wipe off the oil, and let it cool. When you're using a cast-iron pan and some of the food sticks, here's a good way to solve the problem: Heat the pan on the stovetop, rub in some coarse salt with a towel as if you were using sandpaper, wipe the salt out, and let the pan cool. Coat the pan with a thin layer of oil, reheat it until the oil smokes, wipe the pan out, and let it cool again. Never wash the pan with soap and water or scour it with steel wool. Store your pans in a dry area.

*T*his salad holds my most powerful childhood taste memory. I spent the better part of most summers on the Mississippi Gulf Coast fishing, crabbing, swimming, water skiing, and generally wreaking havoc with a most wonderful gaggle of cousins, aunts, and uncles. One day, we caught so many crabs that my Aunt Claire convinced us to help her crack crabs so she could make a marinated crab salad. My mouth waters just thinking about it. This is a mess to eat, but it's well worth it. Frequent finger-licking is encouraged.

1 tablespoon garlic salt

2 heads garlic, cloves peeled and minced

1 tablespoon dried oregano

1 tablespoon dried parsley

1 tablespoon dried thyme

1 tablespoon dried sweet basil

1 cup extra-virgin olive oil

1½ cups vinegar (cane, cider, sherry, or red wine)

2 medium onions, thinly sliced

Kosher salt and freshly ground pepper to taste

12 boiled crabs (buy them cooked, or follow recipe on page 129)

1 pound new potatoes or other small potatoes, boiled, cooled, and sliced

4 Creole or vine-ripened tomatoes, at room temperature, seasoned and sliced

MAKE the marinade in a very large mixing bowl by whisking together the garlic salt, minced garlic, oregano, parsley, thyme, and basil. While mixing, add the olive oil and vinegar. Add the onion slices, and taste, seasoning with salt and pepper if necessary.

CLEAN the crabs by taking off their tops and removing the gills, which surround the cavity that contains the meat. Break the crabs in half, and rinse away any debris. Discard the legs, remove and crack the claws, and add the cracked crab, still in its inner shell, to the marinade.

ADD the sliced potatoes, toss all the ingredients together, and marinate overnight in the refrigerator. Serve over tomato slices. At the table, each diner should pick the crabmeat out of the shells.

Use any variety of crab, although the marinating time may vary with the crab variety. Removing the legs and cracking the claws helps the marinade penetrate into the meat. If you're boiling your own crabs, cook the potatoes in the same water.

 CHEF JAMIE'S TIPS

Fried Catfish and Vinaigrette Coleslaw Salad

MAKES 6 ENTRÉE SALADS

*I*f you can ever find your way to Manchac, Louisiana, and Middendorf's Restaurant, you will have, bar none, the greatest catfish of your life. So we do it the way they do it. The goal is fresh, thin catfish fillets that are never overfried or greasy. We're all big catfish fans—particularly catfish from Des Allemandes, Louisiana, and this is our favorite version. Top it with a tartar sauce and have some vinaigrette coleslaw on the side. The vinegar in the slaw cuts the fat of the fish and tartar sauce.

2 pounds catfish fillets

1 cup buttermilk

1 tablespoon hot sauce, or to taste

3 cups cornmeal, any color

2 cups all-purpose flour

$1/4$ cup Creole Seafood Seasoning (page 294) or any Creole seasoning mix, or to taste

2 to 3 quarts canola or corn oil, for frying

$1/2$ cup Creole Tartar Sauce (page 298)

Coleslaw:

2 pounds cabbage (about half a medium head), sliced paper-thin

1 medium red onion, sliced paper-thin

1 teaspoon celery salt

$1/2$ cup cane, malt, cider, or rice wine vinegar

Kosher salt and freshly ground pepper to taste

TRIM any bones that might still be in the fillets. With a sharp knife, slice the fish on the bias, almost horizontally, as you would slice smoked salmon. It's most essential that the slices be thin—no more than $1/4$ inch thick—and they'll be made thinner as you prepare the pieces. Each piece should weigh about 1 ounce. In a bowl, thoroughly combine the buttermilk and hot sauce, add the fish pieces, stir, and refrigerate for about 2 hours.

MAKE the slaw by combining the cabbage and onion slices, celery salt, vinegar, salt, and pepper in a bowl. Mix well and refrigerate for $1^1/2$ to 2 hours, depending on how thinly the cabbage is sliced. The slaw should be slightly crisp but tender to the bite.

MIX the cornmeal, flour, and seasoning, remove the marinating fish from the refrigerator, and, piece by piece, bread the fish. Here's the best way: Place the bowl with the fish next to the cornmeal mixture and a sheet tray. Pull a piece of fish from the marinade, let any excess milk drip off, and place the fish in the dry mixture, generously coating both sides. With the palm of your hand, flatten the fish fillet into the cornmeal mixture, making the fish piece larger but thinner. Turn the fish piece and repeat. You want to flatten and make the fish as thin as possible without breaking it into pieces. Shake off any excess coating and place the coated fish piece on the sheet pan. Repeat until all fish has been breaded. If the tray fills before you're done, start a second layer, but cover the first layer with plastic wrap or parchment paper to keep the pieces from sticking together.

HEAT the oil to 350°F in a pot large enough so that the oil comes only halfway up. When the oil is ready, fry 8 pieces in a batch, lowering them one at a time into the oil with a slotted spoon. Keep using the slotted spoon to keep the fish from sticking together. Fry for about $1\frac{1}{2}$ minutes, turning and frying until golden brown and crisp. When the fish has curled, especially on its edges, cook for about 30 to 60 seconds more. Remove and set on paper towels to drain. Season with additional Creole seasoning to taste. Fry the remaining fish pieces, eight at a time.

DIVIDE the slaw in the centers of six serving plates, place catfish pieces around the slaw, and spoon the tartar sauce on the fish.

When buying the catfish, look for medium-size fillets, about 6 to 8 ounces each. I prefer wild catfish, but farm-raised is fine.

The goal here is to end up with a curly, crunchy, evenly fried piece of fish. Thin pieces of fish and proper breading procedure help. I prefer the neutral flavors and high smoking points of canola oil or corn oil for frying.

When making the slaw, slice the ingredients as thin as possible. A mandoline, available in kitchenware shops, does the job perfectly.

 CHEF JAMIE'S TIPS

Soft-Shell Crab Salad with Tomato and Sweet Onion

MAKES 4 SERVINGS

*A*mericans are relearning how to eat seasonally. That means getting only ingredients that are fresh and available now—and forgoing canned or frozen versions when they give you only a tasteless food. Louisiana was almost lulled into that nonsense, yet so many of the foods we love most are simply not available year round. Face it: You can't freeze or can a soft-shell crab. But there's a great deal of fun and anticipation involved in eating seasonally. We wait all year for soft-shell season. In this recipe, Jamie explains how to get the legs to stand up straight for a dramatic presentation. The trick is gravity. Let the legs hang in the oil while you fry them.

4 medium to large soft-shell crabs
Creole Seafood Seasoning (page 294) or
    any Creole seasoning mix, to taste
2 cups all-purpose flour, for dredging crabs
3 medium eggs
1 cup milk
1½ cups fine bread crumbs
2 quarts canola oil, for frying

4 large Creole or vine-ripened tomatoes,
    in ½-inch slices
½ large sweet onion, in very thin slices
4 ounces salad greens, cleaned
Kosher salt and freshly ground black
    pepper to taste
1 cup Commander's Ravigote Sauce
    (page 297)

IF YOUR fishmonger will clean the crabs for you, go for it. Otherwise, clean the crab by pulling back the top shell from the point to the center of the crab and removing the gills (the brownish fibrous layer that rests on top of the inner shell). If the top shell has an air sack in the point, gently break it with a finger. Pull off the eyes and mouth. Turn crab over and pull off the apron and intestinal vein, which is in the center of the crab bottom.

IN A BOWL, combine about 1 tablespoon of Creole seasoning and the flour. In a separate bowl, whisk the eggs, milk, and 1 tablespoon of Creole seasoning. In a third bowl, mix the bread crumbs and another 1 tablespoon of Creole seasoning.

PLACE the oil in a large, deep, heavy pan and heat it to 325°F. While the oil is heating, arrange the tomatoes, onion slices, and greens on four large plates, and season with salt and pepper.

LIGHTLY dust the crab with flour, evenly coating the legs, tops and bottoms, and the point where the legs meet the body.

PLACE a crab in the egg wash, remove, and let the excess run back into the bowl. Make sure that the crab is completely coated. Place in the bowl with the bread crumbs, and coat evenly, shaking off any excess crumbs. Repeat with the remaining crabs.

USING tongs, hold a crab into the heated oil with only its legs submerged, and cook for about 30 seconds. Then use the tongs to flip the crab over, allowing the crab to float to the top, possibly with part of the legs sticking up. Cook for about 3 minutes, or until golden brown. Place the cooked crab on paper towels to allow any excess oil to drain, then season with Creole seasoning. Repeat with remaining crabs.

PLACE a cooked crab on top of each salad, and top each with about $1/4$ cup of ravigote sauce. Serve immediately.

CHEF JAMIE'S TIPS

A good reason not to remove the face of the crab with scissors is that scissors can make a hole so large that it and the air sack may fill with oil, leading to a dangerous situation during the cooking process. The air sack can explode during cooking if not broken.

Be careful with hot oil. The safest way to fry is to use a large vessel with plenty of extra room, and to use a thermometer rather than to guess the oil temperature.

One variation we use a lot is to stuff the crabs with our crabcake mixture (page 196) and then fry the crabs. We've also been known to add a shrimp in the cavity.

We serve the crab immediately (it's okay for friends and close relatives to wait while others eat).

I like to use a pungent green tossed with a little oil and vinegar for the salad portion.

SOFT-SHELL CRABS

Soft-shell crabs are a national favorite, and Commander's customers love them, too. They're available only when the weather is warm, which could be into November in New Orleans. But they can be hard to come by. The crab has to be caught just after it has molted its shell but before another crab eats it. One of our suppliers has set up a lamp system behind his house to help Mother Nature along. It means that he and his wife have to check the crabs and rotate them a few times during the night, but if you love soft-shells enough, it's worth the effort.

RÉMOULADE SAUCE

Here's my favorite description of rémoulade: "Good rémoulade sauce, a Creole cook will tell you, is supposed to make you think you look better and younger than you ever have—and if you think you look that way," she will add, "then you will look that way." That's Peter Feibleman, writing in the sadly out-of-print Time-Life book American Cooking: Creole and Acadian.

Rémoulade is such a New Orleans favorite that there are even a restaurant and a television news segment named Rémoulade. And now you have our recipe, too.

*J*ust the sight of some dishes gets your mouth watering. So it is for me with perfectly boiled shrimp coated in a red-orange Rémoulade Sauce. As a youngster, Chef Jamie would devour shrimp cocktail anytime he ate in a restaurant. Shrimp Rémoulade is such a New Orleans favorite that Jamie naturally fell in love with it when he moved to New Orleans. At Commander's, the sauce is very acidic, so slightly undercook your shrimp because the sauce will continue cooking them a little. Miss Ella, as many in the restaurant refer to my mother, says shrimp should never be chilled but should be eaten as soon as possible after boiling.

1/2 cup white vinegar

1/4 cup ketchup

1/4 cup prepared horseradish

1/4 cup Creole mustard

1/4 cup yellow mustard

2 tablespoons paprika (avoid very spicy varieties)

1 teaspoon cayenne, or to taste

6 cloves garlic, peeled

1 tablespoon hot sauce, or to taste

2 tablespoons Worcestershire sauce

6 green onions

3 stalks celery, chopped

3 medium eggs

1 1/2 cups vegetable oil

Kosher salt and freshly ground pepper to taste

COMBINE the vinegar, ketchup, horseradish, mustards, paprika, cayenne, garlic, hot sauce, Worcestershire, green onions, celery, and eggs in a blender or food processor. Process on high speed until smooth. While blending, add the oil in a slow, steady stream until the mixture is thick. Adjust the salt and pepper, and refrigerate. It should keep for at least two weeks, perhaps as long as a month.

SHRIMP is its best partner, but it also goes well with greens and tomato dishes, or all of them together as an entrée or appetizer salad. Try it, too, as a dipping sauce for hors d'oeuvres.

Onion-Crusted Fried Chicken Salad

MAKES 4 ENTRÉE SALADS

Chef Jamie says he has been threatened not to take this dish off the menu. He won't. At about 2:30 P.M., when we haven't eaten all day and we have another 8 hours to go, this is a very satisfying entrée salad with lots of flavor, and it makes a great meal of the day for family and managers. The customers like it, too! The chicken pieces are actually fried with bits of onion in the batter, so on your plate it looks like little fried onion rings are on your chicken. Serve this with sliced onion, Bibb lettuce, and Blue Cheese Dressing.

6 medium chicken breast halves, boneless and skinless

Kosher salt and freshly ground pepper to taste

1 cup buttermilk

1½ medium onions, 1 cut in very small dice, ½ sliced very thin

¼ cup cane, cider, or malt vinegar

2 medium cucumbers, peeled, seeded, and sliced ¼ inch thick

¼ teaspoon crushed red pepper flakes

3 cups all-purpose flour

3 cups vegetable shortening, canola oil, or corn oil, for frying

2 small heads Bibb or Boston lettuce, trimmed, washed, halved, and cored

⅔ cup Blue Cheese Dressing (page 94)

2 roasted red peppers, store-bought or homemade (page 306), sliced

¼ pound blue cheese, crumbled

REMOVE the tenderloin strips from each chicken breast half, and cut each breast half into three long strips. Place the chicken pieces in a large bowl, season with salt and pepper, add the buttermilk, stir, and refrigerate for an hour or two.

PLACE the onion slices, vinegar, cucumbers, pepper flakes, and additional salt and pepper in a small bowl. Toss to combine, and set aside for the cucumbers to marinate.

PLACE the flour, diced onion, and some salt and pepper in a large bowl, and mix with your hands just enough to coat the onion with flour, but don't allow the onions to stick together.

NOW coat the marinated chicken. Take a piece at a time with one hand, shake off excess liquid, and place it in the flour mixture. With your other hand, press the chicken with your knuckles so the onion adheres, then flatten out the chicken. Shake off excess, and repeat with remaining chicken.

IN A LARGE, heavy pot, heat the shortening or oil to 350°F on a deep-fry thermometer. Gently place about 8 strips of chicken in the pot, and cook for 3 to 4 minutes, or until the bottom starts to brown. Turn the chicken over, and cook until the pieces are golden brown and begin to float, another 2 to 3 minutes. Transfer the cooked chicken to a rack that has a sheet pan as an underliner. Repeat until all the chicken is fried.

SERVE with marinated cucumber at the bottom of each plate, some lettuce in the center, and 3 pieces of chicken on each side of the lettuce. Drizzle blue cheese dressing on top of each salad, place some roasted pepper strips on top, and sprinkle with the crumbled blue cheese.

Chicken breasts vary in size, so you may need to adjust the cooking time.

Some Bibb and Boston heads are big, so two heads is only an approximation. You can also substitute hearts of romaine.

A couple wedges of tomato, when they're in season, make a nice addition.

 CHEF JAMIE'S TIPS

Blue Cheese Dressing

MAKES 2⅓ CUPS

*W*e use this dressing with our Onion-Crusted Fried Chicken Salad, but it's great, too, as a dip with pieces of fried chicken, vegetables, or, best of all, with fried frogs' legs. It's a real thick dressing that gets even thicker when chilled.

½ pound good-quality blue cheese
½ medium onion, coarsely chopped
Kosher salt and plenty of freshly ground pepper to taste
¼ cup cane, cider, or malt vinegar

Juice of 1 small lemon
¼ teaspoon hot sauce, or to taste
1 tablespoon Worcestershire sauce
1 cup olive oil

PLACE half the cheese, the chopped onion, salt, pepper, vinegar, lemon juice, hot sauce, and Worcestershire in the workbowl of a food processor. Purée until well blended and liquefied. Slowly drizzle the olive oil into the mixture; then turn off the machine. Crumble in the remaining cheese, and pulse until well blended. There should be lots of small cheese chunks remaining in the dressing. Adjust seasoning. Refrigerate for up to two weeks.

CHEF JAMIE'S TIPS

Use a high-quality, aged blue cheese, but remember that the cheese may be salty, so be careful with added salt. But pepper's another story. Add lots of freshly ground pepper.

Cocktails: Florida Margarita, Cosmopolitan, Sazerac, Plantation Porch Punch, Mint Julip, Brandy Milk Punch

Crab and Corn Johnny Cakes with Caviar

Roasted Gulf Oysters with Artichokes

Whole Baked Fish with Oysters and Shrimp

*T*his is Commander's version of Caesar dressing, something like Caesar but more garlicky. We love it—not only as a salad dressing but as a vegetable dip and on Po' Boys.

2 tablespoons packed anchovy fillets
    (about 12)

12 cloves garlic, peeled

1 medium egg (optional)

¼ medium onion, coarsely chopped

½ cup grated Parmesan cheese

1½ teaspoons coarsely ground black
    pepper

2 tablespoons red wine vinegar

½ cup plus 2 tablespoons olive oil

Kosher salt and additional freshly ground
    pepper to taste

PLACE the anchovies, garlic, egg, onion, cheese, pepper, and vinegar in the workbowl of a food processor. Run the machine and slowly drizzle in the olive oil until all ingredients are fully blended. Taste the dressing, and adjust salt and pepper, if necessary.

This is a very pungent dressing. Personally, I like even more anchovy, but try it this way and add more or less as you prefer.

 CHEF JAMIE'S TIPS

Pulled Chicken and Ginger Pasta Salad

MAKES 8 ENTRÉE SALADS

The chicken in this recipe is rubbed, then boiled, then pulled. It's tightly wrapped with plastic wrap, wrapped again with aluminum foil, then boiled. The secret is keeping the flavor in the chicken, not in the water, and this chicken stays moist and flavorful. This is a light dish with serious flavor that's a lunchtime winner with our regulars.

1 whole chicken, 3½ to 4 pounds

2 to 3 ounces fresh gingerroot (2 medium-size pieces), peeled and chopped

6 cloves garlic, peeled

Kosher salt and freshly ground pepper to taste

¼ cup sesame oil, or oil of your choice

¼ cup soy sauce, any kind

1 cup dry-roasted peanuts

1 tablespoon honey or peanut butter

12 ounces rotini pasta, cooked according to package instructions

1 pineapple, peeled, cored, and cut in large dice

5 ounces mixed baby greens, cleaned and spun dry

3 ounces mung bean sprouts or alfalfa sprouts

1 small onion, cut in half and thinly sliced

BRING about 6 quarts of water to a boil in a large pot.

REMOVE the chicken from its package, save the giblets for another use, rinse the chicken with cold water inside and out, and dry it with paper towels.

MINCE the ginger and garlic in a food processor, remove half the purée, and rub it over all surfaces of the chicken, inside and out. Season the bird generously with salt and pepper.

PLACE several large pieces of plastic wrap on a work surface and wrap the chicken tightly, twice. Place the wrapped chicken on a sheet of aluminum foil, and wrap the chicken tightly again, totally covering the plastic wrap. The idea is to contain the juices until the chicken is cooked.

SUBMERGE the wrapped bird in the boiling water, cover, and return to a boil. Simmer for 1¼ to 1½ hours, or until the chicken reaches an internal temperature of 165°F. If you need to use a meat thermometer to judge doneness, you'll have to puncture the wrapping in one spot. If the chicken is not completely submerged, turn it over after 1 hour. Remove the chicken and place it in an ice bath.

WHILE the chicken is cooking, run the food processor, which already contains the remaining ginger-garlic purée, drizzle the oil and soy sauce into the workbowl, and continue running until emulsified. Add half the peanuts and the honey. Adjust the salt and pepper, keeping in mind that soy tends to be salty. Remove and refrigerate the mixture. You should have about 1 cup.

WHEN the chicken is completely cooled, remove the foil and plastic wrap over a large bowl, saving any broth that might drip. Peel off and discard all the skin. Remove all the meat from the bones, place it in a bowl, and tear the meat into bite-size pieces.

ADD the pasta and the reserved soy dressing. Just before serving, add the pineapple, greens, sprouts, onion, and remaining peanuts. Toss and adjust seasoning to taste.

Peeling fresh ginger works best when you scrape the ginger with the edge of a spoon. Ginger is strong for some palates, so use it judiciously. If you have a favorite dressing, go ahead and use it in place of the one in this recipe.

 CHEF JAMIE'S TIPS

Lagniappe

JAZZ BRUNCH

Looking back, it seemed all too obvious, combining New Orleans' two greatest contributions, food and jazz. The concept of our Jazz Brunch started at Commander's Palace when the family was looking for a way to put a kick into weekend brunches. Dick was on a trip to London when the idea struck him. He called Ella in New Orleans and said that he had an idea. "You're calling me from England? I guess it's a good one." Now it seems strange to even imagine life before Jazz Brunch. Every Saturday and Sunday, bright-colored balloons float above every table while Joe Simon's jazz trio strolls from room to room playing "Do You Know What It Means to Miss New Orleans?" and every jazz great you can fathom. They sing, and a lot of "second lining" goes on. In New Orleans, the "second line" is a little strut you do when you fall "second in line" behind passing bands and parades. Most every weekend, a spontaneous second line breaks out all over Commander's. All the better to sip your milk punch and watch all the "carrying on."

BRUNCH

admit it. Brunch and eggs are my absolute favorites. I *love*

brunch at Commander's Palace. We're open for 14 meals a week at Com-

mander's, but brunch gets its own special menu. The atmosphere crackles

with celebration—of birthdays, of graduations, but most of all, of the New

Orleans good life. And the roving jazz band makes it even more festive.

But as some political types might say, "It's the food, stupid." For

me, the past and the present of Creole cooking come together in glorious

bloom at a Commander's Palace brunch. It could be the simple elegance of

Eggs Sardou, the racy spirit of Eggs Louis Armstrong, the soul-comforting tastes of Eggs Jeannette, the charm of Truffled Scrambled Eggs, or the Granola Parfait of homemade granola, sweetened Creole Cream Cheese, and fresh fruit.

The New Orleans Sunday brunch is thought to have its origins in the nineteenth century, when some enterprising businesses near the French Market began offering midmorning meals to the merchants, fishermen, and the like who would bring their goods to the market by 4 A.M. And because nearly everyone in New Orleans was Catholic and could eat nothing after midnight if they were to take communion later Sunday morning, the tradition evolved to feed luxurious Creole feasts to families leaving church, folks who were nicely dressed with time to relax.

Today, brunch at Commander's Palace is a rollicking affair with some of the best jazz musicians in New Orleans (led by our dear friend Joe Simon) roving from room to room singing "Oh When the Saints," "Bacon Street Blues," and "What a Wonderful World." Everywhere are balloons, kids in their dress-up clothes wanting to meet the turtle they are about to eat, plump poached eggs, and lights being dimmed so a captain can show off the blue-orange flame dripping down his clove-studded orange peel over a hot café brûlot.

Why don't we eat like this all week? Well, we don't, so short of demanding the rights of breakfast lovers everywhere, I wait and wait and then savor my brunches. I'd love to think that part of me was there when my mom was poring over old cookbooks to research the gustatory history of eggs and breakfast. That's how the original "Breakfast at Brennan's" got started, and what a monumental moment in New Orleans' and America's cooking history *that* turned out to be. Mom wanted to dazzle her customers. Between the divinely decadent eye-openers and cocktails (New Orleanians loved being told it was not only okay, but definitely chic to have glamorous drinks in the morning), the daring egg dishes, and the scene-stealing flaming desserts—well, it worked. They were dazzled. Maybe it's my sentimental side, admiring thoughts of her discipline, driving curiosity, and creativity, as well as her naïve amazement at the "line around the block" response that explain my infatuation with brunch.

Nah! It's the food!

*I*t's true, hollandaise can be maddening. How do you get the sauce warm enough without breaking it? Here's how: Use a double boiler and use clarified butter. It's a trick worth learning, because hollandaise is a simple, elegant combination of butter, egg yolks, and lemon juice, and it's a quintessential Creole brunch sauce.

3 tablespoons fresh lemon juice

1/3 cup hot water

6 medium egg yolks

2 teaspoons dry mustard

1 1/2 cups warm clarified butter (see Note)

3 dashes hot sauce, or to taste

Kosher salt and freshly ground black pepper to taste

PLACE 2 tablespoons of the lemon juice and the hot water in a stainless-steel bowl or in the top half of a double boiler set over simmering water. Add the egg yolks, and whisk until the eggs thicken and triple in volume, about 3 minutes. Reduce the heat to very low, add the mustard, and slowly drizzle in the clarified butter, constantly whipping as you add the ingredients. If the sauce seems to thicken and looks ready to break, add the remaining lemon juice; it may not be needed. Keep whisking in the butter until all is incorporated. Add the hot sauce, salt, and pepper. Keep in a warm place until ready to use. Use as directed in recipes using hollandaise.

NOTE: Clarified butter has no milk solids or water and therefore makes the sauce less likely to break. To get this amount of clarified butter, melt about 1 pound of butter in a pot. It will separate. Skim away the foam or solids. The golden liquid remaining is the clarified butter. Pour it off, and discard the water in the bottom of the pan.

CHEF JAMIE'S TIPS

Practice makes perfect. A successful hollandaise is easy when the egg yolks are cooked to perfection, properly thickened, frothy but still very liquid, and warm but not scrambled. If the mixture seems hot and curdles on the edge of the bowl, remove from heat and continue whisking until cool. Then return to the heat.

You will need both hands to whip and drizzle the clarified butter, so stabilize the bowl, which is best done by placing a wet towel between the bottom of the bowl and the pot.

Lemon juice and hot sauce will lighten the texture and add flavor. You can use either one if the sauce becomes too thick, or you can add hot water.

Butter and eggs should be at about the same temperature before being added together.

If the sauce breaks, heat 1 ounce of white vinegar or white wine in a clean stainless steel bowl over boiling water, whisking constantly. Add the broken sauce a little at a time to the bowl, also whisking constantly, until the sauce is completely emulsified.

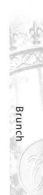

Lagniappe

TRUFFLED EGGS

A lot of food-savvy people guess that our Truffled Scrambled Eggs are flavored with a little truffle oil. Wrong! We place eggs in a sealed jar with truffles and raw arborio rice for about a week and the truffle essence permeates the eggshell. Then we sauté the eggs in truffle butter and top them with shaved Alba truffles. That makes for serious truffled scrambled eggs.

POACHING EGGS

Why do our poached eggs stand so tall and the whites hold together instead of making a stringy mess? Timing and practice are critical, but there are a few tricks. First, use the freshest eggs possible. Ours are local, from Ponchatoula. (A white membrane coating the yolk of a raw egg is the sign of a very fresh egg.) Second, the poaching water should be at less than a boil, even less than a simmer—at 180° to 185°F, depending on your elevation. The right amount of cooking is important—just enough so that the egg holds together but so that the yolk runs when it's pierced, about 3 to 4 minutes. Because we poach several at once, we need a way to hold them before they're sauced and served. We hold them in a bath of ice water with a touch of vinegar and a pinch of salt to keep the egg plump and coagulate it slightly. Before serving, we remove the eggs from the ice water, reheat them in the poaching water, dab them with a kitchen towel, and cover them with the sauce, which is hot enough to warm them. We love poached eggs because they are so elegant, hold sauces so well, and show off the egg flavor of the dish rather than tasting greasy or fried.

MAKES 8 EGGS OR 4 SERVINGS

I love eggs, especially poached eggs. Maybe I have a thing for eggs because we serve so many of them that they paid for most of my education. And not any old eggs. I'm talking about exciting glamorous poached egg dishes—and lots of them—like I had never seen before. I can remember literally hundreds of different egg dishes from my childhood and from our later restaurants. These eggs are great by themselves or as the centerpiece of some of the egg dishes that follow. A poached egg should be big and round and the yolk runny, all the better to melt over your pulled pork, homemade cheese biscuit, and tasso hollandaise (one of my favorite variations on eggs Benedict).

2 quarts water

2¹/₂ tablespoons distilled white vinegar

8 fresh medium eggs

Kosher salt and freshly ground pepper to taste

COMBINE the water and vinegar in a large, shallow pot, and bring to a simmer over medium heat. One at a time, break each egg into an individual cup, being careful not to break the yolks. Gently slide the eggs into the simmering water and let cook 3 to 4 minutes. A poached egg should be soft and have an egg shape to it. If it is hard, it is overcooked.

CAREFULLY remove the eggs from the water with a skimmer. Gently pat dry with a towel, and serve.

IF YOU want to hold eggs for later service, plunge them into ice water to halt the cooking process.

TO REHEAT eggs, season water with salt and pepper over medium heat and bring almost to a simmer. Place the eggs in the water for 1 to 1¹/₂ minutes, until hot. Remove, gently pat dry with a towel, and serve.

Eggs Jeannette

an you improve a classic? Yep. I'd put money on it that we proba-bly have served more Eggs Benedict, the classic brunch dish of poached egg with Canadian bacon and hollandaise, than any other restaurant. But Chef Jamie and my mother, Ella, were lamenting one day that customers were sticking with the old egg dishes and not trying our new versions. Mom loved one of them, "that new egg dish with the sage buttermilk biscuits and the roasted pork loin. It's really better than Eggs Benedict, you know." What did he call it? "Poached Eggs with Roasted Pork Loin," Jamie said. We try not to name too many dishes after people, but Mom thought this should be an ex-ception. "Let's name it after your wife." After all, she said, Jeannette was a great New Orleans name. Now this new classic is a top seller.

Pork loin:

1 pound boneless pork loin

1 ½ teaspoons chopped fresh rosemary

Kosher salt and freshly ground black pep-per to taste

2 tablespoons all-purpose flour, for dusting

2 tablespoons butter

1 large onion, cut in half, thinly sliced

10 cloves garlic, peeled and thinly sliced

2 cups cold water

1 tablespoon hot sauce, or to taste

Biscuits:

2 cups all-purpose flour

½ teaspoon salt

2¼ teaspoons baking powder

1½ teaspoons sugar

¼ teaspoon freshly ground pepper

¼ cup chopped fresh sage

8 tablespoons (1 stick) cold, unsalted butter, cut into 1-inch cubes

¾ to 1 cup buttermilk

½ teaspoon baking soda

For serving:

8 Poached Eggs (page 103)

1 cup Hollandaise Sauce (page 101)

PREHEAT the oven to 400°F. Season the pork with the rosemary, salt, and pep-per, and dust it with the flour over a large bowl to catch any excess seasoning and flour.

PLACE a roasting pan over two burners on the stovetop over high heat. Melt the butter in the pan, being careful not to burn it. Place the loin in the pan fat side down, sear for about 4 minutes, turn the meat, add the onion and gar-lic, and cook for about 8 minutes. Remove the loin.

ADD the excess flour and seasoning from the large bowl to the pan, stir to incorporate, about 1 minute, gradually add the cold water while stirring, and bring to a boil. Return the loin to the pan, and place in the preheated oven. Roast for about 1 hour, or until the sauce seems slightly thickened and the loin is completely cooked. Remove the pan from the oven, and remove the loin from the sauce. Let the meat rest.

WHEN the loin is cool enough to handle, cut it in thin slices (each about $\frac{1}{16}$ of an inch), return the pork to the pan, and simmer about 30 minutes, to get the pork extremely tender. Adjust sauce consistency while simmering. Add the hot sauce and adjust seasoning. Keep warm until serving time.

KEEP the oven at 400°F for the biscuits.

SIFT the flour, salt, baking powder, sugar, and pepper into a large bowl. Add the sage. Gently work the butter into the mixture, being careful to keep the butter pieces about the size of peas. Form a well in the center of the mixture and add $\frac{3}{4}$ cup of buttermilk and the baking soda. Using a rubber spatula, lightly fold the mixture so that it's just sticky and the dry ingredients are just moistened—no longer. Add more buttermilk if needed for the proper feel. The idea is to create layers so the butter will steam and will serve as a leavening agent to help the biscuits rise. The less the dough is handled, the flakier the biscuits will be.

ON A COUNTER lightly dusted with flour, flatten the dough to about $1\frac{1}{2}$-inch thickness. Using a flour-dusted cutter 3 inches in diameter, cut the dough into 4 biscuit shapes. Arrange them in a 9-inch pie tin so that the biscuits are touching; this helps them stay moist while baking. Bake the biscuits for 20 minutes, but do not overbake. Remember: The last 10 percent of the cooking will occur after they're removed from the oven.

TO SERVE, split each biscuit in half horizontally, set two halves side by side in the center of each dinner plate, place about 2 ounces of pork on each biscuit half, top each with an equal amount of sauce from the roasted pork, place a poached egg on each biscuit half, and top each half with about 2 tablespoons of hollandaise sauce.

CHEF JAMIE'S TIPS

Be sure the pork is tender. It can be made in advance and reheated before serving. With a little practice, the biscuits will be perfect. The biscuits could be made with a different herb (marjoram or rosemary, for example), or with none at all.

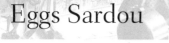

Eggs Sardou

*I*t just wouldn't be brunch at Commander's without Eggs Sardou—a dish with poached egg and creamed spinach. This dish was created by the New Orleans restaurant Antoine's in 1908, in honor of the French playwright Victorien Sardou. It's so popular that we serve a one-egg version (rather than our normal two), so that folks can get their "Sardou fix" and still try another entrée.

1 pound fresh spinach	8 medium to large artichokes
2 tablespoons butter	1 quart water
2 tablespoons flour	1 lemon
1/2 cup heavy cream	2 tablespoons whole black peppercorns
1/2 teaspoon freshly grated nutmeg	8 Poached Eggs (page 103)
Kosher salt and freshly ground pepper to taste	1 cup Hollandaise Sauce (page 101)

RINSE the spinach three times, tear into 3-inch pieces, let drain and set aside. Make a roux by melting the butter in a large pot over medium heat, slowly adding the flour, stirring constantly with a wooden spoon, and cooking for about 2 minutes or until the roux is pale, smells lightly nutty, and has the consistency of wet sand.

STIR in the cream, nutmeg, salt, and pepper. Simmer for about 2 minutes, stirring constantly until smooth. Add half the spinach and stir. Cook for about 3 minutes, then add the remaining spinach, stir, and cook until tender, about 4 to 6 minutes longer. Adjust the seasoning and consistency, either by adding more cream or cooking longer to reduce the liquid.

CUT the stems off the artichokes, and place the artichokes upside down in a pot large enough to accommodate them stacked tightly at least two levels high. Measure the water into a pitcher, slice the lemon, and squeeze its juice into the water. Add the lemon slices, peppercorns, and about 1 teaspoon of additional salt. Stir and pour the water over the artichokes. Place the pot over high heat, cover, bring to a boil, and steam the artichokes for 30 to 40 minutes, until a knife easily pricks the artichoke heart or when large leaves pull off with little resistance. When the artichokes are done, remove them from the pot, run cold water over them to stop the cooking, and peel away the leaves. Scrape out the hairy choke with a spoon.

TO SERVE, place about 1/2 cup of creamed spinach on the center of a hot plate. Place 2 hot artichoke bottoms in the center of the creamed spinach, and a poached egg in the center of each artichoke. Spoon about 2 tablespoons of hollandaise over each egg.

The spinach and artichokes can be prepared in advance. Store cooked artichoke bottoms in water. Be sure to cut each artichoke bottom evenly, so an egg will sit on it.

The plate, spinach, and artichokes should be very hot so that when the eggs and hollandaise are added, the dish will make it to the table hot.

Be careful not to overcook the artichokes.

Drain the artichokes and eggs well, and use a towel to pat them dry before adding the sauce.

Eggs Louis Armstrong

MAKES 4 SERVINGS

For me, this is the King of Egg Dishes, named after the King of Jazz. When we called it Poached Eggs with Red Bean Sauce and Pickled Pork Hash Cakes, we couldn't give it away. But when we renamed it Eggs Louis Armstrong, it started flying out of the kitchen. The salty, almost sweet meat flavor of pickled pork (see Chef Jamie's Tips) is trumpeted by the creamy, spicy red bean sauce, topped by our plump poached eggs. A very jazzy dish! All the more appropriate since Louis signed his name "Red Beans and Ricely Yours."

3 tablespoons butter

2 medium onions, in medium dice

1½ medium bell peppers, in medium dice

15 cloves garlic, peeled and minced

2 stalks celery, in medium dice

1½ jalapeño peppers, in small dice, stems and seeds removed

½ pound dried red beans

1¼ pounds ham or pickled pork, soaked in water overnight to release excess salt

1½ quarts plus 1 cup water

1 bay leaf

1 large russet potato, unpeeled

Kosher salt and freshly ground pepper to taste (see Chef Jamie's Tips)

½ cup flour, for dusting

8 Poached Eggs (page 103)

3 green onions, thinly sliced (green portion only)

Hot sauce to taste

MELT 1 tablespoon of the butter in a Dutch oven or a large, heavy pot over high heat until it starts to smoke, about 2 to 3 minutes, then reduce heat to medium. Add half the onion, bell peppers, and garlic, and all of the celery and jalapeños, and sauté for 8 to 10 minutes, until tender and lightly browned, stirring occasionally.

WHILE the vegetables are cooking, rinse the beans thoroughly, looking for any debris. Drain, and add them and the meat to the pot with the 1½ quarts of water. Stir. Add the bay leaf and the whole potato and bring to a boil, skimming away any impurities that may rise to the top. Reduce the heat, and simmer for about 1 hour. Remove and set aside the potato, and simmer the beans and meat for 1 to 1¼ hours more, until the beans are tender. Turn off the heat. Remove the meat, set it aside, and let it cool.

CUT the meat into small dice. Peel the potato, and cut it into medium dice.

NOW make the hash cakes. In a large skillet, melt 1 tablespoon of the remaining butter over high heat, until it starts to smoke, 2 to 3 minutes. Add the remaining onions, peppers, and garlic. Sauté for about 5 minutes, stirring, until the vegetables start to cook and become tender. While cooking, add the diced meat to the pan, and stir. Reduce the heat to medium, and sauté for about 10 more minutes, stirring occasionally. Add the diced potato, stir, and cook 5 more minutes, stirring occasionally. Add the remaining 1 cup of water, bring to a simmer, and cook 25 to 30 minutes more, stirring frequently. The mixture should become pasty, the meat will start to break up, and all the water will be absorbed. Remove from the heat and refrigerate.

MAKE the red bean sauce: With a hand blender or in a blender or food processor, purée half the beans to a saucelike consistency. Return to the pot and mix with the whole beans. Adjust salt and pepper, if necessary.

DIVIDE the chilled hash cake mixture into four even balls. Roll the balls on a floured sheet pan to fully coat each one, then slightly flatten each ball on the pan. If necessary, flip the cakes to coat again with flour.

MELT the remaining 1 tablespoon of butter in a nonstick skillet or a well-seasoned pan over high heat, about 2 to 3 minutes. Be sure the butter coats the entire surface of the pan. Place the cakes in the pan, and sauté until they start to become brown and crisp, about $2\frac{1}{2}$ minutes; if they are cooking too quickly, reduce the heat. Turn the cakes over, and cook another $2\frac{1}{2}$ minutes, adjusting the heat if necessary, until the cakes are golden brown, crisp, and hot in the center.

BRING the red bean sauce to a boil, adding a bit of water if it's too thick or boiling to reduce if it's too thin. To serve, spoon about 4 ounces of sauce on each of 4 warmed plates and place a cake on top. With your thumbs, make an indentation in each cake big enough for the eggs to stay in place. Place 2 poached eggs on each cake. Serve with green onions and hot sauce.

 CHEF JAMIE'S TIPS

The cakes and the sauce are best made a day in advance. Pickled pork has been cured in liquid brine. It is much like corned beef. Pickled pork is hard to find outside of the New Orleans area. Any well-preserved ham could be substituted, but not smoked ham, which would distort the flavor of the ham and the salt too much.

Whatever you use, don't season the sauce or the cakes until the end. It's very easy to oversalt, especially when you're cooking meat in beans; that mixture extracts the salt into the sauce.

An immersion blender is the best tool to use for blending the sauce, but if you don't have one, use a blender or food processor.

I like my eggs sprinkled with hot sauce at the end.

Lagniappe

MEETING LOUIS ARMSTRONG

Louis Armstrong came home to New Orleans in the early 1950s to present a live television show. Since it meant there would be nationwide viewership, my Uncle Owen Brennan convinced the television people to do the show in front of Brennan's restaurant sign.

But this artist who was the toast of America still wasn't allowed in most hotels and still was not welcome in the heavily segregated South. Louis was hurt, and he stayed only long enough to do the show. But he practiced a little. He stood on the corner of Bourbon and Bienville, in front of the Old Absinthe House, and he started to play. Ella and the staff ran up to the balcony and listened, watching in awe. Word spread fast. People came from everywhere. A huge crowd formed. People were amazed, and Louis did not disappoint. He played his heart out. Ella says it brought tears to her eyes. "His talent was so awesome." And for him to stand on that corner—our corner, his corner, the center of New Orleans in many ways—and play "Do You Know What It Means to Miss New Orleans?"

"Well, it gives me chills just remembering it," Ella recalled. "He was such a gentleman. We told him it was so good to have him home, and he wanted to talk about red beans and rice and all the foods he missed. It's been such fun meeting so many famous writers, musicians, actors, and politicians over the years, but nothing can top meeting Louis Armstrong."

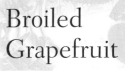

Broiled Grapefruit

*T*his brunch appetizer could fall under the "eat dessert first" theory. Believe me, this is not on your mother's old grapefruit diet—probably because of the brown sugar, dark rum, and cinnamon. But all that combined with a sweet, juicy grapefruit qualifies it as a longtime New Orleans favorite.

2 grapefruits, preferably Ruby Red	1/2 cup packed brown sugar
1/4 cup dark rum	1 teaspoon ground cinnamon

PREHEAT the broiler.

CUT each grapefruit in half across its equator. With a grapefruit knife or paring knife, cut the fruit away from the rind around the circumference of the fruit. Section each segment by running the knife from the center along the membrane to the rind. This will loosen the fruit, making it easy to eat. Place the grapefruit halves in a casserole dish or baking pan.

DRIZZLE 1 tablespoon of rum over each grapefruit half. Poke a few holes in the flesh if the rum does not soak in.

COMBINE the sugar and cinnamon and divide the mixture equally among each of the grapefruit halves. Broil for 4 to 5 minutes, or until the sugar and juice boil and the sugar starts to darken. Serve each grapefruit half in a small bowl, and pour any excess liquid on top of each portion. If desired, splash with a little extra rum before serving.

A grapefruit knife is a curved, flexible, double-edged, serrated knife. It makes it a lot easier to remove flesh from rind and membrane.

CHEF JAMIE'S TIPS

Andouille and Pepper Farmer-Style Omelet

MAKES 8 SERVINGS

Camellia Grill is a diner in New Orleans on the streetcar line where St. Charles Avenue ends. The waiters in their white linen jackets are as full of personality and showmanship as the food. Seated on stools at the long counter, side by side, at 1 A.M. you'll find tired-eyed Tulane students at exam time next to couples dressed in black tie and ball gowns. They're all having omelets—big, fluffy omelets—with all manner of ingredients. Here's our own version. And long live Camellia Grill!

1 pound andouille sausage, in medium dice	18 medium eggs, well beaten
1 green bell pepper, in medium dice	Kosher salt and freshly ground pepper to taste
1 red bell pepper, in medium dice	2 teaspoons hot sauce, or to taste
1 medium onion, in medium dice	1 bunch green onions, thinly sliced
8 tablespoons (1 stick) butter	

PREHEAT the broiler.

COMBINE the sausage, pepper, and onion in a large nonstick skillet over high heat, and cook for about 5 minutes or until the sausage is semi-rendered and the vegetables have begun to brown and tenderize. Remove and set aside half the mixture.

MELT half the butter in the skillet and add half the eggs to the mixture remaining in the pan. Season with salt and pepper, and stir gently with a rubber spatula. Reduce heat to low and cook for 30 to 60 seconds, or until the eggs start to set.

PLACE the skillet under the broiler to completely cook, about 2 minutes or until the eggs start to brown and puff up. Be careful not to overcook the eggs. Slide onto a cutting surface and cut into quarters. Repeat with the remaining eggs and the remaining sausage mixture.

SERVE each wedge with a sprinkle of hot sauce and green onions on top. Lyonnaise Potatoes (page 245) make a great accompaniment.

CHEF JAMIE'S TIPS

Use a nonstick 10-inch frying pan, Teflon-coated or similar, unless you have a heavy well-seasoned aluminum French pan that's used only for eggs.

Timing is important in this recipe, so have all ingredients and equipment ready. The egg mix should be ready to go and the plates should be prewarmed. A skilled egg cook can juggle more than one pan and burner. If you can't do that, encourage the first people served to start eating while you cook the rest of the omelets. But if you don't like that idea, keep the first omelets warm in a 200°F oven while you cook the others. The total time spent should be about 2 1/2 minutes per omelet.

Don't overcook your eggs. Omelets should be bright yellow and fluffy, but hot—not brown, rubbery, and overcooked.

Grillades and Grits

*G*rillades and grits are as common in New Orleans as ham and eggs are elsewhere. Ella and Dottie Brennan, my mother and aunt, served it at the christening brunch for the most recent little Brennan to arrive, Ashley (my godchild and the daughter of my cousin, Brad Brennan, and his wife, Elizabeth). It's another Creole dish invented to use lesser cuts of meat, but when it's done well, serving it in an ornate chafing dish is just right. Alas, too many of today's cooks just don't do it right. The grillades are usually made with veal or pork round steaks, and they're best sliced, stewed down, and served the day after initial cooking. Try to use real stone-ground grits, ground from whole corn kernels and untreated. Ours come from a plantation in South Carolina, where they are fresh ground by 150-year-old granite stones.

Grillades:

1 cup all-purpose flour, seasoned with salt and pepper

2 pounds pork or veal cutlets, about 1 ounce each, pounded thin

Kosher salt and freshly ground pepper to taste

4 tablespoons (1/2 stick) butter

3 medium red bell peppers, thinly sliced top to bottom

3 stalks celery, thinly cut on the bias

2 medium onions, halved top to bottom and thinly sliced

15 cloves garlic, peeled and thinly sliced

1 quart Veal Stock (page 73) or canned chicken broth

2 large tomatoes, peeled, seeded, cored, and chopped

1 bunch green onions, thinly sliced

Grits:

2 quarts milk, any kind

Kosher salt and freshly ground pepper to taste

2 cups quick grits, any color

2 tablespoons butter

TO PREPARE the grillades, place the seasoned flour in a bowl. Sprinkle the cutlets with salt and pepper, and dust them with the seasoned flour, shaking any excess back into the bowl. Some of the remaining seasoned flour will be used later.

BROWN but don't burn 2 tablespoons of the butter for about 2 minutes in a heavy pot or Dutch oven over high heat. Sauté a quarter of the floured cutlets for 2 to 2 1/2 minutes, or until brown. Turn the meat and cook the second side until brown, about 1 1/2 minutes. Remove the grillades, and scrape the pan with a wooden spoon to remove any particles from the bottom. Cook the remaining meat in three batches in the same manner, adding the remaining 2 tablespoons of butter between the second and third batches.

ADD the peppers, celery, onions, and garlic to the pan, and stir, scraping the bottom of the pan with a wooden spoon. Season with salt and pepper, cover, and cook for about 8 minutes, or until the vegetables start to become tender and brown. Add ¼ cup of the reserved seasoned flour to the vegetables. Stir and cook for about 1½ minutes, or until any liquid is absorbed and the vegetables start turning a darker brown. Scrape the bottom of the pan with a wooden spoon to cook the flour and give the sauce some color.

GRADUALLY stir in the stock, again scraping the bottom of the pan with a wooden spoon. Bring to a boil. Return the cooked grillades to the pan, and return the contents of the pan to a boil. Add the tomatoes, bring to a boil again, then reduce to a slow simmer. Season and cook for 30 to 45 minutes, until the meat is tender and the sauce coats the back of a spoon.

TO COOK the grits, put the milk in a large pot over medium-high heat and season with salt and pepper. Bring to a simmer, stirring occasionally and being careful not to let the milk boil over or scorch on the bottom of the pan. Add the grits, stir thoroughly to blend with the milk, boil for about 2 minutes, reduce the heat, and simmer for 2 to 3 minutes, stirring frequently until the grits mixture thickens. Cover, turn off the heat, and let rest for 10 minutes. Stir in the butter, and adjust salt and pepper.

TO SERVE, place 4 pieces of meat on each plate with a portion of the vegetables and sauce. Sprinkle with green onions, and spoon a portion of grits in the center of the plate.

 CHEF JAMIE'S TIPS

The meat can be prepared and kept refrigerated up to 3 days in advance.

When you scrape the bottom of the pot, you release what's called the fond—starch from flour and meat that has caramelized and turned to sugar. You want to release this from the bottom of the pan to keep it from burning, from becoming bitter, and from putting black specks in the sauce. The fond is an important part of the sauce, giving it color and sweet flavor.

You can always adjust the consistency of the sauce by cooking it longer to thicken it or by adding water to thin it.

Pain Perdu (or French Toast)

MAKES 8 SERVINGS

*Y*ou haven't had real French toast until you make it with stale French bread. Regular sandwich bread will do, but try it this way. The French called it "lost bread" or "pain perdu" because it was a great way to use leftover, stale bread. In fact, the more stale the bread, the better the French toast. Try it with the traditional cane syrup, jam and/or powdered sugar, or with honey mixed with melted butter. When your household is sleeping a little too late, get a pan of this going and they'll appear out of nowhere, like New Orleans kids at a King Cake party.

12 medium eggs

1 cup milk

1 tablespoon vanilla extract

$\frac{1}{3}$ cup packed light brown sugar

1 tablespoon ground cinnamon

$\frac{1}{2}$ teaspoon freshly grated nutmeg

Kosher salt and freshly ground pepper
    to taste

16 slices day-old French or Italian bread,
    cut $\frac{3}{4}$ inch thick on the bias

4 tablespoons ($\frac{1}{2}$ stick) butter

$\frac{1}{4}$ cup powdered sugar

$\frac{1}{2}$ cup cane syrup, molasses, or honey
    butter (see Chef Jamie's Tips)

CRACK the eggs into a large bowl and whisk with the milk and vanilla until well incorporated. In a separate bowl, combine the sugar, cinnamon, nutmeg, salt, and pepper, add to the egg mixture, and whisk until well blended.

PLACE 4 pieces of the bread into the egg mixture, soak for 5 seconds on each side, and allow any excess to drain back into the bowl. Melt 1 tablespoon of the butter over high heat in a nonstick skillet. When the butter starts to turn brown and coats the bottom of the pan, about 2 minutes, place the soaked bread slices into the pan and reduce the heat to medium-high. Cook for 1 to 1$\frac{1}{2}$ minutes on each side or until done. Both sides should be brown and the egg should be cooked and hot all through the bread.

REMOVE the slices from the pan and keep warm. Wipe the pan with a paper towel, melt another tablespoon of the butter, and repeat until all the bread has been cooked.

IN THE restaurant, we'll dust the finished slices with powdered sugar and serve them with cane syrup, molasses, or honey butter (a mixture of 2 parts honey and 1 part melted butter). Maple syrup would be fine, too.

It's important to use day-old bread to keep the toast light when battered. In Commander's kitchen, we like to use our homemade brioche for this recipe. It makes an outstanding, rich dish.

There are lots of ways to serve this. Fresh fruit or a homemade jelly (mayhaw and muscadine are popular in the South; fig and strawberry are more widely available) make great toppings, as well as the maple syrup so popular everywhere.

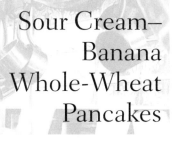

Sour Cream–Banana Whole-Wheat Pancakes

MAKES ABOUT 20 PANCAKES,
OR 6 TO 8 SERVINGS

*Y*ou like big, light, fluffy pancakes? Whip your egg whites thoroughly and watch these pancakes stand tall. This is such a favorite with kids that we often put these on the menu for Mother's Day and Easter, when we know we'll have lots of little customers. We like to break them in young.

3½ cups whole wheat flour

4 teaspoons baking powder

2 tablespoons sugar

1 pint sour cream

1½ teaspoons vanilla extract

8 tablespoons (1 stick) butter, melted

2 large ripe bananas, peeled and thinly sliced (about ½ pound)

8 medium egg whites

½ teaspoon kosher salt

1 cup chopped pecans

½ cup honey

COMBINE the flour, baking powder, and sugar in a large bowl and stir lightly. In a separate bowl, lightly mix the sour cream, vanilla, and 2 tablespoons of the melted butter. Add the banana slices and mix. Stir the banana mixture into the flour mixture, incorporating all ingredients thoroughly.

PLACE the egg whites and salt in a large bowl and whip the whites to a medium peak (not quite a stiff peak). Fold into the pancake batter. Be sure the ingredients are well incorporated, but don't overwork the mixture as you fold in the egg whites.

PLACE a nonstick skillet or a griddle over medium-low heat, brush with about ½ tablespoon of the remaining melted butter, and continue heating about 2 minutes, until the pan is moderately hot or until the butter starts to bubble and brown. With a spoon or measuring cup, drop about ¼ cup of the mixture onto the pan for each cake, leaving about half an inch between the cakes. You'll fit about 5 cakes, fairly thick as pancakes go, in a large skillet. Cook slowly, until the underside of each cake is brown (about 2 to 2½ minutes) or until bubbles begin to break through the surface around the edges. Then flip the cakes and cook them on the second side until brown and cooked all the way through (about 2 more minutes). Remove the cakes and wipe the pan clean. Brush with more of the melted butter and continue until all the batter has been used.

HEAT any remaining butter—probably about 4 tablespoons—in a small saucepan, add the pecans, and bring to a simmer. Add the honey and bring to a simmer again, then remove from the heat.

SERVE the pancakes immediately with the pecans, or keep them warm in an oven, uncovered. You can keep the first cakes warm in the oven while you cook the later batches, but don't let the finished pancakes sit more than 15 minutes or they will become dry and tough.

Whip the egg whites and add them just before cooking. Don't give them time to deflate. Cook the pancakes slowly and without using too large a dollop of batter. If the cakes bubble very quickly around the edges, they are cooking too fast.

If you don't want a whole-grain pancake, substitute 3 cups of all-purpose flour.

You can make this a more healthful dish by substituting a little oil for the butter, light sour cream for regular sour cream, and jelly for pecans.

 CHEF JAMIE'S TIPS

Sour Cream Pecan Coffee Cake

MAKES 10 TO 12 SERVINGS

I've always loved figuring out how different flavors work together to enhance, overpower, or even cancel each other out. Sweetened sour cream and pecans are a good example of two distinct flavors that together just soar on your palate. The pecan is great alone but is intensified by the contrary tastes of the sugar and the cream. Together, they make this cake a perfect dish—made the day before, too—when you have people coming over for brunch.

½ pound (2 sticks) plus 1 tablespoon butter, softened

2 cups all-purpose flour, plus additional for preparing pan

3 cups sugar

1½ tablespoons vanilla extract

2 medium eggs

1 tablespoon baking powder

Pinch of salt

1½ cups sour cream

1½ cups coarsely chopped pecans

1 tablespoon ground cinnamon

PREHEAT the oven to 350°F. Grease a 10-inch Bundt pan with the 1 tablespoon of butter and dust the pan thoroughly with flour.

CREAM the ½ pound of butter, 2 cups of the sugar, and the vanilla extract until smooth in the large bowl of an electric mixer at medium speed. Scrape the bowl, add the eggs, mix for about 30 seconds, and scrape the bowl again. Sift together the flour, baking powder, and salt, and add to the mixer over low speed until the ingredients are well incorporated. Scrape the bowl and mix for a few seconds more. Don't overmix. Fold in the sour cream by hand, again being careful not to overmix. Combine the remaining sugar, the pecans, and the cinnamon in a separate bowl.

SPOON two-thirds of the batter into the prepared Bundt pan. Smooth the batter, and carefully place the pecan mixture atop it, pressing some into the batter with your fingers but leaving most of it on top.

TOP with the remaining batter, smooth it out, and bake on the middle rack of the preheated oven until done, about 60 to 70 minutes or when a toothpick inserted into the middle comes out clean. Let cool for 1 hour, then remove cake from pan.

SERVE with fresh fruit and your choice of Crème Fraîche (page 308), Creole Cream Cheese (page 309), or whipped cream.

The sour cream is folded in by hand to prevent the cream from breaking down, resulting in a lighter cake. The small amount of flour also contributes to the lightness.

 CHEF JAMIE'S TIPS

Beignets with Mississippi Blueberry Sauce

MAKES 6 SERVINGS

*B*eignets are as much a part of our culture as good jazz and serious hurricanes. *Beignet* comes from the French word for fritter. It's a yeasty, deep-fried type of doughnut, usually served with powdered sugar. This recipe is for a Commander's beignet, and it works as a savory beignet as well as a sweet one. And if you've never been to Café du Monde in New Orleans, well, you've got some living left to do. Café du Monde, which is packed with customers 24 hours a day, serves a more classic beignet—and the powdered sugar flies, literally.

Blueberry sauce:

2 pints fresh blueberries

3/4 cup granulated sugar, approximately

1 cup water

Beignet batter:

3 cups all-purpose flour

2 tablespoons baking powder

1 teaspoon kosher salt

1/2 cup granulated sugar

1 cup water

1 cup milk

1 medium egg, beaten

For cooking and serving:

2 1/2 quarts vegetable oil, for frying

1/3 cup powdered sugar

COMBINE the blueberries, the 3/4 cup of sugar, and water, purée in a food processor, and pass through a fine sieve. Taste, and add more sugar if necessary. Set aside.

TO MAKE the beignets, combine and sift together the flour, baking powder, salt, and 1/2 cup of sugar in a large bowl. Combine the water, milk, and egg in a small bowl. Add the wet ingredients to the dry ingredients, and combine thoroughly.

HEAT the vegetable oil in a large pot over medium-high heat until it reaches 325°F on a deep-fry thermometer.

USE 2 teaspoons, one in each hand. Lift a spoonful of batter with one spoon, and push the batter into the hot oil with the other. Fry no more than 10 beignets at a time; crowding the pot will reduce the oil temperature and cause the beignets to be greasy and soggy. Adjust the heat to maintain the

122

temperature at 325°F. Fry each batch for 6 to 7 minutes, until golden brown and cooked all the way through. Check for doneness by splitting one open. Drain on a rack or paper towels. Soon after removing the beignets from the oil, place the powdered sugar into a sieve and generously dust the beignets with the sugar.

LADLE equal portions of the blueberry sauce onto each of 6 plates, and arrange 5 beignets around the sauce.

Granola Parfait

This is a granola mix. That's all. But we make it special by adding sweetened Creole Cream Cheese and fresh fruit. It's very addictive. The nutty granola flavor seems to intensify the sweet cream cheese, and the contrast between the smooth, liquidy cheese and the crunch of the granola just sends me to the moon. Because most of it can be prepared a day (or more) before, this is a perfect brunch dish. Just spoon it all together the morning of your party and serve preceded by some fresh juice or mimosas. Your hosting prowess will be legendary.

Granola:

2 cups old-fashioned rolled oats (not instant)

$1/4$ cup sunflower seeds

$1/2$ cup coarsely chopped pecans

$1^1/2$ tablespoons butter, melted

$1/3$ cup honey

$1/2$ teaspoon ground cinnamon

$1/4$ teaspoon grated nutmeg

$1/4$ teaspoon kosher salt

1 teaspoon vanilla extract

$1/2$ cup raisins

For the Parfait:

$2^1/2$ cups Creole Cream Cheese (page 309) or Crème Fraîche (page 308)

$1/2$ cup sugar

$1^1/2$ quarts fresh strawberries, stemmed and thinly sliced, the 8 best reserved for garnish

PREHEAT the oven to 300°F. Lightly oil a baking sheet or line it with parchment paper.

COMBINE the oats, sunflower seeds, and pecans in a large bowl. Combine the melted butter, honey, cinnamon, nutmeg, salt, and vanilla in a small bowl, and pour the mixture over the oats. Stir the two mixtures together thoroughly and spread onto the baking sheet. Bake until golden brown, about 40 minutes, stirring after 15 minutes and again after 30. Let cool, then stir in the raisins.

GENTLY stir the Creole cream cheese with the sugar in a small bowl. Place a heaping tablespoon of the granola mixture in each of 8 large wine glasses, and drizzle about 2 tablespoons of the Creole cream cheese on top. Layer the strawberry slices over the cheese. Repeat. Top with the remaining cheese and sprinkle with remaining granola.

SLICE each of the reserved strawberries vertically down the middle and press them onto the rim of each glass as a garnish.

When it comes to making the granola, you can get creative and substitute any type of nut for the pecans or your favorite dried fruit for the raisins. This recipe works with almost any type of fresh fruit, too, so use what's in season where and when you make this.

The Creole Cream Cheese or Crème Fraîche are our choices, but you could use yogurt or sour cream as substitutes.

6

SEAFOOD

From the air, Louisiana often looks like a soggy web spun by a drunken spider. Even though the water is usually shallow, the earth below is so soft that it swallows intruding objects, often forever. The Mississippi River rumbles with power and majesty, scouring an ever deeper, darker river bottom peeking at the French Quarter and the business district past bustling wharves and a man-made levee.

The Mississippi is the third-longest river in the world. It rages past us, giving life to the lush land, connecting waterways, and the world's third-largest port. Lake Pontchartrain, which bounds the northern edge of the city, feeds scores of twisting waterways and bayous. For centuries, New Orleanians have made their living from waterways and provided Louisiana cooks with tuna, snapper, flounder, catfish, redfish, crabs, oysters, shrimp, turtle, alligator, and more. We in turn have stuffed, marinated, sautéed, fried, boiled, seared, baked, and grilled what they've given us.

As we have continued to push the boundaries of Creole cooking, our vibrant community of modern-day fishers, hunters, and trappers have continued to present us with seafood previously shunned. In fact, the array of premium Gulf fish that we now look forward to sharing with our guests has grown so much in recent years that we've shared our own "fish tasting" results (pages 150–151) to help guide you.

In this chapter, you'll find Broiled Snapper, Catfish Pecan, Crispy Snapper, Stuffed Deviled Crab, and, what for me is the queen of Creole luxury, Whole Baked Fish with Oysters and Shrimp. As you work with these recipes and you use the freshest seafood and best stocks that you can make or find, remember some simple advice I once heard my mother give a young cook: "If it's fresh it won't smell fishy or past its prime. But work with it. Don't overpower it. Seafood should taste like the sea."

*W*hen you want just a few friends over to boil a few crabs, this is the recipe for you. Use this recipe alone or for Miss Claire's Marinated Crab Salad (page 85). But it's messy, so be armed with lots of napkins.

10 quarts water
3¼ cups Creole Seafood Seasoning
    (page 294)

5 bay leaves
24 live blue crabs, rinsed (see Chef Jamie's
    Tips)

PUT the water in a large pot with the Creole seafood seasoning and bay leaves, and bring to a boil. Boil for about 5 minutes. Add the crabs in batches, about 6 at a time. Cook each batch for about 4 to 4½ minutes, turn off the heat, and let the crabs soak for 5 minutes. Remove the crabs, return the water to a rolling boil, and repeat with the next batch of crabs until all the crabs are cooked. The finished crabs need no special treatment while you cook the rest.

THIS MAKES for a messy meal, so be prepared with newspapers, napkins, and a tool for cracking shells. A tomato-onion salad is a great accompaniment, as are corn and potatoes, which would be especially good cooked in the same liquid.

CHEF JAMIE'S TIPS

Use a lot of water to minimize the temperature drop when you add the crabs. Too much of a drop can result in broken claws and mushy crabmeat.

Instead of the Creole seasoning and the bay leaves, you can substitute Crab Boil (page 296) plus 2¼ cups of salt. Live crabs can be hard to find, but they're a treat to eat. When buying crabs, be sure to lift them. They should have some weight to them. Crabs that feel light probably have very little meat.

Blue crabs are the variety found on the East Coast and Gulf Coast, but any variety of crab would be fine. Remember, though, that larger crabs could change the cooking time.

Crawfish Boil

The crawfish boil is the New Orleans version of a picnic or a clambake. This recipe works best in a park or a backyard when you're serving a large group. You lay down some newspaper and dump mounds of steaming crawfish, corn, and new potatoes in a heap. Then everyone gathers 'round, peels, and eats. The best flavor in the crawfish is in the fat in the head, so sucking it out is efficient and authentic. Peel the tails by "pinching" the very end and letting the crawfish pop out. Being a good crawfish boiler in New Orleans means you're someone with the right knack for mixing seasonings, and that means the aroma will draw people from around the neighborhood. It'll amaze you how many neighbors will return a borrowed item at just that moment.

1 sack of live crawfish (40 to 45 pounds)	15 bay leaves
8 cups salt	12 lemons, halved
12 gallons water	12 heads garlic, peeled, each head cut in half
6 cups Creole Seafood Seasoning (page 294) or any Creole seasoning mix	10 onions, peeled and quartered
2 cups cayenne pepper	3 pounds small new potatoes, scrubbed, skin on
2 cups whole black peppercorns	12 ears corn, shucked and halved

FILL a washtub or ice chest with water and 2 cups of the salt, stir, and place the crawfish in the mix. As they swim around, the salt will cause them to purge themselves of impurities and cleanse their outer shells. (Let them purge for 30 to 40 minutes; they need to stay alive until you're ready to cook them.)

WHILE that's happening, pour the 12 gallons of water into a 20-gallon pot. Add the remaining salt, the seasoning, cayenne pepper, black peppercorns, bay leaves, and lemons. Boil for 15 minutes. In a basket insert, place half the garlic, half the onions, and half the potatoes. Place the basket in the water and cook for 4 to 5 minutes. Add half the corn and return the water to a boil.

DRAIN the crawfish from their purging water, add half of them to the basket, and bring to a rolling boil. Turn off the heat and let soak for 10 minutes. Pull out the basket, drain, and dump the basket's contents onto a newspaper-lined table. Repeat with the remaining ingredients.

SERVE crawfish, corn, onions, and garlic to each person.

NOTE: You certainly can boil a small amount of crawfish in a smaller vessel, do it indoors, and serve it to a smaller gathering, but in New Orleans, this is for an outdoor bash. Instead, consider Boiled Crabs (page 129) for a smaller, indoor dinner.

 CHEF JAMIE'S TIPS

Be sure to have a large pot, at least 20 gallons, with a basket and a lid, which helps the boil to boil faster. You'll probably use a propane tank, so be sure to have enough fuel. Also, place the pot on the burner before you add the water or it will be too heavy to lift.

Instead of the Creole seasoning, cayenne, peppercorns, and bay leaves, you can substitute a double recipe of Crab Boil (page 296) with 4 cups of salt.

When buying crawfish, make sure they are lively.

You also can have a lot of fun personalizing your boil by adding sausage, mushrooms, artichokes, etc.

Boiled Shrimp

We're having a seafood boil after the parade, hope y'all can stop by!" If I close my eyes, I can see it right now—someone's backyard, or deck, or City Park, or on the lakefront; kids running around, tubs of ice-cold Abita beer, and picnic tables covered in newspaper and piled high with mounds of steaming food. While you peel shrimp, crack crabs, and pinch crawfish tails, you visit with friends and family. And if any shrimp are left over, a shrimp ré-moulade (sauce on page 91) will be in order the next day.

10 quarts water

3¼ cups Creole Seafood Seasoning (page 294) or any Creole seasoning mix

5 bay leaves

3 pounds shrimp, heads off, unpeeled

IN A LARGE POT, bring the water, 2¾ cups of the seasoning, and the bay leaves to a boil, and cook for 5 minutes. Add the shrimp and cook for 3½ to 4 minutes; the exact timing will depend on the size of the shrimp. (The shrimp should turn bright orange and feel firm to the touch.) Drain off all but 2 quarts of the liquid, and add the remaining seasoning and enough ice to chill it quickly. Let shrimp soak for 5 minutes. Drain, peel, and serve.

CHEF JAMIE'S TIPS

Using a large amount of water prevents the temperature from plunging too much when you add the shrimp. It's best to cook the shrimp in their shells and peel them after they're cooked. New Orleanians like their shrimp cooked medium, tender, easy to peel, and served at room temperature.

Instead of the Creole seasoning and the bay leaves, you can substitute Crab Boil (page 296) plus 2¼ cups of salt.

Boiled shrimp are wonderful with rémoulade or cocktail sauce.

AUNT ADELAIDE AND CHARLIE GRESHAM

Charlie Gresham was our decorator. He was a rather large British gentle-man, ever so proper in attire and in manners, and he was magnificent. Like Aunt Adelaide, he was partial to a risqué joke and a good martini. About twice a week he would arrive at my house to pick up Aunt Adelaide, who did not drive, for an afternoon of searching out antiques or a new fabric. The restaurant always seemed to need refurbishing.

These two were not particular about time. Charlie could easily arrive an hour before, or an hour after, the appointed time. Regardless, the routine was the same. Aunt Adelaide was not ready. Charlie never seemed to mind. I or my brother would let him in, he would proceed to the bar to make himself a martini, then he would pick a room and sit and wait. Eventually, Aunt Adelaide would descend the staircase in some smashing outfit. "Well, hello, Charlie." "Hello, Adelaide, you look beautiful today." And off they'd go. It was Adelaide and Charlie who painted Commander's aqua blue and made a zillion other perfect touches.

Stuffed Deviled Crab

MAKES 8 APPETIZERS
OR 4 ENTRÉES

*C*rabcakes rarely appear on the menus of first-class restaurants." So says the original Commander's Palace cookbook of 1984. Now *that's* a testament to the fast and furious changes in the landscape of American cooking between 1984 and now. They're everywhere! Crabcakes, like grits, were long considered pedestrian. But with fewer and fewer people cooking regularly at home, we all clamor for these "just plain good" dishes in restaurants. Deviled crab turns the heat up; hence, the "deviled" in the name.

8 tablespoons (1 stick) butter

1 bell pepper, any color, in small dice

1 small onion, in small dice

2 stalks celery, in small dice

8 cloves garlic, peeled and minced

2 bay leaves

2 teaspoons celery salt or celery seed (optional)

1 teaspoon dried thyme

1 teaspoon dried basil

1 teaspoon grated nutmeg

Cayenne pepper to taste

1/4 cup grated Parmesan cheese

1/2 cup milk

3 medium egg yolks

1 cup bread crumbs (see Chef Jamie's Tips)

1 pound jumbo lump crabmeat (or any variety), picked clean of shell

1/2 bunch parsley, cleaned and chopped

Kosher salt and freshly ground pepper to taste

1 tablespoon paprika

PREHEAT the oven to 350°F.

PLACE 6 tablespoons of the butter in a large skillet over medium heat. Let the butter melt but not brown. Add the bell pepper, onion, celery, and garlic, and sauté for about 5 minutes. Be careful not to brown. Add the bay leaves, celery salt, thyme, basil, nutmeg, and cayenne pepper. Sauté for 30 seconds more. Turn off the heat, add the Parmesan cheese, and stir. Add the milk, then stir in the egg yolks until well blended. Stir in half the bread crumbs and mix well.

FOLD in the crabmeat and the parsley. You don't want the crabmeat to break up, so be careful not to overwork the ingredients as you combine them. Season with salt and pepper.

IN A separate small sauté pan, melt the remaining 2 tablespoons of butter over low heat, stir in the remaining half cup of bread crumbs, and add the paprika.

FILL 8 cleaned crab shells or molds with the stuffing, and gently coat the top with the sautéed bread crumbs. Arrange the shells on a baking sheet and bake for about 20 minutes, or until hot and light brown.

THIS would go well with creamed corn or a lemon-butter sauce.

Whole Baked Fish with Oysters and Shrimp

MAKES 6 SERVINGS

Fish tastes best when it's cooked on the bone. With this dish, it's not only best to leave the fish on the bone but also to cook all the ingredients in a single pan and serve them together. It makes for a beautiful presentation for a dinner party.

1 whole fish, such as redfish, snapper, speckled trout, sea bass, flounder, or sheepshead, gutted and scaled, 3½ to 4 pounds

Kosher salt, freshly ground black pepper, and cayenne pepper to taste

2 tablespoons olive oil

2 large onions, in medium dice

8 stalks celery, in medium dice

1 medium head garlic, cloves peeled and thinly sliced

8 medium tomatoes, cored, peeled, and seeded, in medium dice

4 green bell peppers, roasted, peeled, and seeded, in medium dice

3 bay leaves

Pinch of saffron

1 pound medium shrimp, peeled

1 lemon, sliced

1 pint shucked fresh oysters, with their liquor

1 bunch fresh parsley, chopped

2 recipes Boiled Rice (page 252)

RINSE the fish thoroughly under cold running water. With a knife, score the fish once behind the pectoral fin (that's the fin on the side, nearest the head). Pat dry with a paper towel and season with salt, black pepper, and cayenne. Set aside.

PREHEAT the oven to 450°F.

PLACE a large roasting pan that has a lid over two burners of the stove turned to high heat. Add the olive oil and heat for about 30 seconds. Add the onions, celery, and garlic. Sauté for about 10 minutes or until lightly brown and tender. Add the tomatoes, bell peppers, bay leaves, and saffron. Bring to a boil, and season with salt and pepper. Place the fish and shrimp in the pan, arrange the lemon slices on top of the fish, and cover the pan. Roast in the oven for about 15 minutes, then add the oysters and the chopped parsley. Cover, and cook 5 minutes more, or until the edges of the oysters curl and the fish is done. The internal temperature in the thickest part of the fish should read 130°F. Adjust seasoning to taste. Cut as you would the Salt-Crusted Whole Baked Redfish (page 206), and serve with Boiled Rice.

Use a white, flaky fish. Scoring the meat next to the pectoral fin helps the fish cook evenly. Be sure the fish is completely scaled. Fillets can be substituted, but the sauce and fish taste best when the fish is cooked with its bones. Using fillets would probably reduce the cooking time.

You might want to use a pan that can go directly on the table, because it is difficult to transfer a whole fish to a platter.

Catfish Pecan with Lemon Thyme Pecan Butter

MAKES 6 SERVINGS

Trout amandine has nothing on catfish pecan, nothing. "This is just plain good," says Chef Jamie. Dickie Brennan, my cousin and a big fan of this dish, says, "I've never seen an almond tree around here." But pecan trees are everywhere in New Orleans. I have to work hard to beat my neighbors and my dog to the pecans from the tree in my front yard. Jamie's version of this dish uses browned butter and browned pecans surrounding the steaming catfish.

3 cups (10 ounces) pecan halves
1½ cups all-purpose flour
Creole Seafood Seasoning (page 294) to taste, or your favorite Creole seasoning
1 medium egg
1 cup milk
6 catfish fillets, 5 to 7 ounces each (or use flounder, trout, bass, or any thin,

smaller, nonoily fish), free of bones and scales
12 tablespoons (1½ sticks) butter
3 lemons, cut in half
1 tablespoon Worcestershire sauce
6 large sprigs fresh thyme
Kosher salt and freshly ground pepper to taste

PLACE half the pecans, the flour, and the Creole seasoning in the workbowl of a food processor, and process until finely ground. Transfer the pecan flour to a large bowl.

WHISK the egg in a large mixing bowl and add the milk. Season both sides of the fish fillets with Creole seasoning. One at a time, place the fillets in the egg wash.

REMOVE one fillet from the egg wash, letting any excess fluid drain back into the bowl. Dredge the fillet in the pecan flour and coat both sides, shaking off any excess. Transfer to a dry sheet pan, and repeat with the remaining fillets.

PLACE a large sauté pan over high heat and add 2 tablespoons of the butter. Heat for about 2 minutes, or until the butter is completely melted and starts to bubble. Place three fish fillets in the pan, skin side up, and cook for 30 seconds. Reduce the heat to medium, and cook for another 1¾ to 2 minutes, or until the fillets are evenly brown and crisp. Turn the fish over and cook on the second side for 2 to 2½ minutes, or until the fish is firm to the touch and an even brown. The most important factor in determining the ideal cooking time is the thickness of the fillets you are using.

REMOVE the fish, place on a baking rack, wipe the pan clean with a paper towel, add another 2 tablespoons of butter, and repeat with the three remaining pieces of fish.

WHEN all the fish fillets are cooked, wipe the pan clean and return the heat to high. Melt the remaining 8 tablespoons of butter and, just as the butter turns brown, add the remaining 1½ cups of pecans and sauté for 2 to 3 minutes or until the nuts are toasted, stirring occasionally. Put the lemons face down in the pan, first squeezing a little juice from each piece. Add the Worcestershire and the fresh thyme, season with salt and pepper, and cook for 30 seconds more, or until thyme starts to wilt and becomes very aromatic.

PLACE one fish fillet and a lemon piece on each of six dinner plates, spoon some pecan butter around each piece of fish, and use the wilted thyme to garnish each plate.

Creole seasoning is used in the coating, the egg wash, and directly on the fish fillets to give this recipe its zest. The amounts are to your taste, but you want to give color and flavor to this recipe.

 CHEF JAMIE'S TIPS

When making the browned butter with pecans, don't brown the butter too much or it will become bitter.

The thickness of the fish determines the actual sauté time. If the fillets are especially thick, you can finish cooking them in the oven to keep from burning the crust.

HOMEMADE   WORCESTERSHIRE

Broiled Snapper with Chardonnay-Steamed Crabmeat and Spinach

MAKES 6 SERVINGS

*T*his dish is about the art of broiling and simple ingredients treated with care. Use lots of liquid (we use Chardonnay), keep the snapper fillets close together and seasoned well, cover the crabmeat and steam just until it's done—and don't overdo it (either with cooking or seasoning). Any delicate fish works well in this recipe. Serve in a bowl with the liquid from the spinach and the crabmeat. Good French bread for dipping will guarantee that you don't miss a drop of flavor.

6 snapper fillets, each 6 to 7 ounces (or use flounder, redfish, or grouper), scales and bones removed

1 medium head garlic, cloves peeled and minced

Kosher salt and freshly ground pepper to taste

1 cup white wine (a buttery Chardonnay works well)

1 lemon, ends removed, cut crosswise into 6 slices

$\frac{1}{3}$ cup extra-virgin olive oil (5 tablespoons of butter can be substituted)

1 medium onion, in medium dice

3 pounds fresh spinach, washed and dried, stems removed and large leaves torn

2 bunches green onions, thinly sliced

1 pound jumbo lump crabmeat, picked free of shell (you can use a different variety of crabmeat)

PREHEAT the broiler.

SEASON the fish fillets with half the minced garlic and the salt and pepper. Put half the wine in a medium-size baking pan, and arrange the fish tightly in the pan skin side down with a lemon slice over each fillet. Sprinkle with 2 tablespoons of the olive oil.

PLACE the pan under the broiler and cook, without turning, until the fillets are done, about 5 minutes. The fish should be firm and white and should not spring back when touched.

WHILE the fish is cooking, heat about $1\frac{1}{2}$ tablespoons of the olive oil in a large pot for about 2 minutes. Over high heat, add the remaining garlic and the diced onion. Stir and cook for about 1 minute. Add half the spinach and cook for about 1 minute, or until the spinach starts to shrink. Add the remaining spinach, cook for about 1 minute, stir, and cover. Cook until spinach is tender, about 3 to 5 minutes. Adjust salt and pepper, and set aside. Keep covered and warm.

PLACE the remaining olive oil in a sauté pan over high heat for about $1\frac{1}{2}$ minutes, or until you can smell the oil cooking. Add the green onions, and cook for 1 minute. Add the crabmeat, and cook for 30 seconds without stirring or shaking the pan. Add the remaining wine, season, and cover. Steam until the crabmeat is hot and the liquid is boiling, about 2 to 3 minutes.

TO SERVE, divide the spinach evenly among 6 soup bowls or deep dinner plates. Place a fish fillet on each dish, remove the lemon slice from each, and divide the crabmeat among the 6 plates. Spoon any juices from the fish and crabmeat on top. If desired, use the lemon slices as a garnish.

The fish will cook more evenly if it is cut evenly. I usually cut the fillets into squares and use 2 per serving, about 7 ounces total.

Keeping the fish close together when it's broiling helps it stay moist. Broilers vary greatly, so the cooking time will vary, too. Just be careful not to overcook. You're looking for firm, pearl-white flesh. Small amounts of white foam seeping from the flesh mean the fish is done.

Remember, the crabmeat has already been cooked. You're mainly reheating it. Crabmeat is very delicate, so don't break it up by stirring and tossing.

This dish does not require a complex sauce because the liquid from the crab and fish gives you an outstanding flavor of sweet seafood, good olive oil, and wine.

CHEF JAMIE'S TIPS

Lagniappe

HAUTE CREOLE

Commander's Palace is always looking to capture, intensify, and complement the flavor of food—never to mask it. We call our cooking style Haute Creole, and our mission is to constantly push the flavor envelope. You can see it in lots of dishes.

Our Broiled Snapper with Chardonnay-Steamed Crabmeat and Spinach (page 140) reenergizes a method as basic as broiling, and by seasoning the fish well and keeping the ingredients close, we save all the flavorful liquid for the dish. Or consider our many fried dishes. A properly fried oyster tastes like the sea, not like oil. Or our Shoestring Potato–Crusted Lyonnaise Fish (page 200). Yes, the potatoes are loaded with moisture, but we steam the fish with that moisture while the juices stay inside. Or our Creamed Corn with Jalapeño and Thyme (page 248), which preserves the corn flavor by cooking the scraped corncobs with the sauce. And the chicken from our Pulled Chicken and Ginger Pasta Salad (page 96) isn't merely well seasoned; it's wrapped twice to lock in flavor and moisture, then slow-cooked.

These are examples of our never-ending effort in the pursuit of flavor.

*T*his light, heart-healthy dish is a favorite of Ella Brennan, my mother. Heart-healthy though it may be, she loves it because it tastes good. It's similar to shrimp creole but without the roux, and it's a great summertime dish. Serve it over pasta or boiled rice.

6 large Creole or vine-ripened tomatoes, cored, peeled, seeded, and coarsely chopped

1 medium sweet onion, in medium dice

3 medium stalks celery, in medium dice

3 jalapeño peppers, stemmed, seeded, and minced

1 tablespoon light corn syrup (optional)

¼ cup white vinegar

10 cloves garlic, peeled and thinly sliced

Kosher salt and freshly ground pepper to taste

1½ pounds medium or large shrimp, peeled and deveined

1 tablespoon chopped fresh basil (thyme or oregano could be used, too)

Boiled Rice (page 252) or cooked pasta

¼ cup chopped fresh parsley or green onions (optional garnish)

PLACE the tomatoes, onion, celery, jalapeño, corn syrup, vinegar, garlic, salt, and pepper in a large pot over medium-high heat and cook for 10 minutes, stirring occasionally. Reduce to a simmer, cover, and cook for about 1 hour, checking occasionally to make sure the mixture is not drying out or burning (add water if it is).

ADD the shrimp and the herbs, and simmer uncovered for 7 to 10 minutes, depending on the size of the shrimp, or until the shrimp are firm and fully cooked. Adjust seasoning and serve over boiled rice or pasta.

GARNISH with parsley or green onions, if desired.

CHEF JAMIE'S TIPS

Try to use vine-ripe tomatoes, but if you substitute canned tomatoes, use about a quart of tomatoes with their liquid.

When you core, peel, seed, and coarsely chop tomatoes, you are preparing what's called a tomato *concassée*. After removing the core, score an X in the bottom with a paring knife, drop the tomatoes in boiling water a few at a time for 10 seconds, then cool in cold water and peel the skin off with a knife. Cut them in half horizontally, then gently squeeze out the seeds and coarsely chop the flesh. If you can't get fresh herbs, use a small amount of dried herbs and add to the tomatoes at the beginning of the recipe.

Crispy Snapper with Sour Cream Potato Salad and Peas

MAKES 6 SERVINGS

Because you never turn the fish in this recipe, it sears on one side only. The other side is steamed and moist for a great contrast. This is a great, light dish that we serve in the spring when snapper is running and the peas and fingerling potatoes are in season. We like to use fingerling potatoes for this dish because we find them to be creamier.

Potato salad:

2 pounds small potatoes, washed

1 tablespoon kosher salt

Additional salt and freshly ground pepper to taste

1½ cups sour cream

1 small red onion, halved top to bottom and thinly sliced

1 cup chopped fresh parsley

Fish:

6 snapper fillets, 6 to 7 ounces each, skin on but scales off and all bones removed (any thin fish, such as bass, trout, or redfish, can be substituted)

Kosher salt and freshly ground pepper to taste

2 tablespoons cornstarch

8 tablespoons butter (1 stick), clarified, or ½ cup olive oil

Peas:

4 tablespoons (½ stick) butter, or ¼ cup olive oil

2 lemons, quartered

Kosher salt and freshly ground pepper to taste

1½ pounds fresh peas, shucked

1 tablespoon chopped fresh thyme (substitute basil, oregano, or chives, if you wish)

PLACE the potatoes in a pot, cover with cold water, and add the 1 tablespoon of salt. Bring to a boil over high heat, and cook for 10 to 12 minutes, or until a paring knife easily pierces a potato. Drain the potatoes immediately and let them cool in a large colander. When cooled, peel them.

PLACE the peeled potatoes in a large bowl and season with additional salt and pepper. With a potato masher or a wooden spoon, mash the potatoes until they are well broken up but not creamed. Add the sour cream and onion, stir until lightly creamy, and stir in the parsley. Set aside and leave at room temperature.

SEASON the fish with salt and pepper on both sides, and sprinkle the skin side of each fillet evenly with the cornstarch, shaking off any excess.

OVER medium to high heat, melt half the clarified butter in a large nonstick skillet. When the butter starts to smoke, place 3 pieces of the fish, skin side down, in the pan. Cover the pan, and cook for 6 to 8 minutes, or until the fish is white and firm to the touch and does not spring back. Look for the skin to be crispy but not burned. If the fish is thick, you may have to turn down the heat. Remove fish, flip, set aside at room temperature, wipe the pan clean, and repeat with the remaining butter and fish.

AFTER removing the second batch of fish from the pan, wipe the pan clean to begin cooking the peas. Melt the 4 tablespoons of butter over high heat, but do not let it burn. Add the lemon quarters and season with salt and pepper. Add the peas and cook until they are bright green. Add the thyme, adjust the salt and pepper, and remove from the heat.

TO SERVE, place a portion of the potatoes in the middle of each dinner plate, and a piece of fish, skin side up, over the potatoes. Scatter some peas around the fish and potatoes. Be sure to get a little butter on each plate, too. Garnish each plate with a piece of lemon.

 CHEF JAMIE'S TIPS

Use fresh potatoes. Don't overcook them or let them sit in water after they cook or they will absorb water and lose flavor. This is a room-temperature salad, so do not chill the potatoes.

Cook the fish in a nonstick pan. Do not turn the fish or the skin will not be crisp and the meat will not be moist. If the fish seems close to burning on the skin side, finish the cooking under the broiler.

Skillet-Grilled Tuna with Fresh Legumes and Onion Marmalade

MAKES 8 SERVINGS

*W*e love tuna. It's very tender and flavorful, but it can stand up to seasoning, grilling, and even a glass of red wine. At Commander's, we use the best tuna—sushi-grade, sometimes called No. 1. And if you switch the butter in this recipe to olive oil, you've made it heart-healthy, too.

2 pounds shelled fresh legumes (see Chef Jamie's Tips) or fresh frozen

10 tablespoons (1 stick plus 2 tablespoons) butter

1 small onion, in small dice

2 tablespoons chopped fresh tarragon (you can substitute any other herb)

Kosher salt and extra-coarse black pepper to taste

8 tuna steaks, each weighing 8 to 8½ ounces and about 2 to 2½ inches thick

2 cups Onion Marmalade (page 310)

BLANCH the legumes in boiling salted water for about 10 minutes, or until tender (actual cooking time will depend on the type of bean). Drain the legumes, and plunge them into ice water to stop the cooking.

ROUGHLY chop the stick of butter into 8 pieces and melt but do not brown it in a large sauté pan over high heat for about 30 to 45 seconds. Add the diced onion and cook until tender, about 3 minutes, stirring occasionally. Add the beans, and cook for about 5 minutes or until the liquid remaining in the pan is boiling. Turn the heat off, stir in the the remaining chunk of butter, add the tarragon, season with salt and pepper, and set aside to keep warm. (If the legumes cool before serving, reheat them at the last minute.)

PREHEAT a large, cast-iron skillet for about 4 to 5 minutes over high heat. Be sure the skillet is well seasoned (page 84) so that no oil will be needed to cook the fish. Generously sprinkle all sides of the fish with salt and pepper. When the pan is hot, add 4 fish steaks. Let them sit undisturbed. The fish will stick at first, and it will generally smoke a lot, so you'll need good ventilation. When the fish seems to be completely seared, it will release from the pan, should appear somewhat blackened, and should have a good crust. After about 3 minutes, turn the fish over, and cook the same way on the second side, also for about 3 minutes. The fish should be rare to medium-rare when seared. If you prefer your fish medium or well done, continue cooking until it reaches the desired doneness. Remove fish steaks, and repeat with the 4 remaining steaks.

TO SERVE, mound some legumes in the center of each plate, and place the fish on top. Place about ¼ cup of onion marmalade on top of each serving.

At Commander's, we use many different legumes, such as purple hull peas, baby limas, black-eyed peas, pink-eyed peas, snap beans, red beans, large butter beans, and even English peas, depending on what is available. Certain beans take different cooking times. English peas, for example, might not need more than a few seconds, depending on their age. If you're using a combination of beans that need different cooking times, you might want to blanch the different kinds separately. For 2 pounds of shelled peas or limas, you will need 4 pounds in the shell, or 3 (10-ounce) packages of frozen.

Fresh tuna should be bright red and odor-free. The dark blood line should be removed. I like the fact that this fish can be cut like a filet mignon and treated like a steak—including serving it with a red wine. Tuna also goes great with Lyonnaise Potatoes (page 245) and the seasoned butter in the recipe for Pan-Seared Crusted Sirloin Steak with Cayenne Butter (page 156).

CHEF JAMIE'S TIPS

*S*ince the 1970s, the type of fish New Orleanians eat has changed a great deal. Some fish from our Gulf waters were "overfished," meaning that they had become so desirable all over the country that the price shot up, forcing us to consider eating fish that we had always thrown back. It's hard to imagine now, but my mother remembers when no one ate redfish because it just wasn't considered desirable.

Back when Ella and Paul Prudhomme, who was then the chef at Commander's Palace, were talking about some new ways to prepare fish, they decided to ask one of the cooks, who was known as a serious hunter and fisherman, how he would cook fish he had just caught if he was camping. He said he would make a fire right there, get his black iron skillet very hot, put some seasoning on the fish, and sear it real fast to crisp the skin but keep the moisture in. They asked him to go into the kitchen and try it, right then. He did, and it worked. For a long time, Commander's called it "seared fish." Later on, Paul would dub it "blackened fish," and thus was born a dish whose popularity would spread all over the country and almost wipe out our supply of redfish.

Until then, it seemed that all we ate was trout, pompano, and flounder.

Today, the lineup has changed drastically—so much so that for our benefit and yours, Chef Jamie and his gang put together a fish tasting for us. It was just like a wine tasting: We lined them up next to each other, and we compared. They were all prepared the same way—pan-sautéed with only a bit of salt and pepper—so that we could more easily make comparisons. Because all the new fish can be so confusing, we wanted to share the results with you. We limited our tasting to fresh Gulf fish, with the exception of the popular Atlantic salmon. There were some surprises. For example, there was an almost unanimous new favorite: Hake. Read on.

A FISH TASTING

FISH	BEST WAYS TO PREPARE	DESCRIPTION	OTHER INFORMATION	TASTING COMMENTS
Swordfish	Grilled, poached with olive oil	Consistency of beef; some oil	Available year-round; longline; good price; fish under 100 pounds should be thrown back, according to Greenpeace	Treat it like a steak, even eating it with red wine; grills well; good for kabobs
Yellowfin tuna	Grilled to medium-rare; steamed; raw	Oily, beefy	Longline (caught with fishing lines, not nets); good price; very popular	We all like medium-rare or rare; can treat it like a steak; has the consistency of a fine piece of veal
Redfish	Sautéed, grilled, poached, broiled, baked, deep-fried	White, flaky; strong flavor; big, white flakes	Most popular; farm-raised in La.; longline and gillnet; seasonal	Very versatile with our cooking style; mild, firm, medium oiliness, not "fishy"
Pompano	Sautéed, grilled, steamed in bag	White, flaky; strong flavor; oily; most oily when seared skin is on	Line and gillnet; expensive; in small fish, bones are a problem; very popular	Stands up to cream sauce, with which it's often served; hard to overcook; stays moist because of oil
American red snapper	Baked, pan-seared, broiled, poached, whole-roasted, pan-roasted	Shellfish flavor, sweet like lobster; troutlike texture; white	Expensive, seasonal; longline	Very versatile; high sugar content, so it caramelizes easily; elegant, particularly a pan-roasted presentation; prone to drying out because of low oil content; a favorite of Chef Jamie
Atlantic salmon	Seared, grilled, smoked, raw, sautéed, pan-seared, poached medium-rare to well, smoked	Oily, firm, large flakes	Popular; well-priced; can be farm-raised	Distinctive flavor; oily; flavor of a fresh-water fish but large size of a saltwater fish

FISH	BEST WAYS TO PREPARE	DESCRIPTION	OTHER INFORMATION	TASTING COMMENTS
Amberjack	Sautéed, grilled	Oily, greasy, firm, dry, large flake	Longline and gillnet; we use only La.	Good for outside grill and for sandwiches
Sheepshead (sea bream)	Poached, seared, pan-roasted, sautéed, hard to grill	Flaky, white; not oily	Gillnet; inexpensive; locals like it; has funny teeth from eating barnacles	Elegant but versatile; like trout and flounder but a bit firmer than trout
Puppy drum (small black drum)	Sautéed and grilled	Flaky	Gillnet or line-caught; large drum can have worms, so use small only; use fish under 4 pounds; can be tough	Good substitute for redfish or trout; very similar to redfish but with firmer flake
Hake	Poached, sautéed, pan-seared	Pinkish exterior; soft, tender, juicy, and moist	"The fisherman's fish"; deep-water fish	Sweet, buttery like monkfish; juicy; everyone's new favorite
Flounder	Poached, baked, sautéed, broiled	Fine flake; soft, tender	Gillnet and longline; hard to get	Baked with lemon and butter is a favorite; carries whatever flavor you put with it
Speckled trout	Sautéed, pan-seared, broiled, baked whole	Small flake; elegant; mild	Line-caught; gillnet, but not in La.; expensive	Customer favorite; if it tastes "fishy," it's not fresh
Black grouper	Charcoal-grilled, broiled, baked, pan-seared	Extremely tender	Line-caught from clean, salty water; don't buy over 12 pounds	Like hake, juicy with large white flakes; more popular than red grouper
Red grouper	Charcoal-grilled, broiled, pan-seared	Beefy, white flakes; firm	Similar to black grouper; line-caught	Makes best sandwiches
Cobia (lemon fish, ling)	Grilled	Good oiliness; meaty texture; consistency of canned tuna	Line-caught	Not too popular at our tasting, but Chef Jamie likes it; excellent for grilling

MEAT, GAME, AND BIRDS

eal Chop Tchoupitoulas, Osso Buco, Venison Stew, Onion-Crusted Rabbit, Veal Daube Creole. Some have said that these favorite dishes sound not only exotic but almost as if they were part of a foreign language. But not to New Orleanians. These dishes range from elegant Creole banquet fare to more plebeian farmhouse-style, but they are familiar enough to be considered comfort food to many.

Game is so fundamental to Louisiana life that our license plates carry the legend "Sportsman's Paradise." In fact, my brother, Alex, and his cousin had their own "duck lease," marshland leased out to hunters, 45 minutes from home. They would go there to hunt in the morning, before high school. And if you don't have access to fresh wild game, do what has made Louisiana cooks legendary—adapt. Cajun and Creole cooking has always been about making the most of supposedly "lesser cuts" of meat and of using products such as squab, looked down upon by folks who just don't know better. It has become relatively easy to find fine farm-raised quail, pheasant, turkey, ducks, or Cornish hens, and so many of these recipes will do beautifully with them. As restaurateurs, though, we do try to find the very best products and to prepare them with all the technique and finesse that we have learned over the years.

If there's one product that we'd single out, it's steak. Seek out the very best that you can find. The quality of beef has never varied more than it does today. Seek out the best butcher in your area and get to know him. Then, the recipe for Pan-Seared Crusted Sirloin Steak with Cayenne Butter may give your feeling about steak a whole new dimension. For us, this is the way to eat steak.

Honey Mustard Pork Tenderloin

MAKES 6 SERVINGS

*Y*ou want a serious barbecue meal? Try this, along with some Fig Habañero Barbecue Sauce and our Corn Cakes with Sour Cream and Green Onions. We find pork to have more flavor than veal, especially if you cook it to a rosy pink medium and no more.

4 pork tenderloins, 12 ounces each after trimming
$^3/_4$ cup honey
$^1/_4$ cup mustard seed, cracked (see Chef Jamie's Tips)
$^1/_4$ cup kosher salt
$^1/_4$ cup freshly cracked black pepper
$^1/_4$ cup vegetable oil

PLACE a large cast-iron skillet over medium heat. Brush the pork generously with honey. Mix the mustard, salt, and pepper in a small bowl, and spread evenly over the loins. Put half the oil in the pan, heat for about 30 seconds, taking care not to let the oil smoke, and place two loins in the pan. Sear the pork until an even, brown crust appears, about 4 minutes. Turn and repeat. Continue until all sides are brown and the loin is medium-rare to medium. Remove from the pan and set aside. Wipe out the pan, add the remaining oil, and repeat with the other two loins.

AFTER the meat has cooled, about 3 minutes, cut slices on the bias to a thickness of about a third of an inch.

SERVE with some Fig Habañero Barbecue Sauce (page 303) and two Corn Cakes with Sour Cream and Green Onions (page 246).

CHEF JAMIE'S TIPS

An easy way to crack mustard seeds is to place seeds on a work surface and gently smash them with a small sauté pan.

Pork tenderloins vary in size, so check the weight after trimming. You want about 8 ounces per serving.

Pan-Seared Crusted Sirloin Steak with Cayenne Butter

MAKES 6 SERVINGS

*P*rime sirloin is the best cut of meat in the world. It's by far our family's favorite. Dick Brennan Sr., a Commander's culinarian, has literally searched the world for the best cuts of meat (even trying to import beef from Ireland). This man is a serious steak connoisseur and this preparation of sirloin, with its seared crust and flipped only once, is, for him, the ultimate. The trick, as he likes to say, is to learn not to "mess around with the steak." Lock in the juices and don't give them any chance to escape by needless toying with the steak. But to do this, you must use a heavy, cast-iron skillet.

Seasoned butter:

½ pound (2 sticks) butter, at room temperature and cut into 16 pieces

3 fresh cayenne or other small hot chile peppers, or to taste, seeded and minced (substitute 1 tablespoon dried cayenne pepper, if you wish)

1 tablespoon additional ground dried cayenne pepper, or to taste

20 cloves garlic, peeled and minced

½ bunch parsley, chopped

Kosher salt and freshly ground black pepper to taste

Meat:

6 sirloin steaks, each about 14 ounces and about 1½ to 1¾ inches thick

Kosher salt and freshly ground pepper to taste

TEAR off an 18-inch-long sheet of wax or parchment paper, or plastic wrap, and fold it about a quarter of the way up. Thoroughly combine the butter with the fresh and dried cayenne pepper, garlic, parsley, salt, and black pepper in a bowl, and spoon the mixture evenly along the fold, leaving a few inches on either side. Roll the paper so the seasoned butter forms a cylinder about 12 inches long with the circumference of a 50-cent piece. Twist the ends of the paper in opposite directions to form a package almost like a wrapped piece of taffy. Refrigerate.

PAT the steaks dry with a clean towel, and generously season all surfaces of the meat with salt and pepper. Let the meat sit at room temperature for 20 to 30 minutes.

PUT a large cast-iron skillet over high heat on the stove. After 3 to 5 minutes, when the pan is very hot, place 3 steaks in the pan with opposite ends to each other. Cook about 2½ minutes so that the steaks are browned but not burned. Reduce heat to medium and cook for 4½ minutes more. Turn the steaks, return the heat to high, and cook on the second side for 2½ minutes. Again reduce the heat to medium, and cook for an additional 4½ minutes, or until the steaks are medium rare. It is very important for proper crispiness, a caramelized flavor, and to seal in juices that the steaks be turned only once.

REMOVE the cooked steaks, wipe the pan clean, and repeat with the remaining steaks.

UNWRAP the cayenne butter, cut it into ¼-inch-thick pieces, and place a piece on top of each steak. We also serve these steaks with Lyonnaise Potatoes (page 245).

CHEF JAMIE'S TIPS

Pick steaks that are well-aged, trimmed, and have great marbling. My favorite is USDA Prime. A 14-ounce steak is usually just thick enough, depending on the size of the loin.

A 10-inch black iron skillet is best. If the pan is too big, it won't be the right size for the stove burners and the steaks will not cook properly. Be sure to have a well-ventilated area. Do not poke the steaks, pick them up, or press down on them, or you'll squeeze out the juices and make the meat dry and unevenly cooked.

Cooking steaks to the desired temperature takes some practice. If you like your steaks cooked more or less, add or subtract 30 seconds per side to or from each stage of the cooking times in the recipe. (Using the recipe as an example: Medium steaks would cook for 2½ minutes on high heat and 5 minutes on medium on the first side, and a total of 7½ minutes on the second side.)

Let the meat rest before cutting or serving it, so that juices do not run out.

Veal Chop Tchoupitoulas

MAKES 6 SERVINGS

This is one of about five signature dishes that have been on the Commander's menu for 15 years or more. New Orleanians enjoy teaching out-of-towners how to say Tchoupitoulas (CHAH-pa-TOO-las). We owe this dish's popularity, at least in part, to local food guru and friend Tom Fitzmorris. Tchoupitoulas, by the way, is the name of a major street along the Mississippi River and of a Louisiana Indian tribe.

3 quarts Veal Stock (page 73)

1/3 cup vinegar

1/3 cup honey

1 tablespoon green peppercorns (fresh packed in brine), rinsed

1 roasted red bell pepper, cut in small dice (store-bought, or from page 306)

Kosher salt and freshly ground black pepper to taste

1 tablespoon butter

6 veal chops, each about 12 to 14 ounces and 1 1/4 to 1 1/2 inches thick

Creole Meat Seasoning (page 293) or your favorite meat seasoning to taste

2 tablespoons vegetable oil

BRING the veal stock barely to a boil in a large pot over high heat. Skim away any impurities that might float to the top. Reduce the heat and barely simmer to reduce sauce. Skim occasionally and cook to a saucelike consistency, about 1 3/4 hours to 2 1/4 hours. You'll be left with 1 to 2 cups. Strain through a fine sieve and set aside.

COMBINE the vinegar and honey in a small saucepan, stir, bring to a boil over high heat, then simmer for 10 to 15 minutes, until it is reduced by about half. Add the reduced stock, bring to a boil, and skim if necessary. Reduce the heat and simmer until the sauce coats the back of a spoon, about 10 to 15 minutes. Add the green peppercorns and diced red pepper, season with salt and black pepper, and stir in the butter. Set aside and keep warm.

BRING the veal chops to room temperature. Place a large cast-iron skillet over high heat. Season the chops generously with meat seasoning. Place half the oil in the pan, bring to the smoking point, about 2 to 3 minutes, and place three chops in the pan. Cook 4 to 5 minutes, until the chops are golden brown. If the chops cook too fast, reduce heat. Turn the chops and cook 4 to 5 more minutes, which will bring them to medium rare. (Cook chops of this thickness for 3 1/2 to 4 minutes per side for rare, 4 to 5 minutes for medium rare, 6 to 7 minutes for medium, 8 to 9 minutes for medium well, and 10 minutes for well done.) Keep warm. Add the remaining oil to the pan and cook the remaining chops. Serve with a bit of sauce over each chop.

Meat, Game, and Birds

When you make a reduction sauce, such as the one in this recipe, never let the stock boil. Reduce slowly and always skim away any impurities that float to the top. Depending on the stock, your reducing time and yield will vary. Don't over-reduce. A sauce that's too thick will become bitter.

Season at the end, not the beginning. Peppercorns will make the sauce spicy. As the sauce reduces, salt is more prevalent. Rinse the brine off the green peppercorns before adding them to the sauce. This sauce can keep for about 10 days in the refrigerator.

Professional cooks learn to associate feel and doneness. If you press a finger into medium-rare meat, it will spring back a bit. The longer the meat has cooked, the firmer will be its feel.

Chops are especially good cooked on a grill or under a broiler.

Veal Daube Creole

lowly braised in a tightly covered pot, this is an old French dish that you can put on the stove while you go about your business. You'll wind up with "falling-off-the-bone" tender meat and vegetables to serve over rice or pasta. This is a real Brennan family one-pot cooking favorite.

1 boneless veal roast, 3½ to 4 pounds (use a lean but inexpensive cut, such as a shoulder)

Kosher salt and freshly ground pepper to taste

4 tablespoons (½ stick) butter

3 medium onions, in medium dice

4 medium carrots, in medium dice

4 stalks celery, in medium dice

15 cloves garlic, peeled and minced

1 quart Veal Stock (page 73), Chicken Stock (page 71), or water

6 large tomatoes, peeled, seeded, cored, and diced

2 bay leaves

1 pound cooked pasta or 2 recipes Boiled Rice (page 252)

SEASON the roast generously with salt and pepper. Melt the butter over high heat in a large pot until the butter starts to smoke, about 1½ minutes. Brown the roast for about 5 minutes per side. Each side should have a dark, crisp crust.

ADD the onions, carrots, celery, and garlic to the pot, season with additional salt and pepper, stir, and cook for about 7 minutes, or until the vegetables begin to brown. Add the stock, bring to a boil, add the tomatoes and bay leaves, and return the mixture to a boil. Reduce to a slow simmer, cover, and cook for 6 to 8 hours, until the meat is falling apart and the sauce is thin but not watery. Check the roast every hour to be sure that it is neither cooking too hard nor not cooking at all. Adjust seasoning. Serve with pasta or over rice.

CHEF JAMIE'S TIPS

The beauty of this dish is that most of the cooking is untended. The long cooking time allows a tough cut to tenderize, so this is a very economical recipe for an eye or shoulder roast. Just look for lean meat. Be sure the meat cooks very slowly, barely at a simmer. Stir occasionally. Remember, when you use a gas stove at such a low simmer, the flame will sometimes go out. Don't cook at a higher temperature because the sauce and meat can burn and the sauce can become too thick. I use a Dutch oven or a cast-iron pot. Whatever you use needs to be heavy, with a lid that fits.

After you cover the meat, check it occasionally. The lid will prevent the heat from escaping, possibly elevating the temperature and causing the meat to cook harder than you want. You will know when the meat is done because it will fall apart when you pierce it with a fork.

This dish can be made up to three days in advance and reheated gently.

Osso Buco

We'll do almost anything to make a Commander's Palace customer happy. For one of our regulars, that means serving him osso buco, whether it's on that day's menu or not. Why is osso buco so popular in New Orleans? Because New Orleanians love one-pot cooking and long-simmered dishes. Why was it such a favorite of John Brennan? Because it's so good.

4 large meaty veal shanks, about 20 ounces each, cut into 2½-inch lengths

Kosher salt and freshly ground pepper to taste

1 cup all-purpose flour seasoned with salt and pepper, for thorough dusting

8 tablespoons (1 stick) butter

6 shallots, halved (or 12 pearl onions)

4 large carrots, cut in 3 pieces

16 large cloves garlic, peeled

1 pound new potatoes, halved (quartered, if large)

½ cup brandy

1 tablespoon chopped fresh rosemary

2 bay leaves

¾ cup dried morels, rehydrated in 1 cup warm water

¼ pound fresh wild mushrooms, stemmed and brushed clean

4 orange slices, ¼ inch thick

GENEROUSLY season the shanks with salt and pepper, and dust them with seasoned flour. Preheat the oven to 350°F.

PICK a heavy-gauge ovenproof pot or lidded roasting pan that can hold the 4 shanks flat. On the stovetop, melt the butter over high heat until it's brown and about to smoke and sear the shanks until they have a good crust and are very brown, about 4 to 5 minutes. Turn them over and sear until a crust appears, again about 4 to 5 minutes. Remove from the pan and set aside.

ADD the shallots, carrots, garlic, and potatoes to the pan, cover, and cook until the vegetables are browned, 10 to 12 minutes, stirring every few minutes. Remove the vegetables and pour off any excess fat. Return the shanks and vegetables to the pan, add the brandy, and cook for a few seconds. Add the rosemary, bay leaves, morels, and the morel soaking liquid (don't add any of the sediment at the bottom of the soaking liquid). Add the fresh mushrooms and enough cold water to come to the top of the shanks, about 4 cups. Place 1 orange slice on each shank, bring to a boil, cover, and place in the oven. Bake for about 2 hours, until very tender. Skim off any excess fat that accumulates during the cooking process.

GENTLY remove the shanks and vegetables with a large slotted spoon. Set aside and keep warm. Pour the cooking liquid into a container and place the container on ice for about 20 minutes. Remove and discard the fat that rises to the top and return the stock to the stove. Heat and season it.

PLACE the shanks in individual pasta bowls, each with a portion of the vegetables. Spoon a portion of the heated stock onto each shank and serve. Provide each diner with a marrow spoon or a utensil that will remove the marrow from the shank.

CHEF JAMIE'S TIPS

The orange works as a tenderizer and flavor additive. The citric acid helps break the meat down. If the veal stock or sauce does not seem fatty, then skip the last defatting step.

Be sure your guests get to eat the marrow. It's the best part.

Braised Lamb Shanks with Merlot Mushroom Sauce

MAKES 6 SERVINGS

When cousins Dickie, Lauren, and Brad Brennan and I opened Palace Café in 1991, braised lamb shanks were on our menu. Some of New Orleans' best cooking is based on great techniques that enhance what some may naïvely consider lesser cuts of meat. These shanks are an example. Try them with a red bean succotash and a smooth American Merlot, like Rutherford Hill.

6 lamb shanks, 14 to 16 ounces each, trimmed

Kosher salt and freshly ground pepper to taste

1/2 cup all-purpose flour, for dredging

1/4 cup olive oil

3 medium turnips, peeled and quartered

3 medium potatoes, peeled and quartered

3 large carrots, each peeled and cut crosswise into 4 pieces

12 shallots (any small onion can be substituted), peeled

1 small head garlic, cloves peeled

1/2 pound wild mushrooms, any variety, cleaned

1 bottle (750 ml) Merlot wine

3/4 ounce dried morel mushrooms

1 quart water

1/4 cup fresh rosemary, chopped, or 2 tablespoons dried, finely chopped

1/4 cup fresh parsley, chopped (optional garnish)

PLACE a large, heavy-gauge roasting pan with a tight-fitting lid over two burners. Preheat the oven to 375°F. Season the lamb shanks with salt and pepper and dredge them with flour.

HEAT 3 tablespoons of the olive oil in the pan over medium heat and brown all sides of the lamb, turning the shanks as needed, for about 13 to 15 minutes. Remove the shanks, and place them on a sheet pan. Add the turnips, potatoes, carrots, shallots, and garlic to the roasting pan, season with additional salt and pepper, and sauté until the vegetables brown lightly, about 15 minutes. Transfer the vegetables to the sheet pan with the meat. Discard any excess fat.

SAUTÉ the wild mushrooms in the remaining tablespoon of oil for 3 minutes, season with salt and pepper, add the wine, and scrape any browned bits from the bottom of the pan. Add the dried morels, and turn off the heat. Put a rack in the pan over the mushroom sauce, and arrange the shanks and vegetables on the rack. Place the shanks with their tops and bottoms alternating. Then arrange all the turnips together, all the potatoes, the carrots, the shallots, and the garlic. This makes it easier to portion out vegetables when serving, protects the vegetables from breaking apart, and looks great.

Turn the burners back on, add the water, sprinkle the rosemary on the vegetables, and cover the pan tightly. Bring the pan contents to a boil and place the pan in the oven. Bake for 1 to 1½ hours, or until the shanks are fork-tender. Place the shanks on a large platter or individual serving plates, surrounded by the vegetables.

REMOVE the rack, place the pan on the stovetop, and adjust the sauce for seasoning and consistency. If it's too thin, bring to a boil and reduce to the desired consistency. If it's too thick, add a little water. Serve the sauce over the meat or on the side, and garnish the shanks and vegetables, if you wish, with the chopped parsley.

Roast Pork Loin and Winter Root Vegetables

MAKES 8 SERVINGS

*T*he trick here is removing the bone to season the pork properly, then tying the bone back on to protect the meat from drying out. Remember, food cooks even after you remove it from the heat, so slight undercooking in the oven leads to perfect doneness at the table. The juices from the pork loin also caramelize the vegetables, making this a winter favorite that we'll often serve on holidays. Onion Marmalade (page 310) is a good accompaniment.

1 center-cut pork loin, about 6½ pounds and 12 inches long, ribs intact, backbone or chine bone removed but kept for later use, shoulder-blade bone removed

¼ cup chopped fresh rosemary

3 tablespoons kosher salt or to taste

3 tablespoons freshly ground coarse black pepper or to taste

2 tablespoons clarified butter

8 large carrots, peeled and halved

4 small turnips, peeled and quartered

4 small onions, peeled and halved top to bottom

24 large cloves garlic, peeled

PREHEAT the oven to 450°F. Place the pork loin on a cutting board and trim away any excess fat, although one side should have a fat cap.

COMBINE the rosemary, salt, and pepper in a small bowl, and rub generously on all sides of the loin, almost creating a crust. Turn the loin fat side down with one end toward you. Return the chine bone to where it had been cut off, placing it on top of the seasoning. Cut four long pieces of butcher's twine, and tie the backbone in place with the twine tied securely at even intervals (starting 1 inch in from each end).

PLACE the clarified butter in a large roasting pan over two burners of your stove over high heat. When the butter starts to brown, sear the loin, fat side down, for about 5 minutes. When the fat is golden brown, remove the roast from the pan. Place the carrots, turnips, and onions, cut sides down, in the pan, add the garlic, season with additional salt and pepper, and cook until the cut surface of the onion is golden, about 10 minutes.

PLACE the meat, rib side down, on top of the vegetables, and place in the oven for 20 minutes, or until the roast is completely brown. Reduce the oven temperature to 275°F and roast for about 40 to 55 minutes more, or until the internal temperature of the meat is about 160°F. Transfer the meat to a cutting board and let it rest while you arrange the vegetables on a serving platter. Keep both in warm places. Gently remove as much fat as possible from the pan, pour the remaining meat juices into a medium saucepan, let rest for 10 minutes, and remove any additional fat. Season the juices with salt and pepper, and keep warm over low heat.

AFTER the meat has rested for about 20 minutes, cut and remove the twine and the chine bone. Cut the loin into 8 even portions (some portions might cut between two ribs; others might have two ribs) and serve with juices on the side.

Removing the chine bone makes it possible to cut the chops and makes it a lot easier to season the meat correctly. It's best to pre-order the meat from your butcher so that the roast won't be pre-cut and the bone discarded. (Also, your butcher might give you the twine you need to truss your roast.) If you do this without the chine bone, the total cooking time will probably be less.

When checking the internal temperature of the meat, be sure to place the thermometer in the thickest end, completely into the center.

CHEF JAMIE'S TIPS

Venison Stew

*I*f you live in Louisiana, either you hunt, or your husband, brother, or father hunts, or you all do. That means you usually have some game in the freezer, and that's perfect for this versatile stew. So on a rainy day, defrost some of the meat and try this one-pot recipe. Just let it simmer all day while you do housework or watch a ball game. By dinnertime, you'll have a tender, flavorful stew that will be perfect with a glass of red wine.

2 pounds venison stew meat, cut into 1-inch cubes

Kosher salt and freshly ground black pepper to taste

1/3 cup all-purpose flour

1/3 cup vegetable oil (any variety with a high smoking point)

20 cloves garlic, peeled, halved if large

6 medium carrots, in 2-inch pieces

4 small onions, quartered but with core intact to keep pieces together

2 large turnips, peeled and cut into 6 equal pieces

1 pound small potatoes, peeled and halved

1/2 pound white mushrooms, stemmed

1/2 pound green beans, stemmed and cut in half

1 bottle (750 ml) red wine, any variety

3 bay leaves

1 tablespoon chopped fresh rosemary

PAT the venison dry with a paper towel, place in a large bowl, and season generously with salt and pepper. Add the flour, and toss the meat to lightly dust it with the flour. Heat the oil in a heavy pot or Dutch oven.

WHEN the oil comes to the smoking point, add the meat evenly so that it all sears on the bottom. You may need to do this in batches. Cook for about 5 minutes, or until the meat is browned and crisp on one side. Using tongs, turn each cube so that all sides of each piece get browned and crisp. Using a slotted spoon, remove the meat from the pot and set aside. Repeat until all the meat is browned.

PLACE the garlic, carrots, and onions in the pot, stir, and brown for about 8 minutes. Using a slotted spoon, remove the vegetables and reserve them. A little oil should remain in the pot, but if not, add about 1 tablespoon and bring it to the smoking point. Add the turnips, potatoes, mushrooms, and green beans, stir, and cook for about 8 minutes, or until the vegetables are golden brown.

POUR the wine into the pot and stir to free any flavorful bits clinging to the bottom. Add the seared meat and reserved vegetables, and cover completely with water (you may need 2 or 3 quarts). Bring to a boil, skimming off any impurities or fat. Add the bay leaves and rosemary. Reduce the heat to a very low simmer, cover, and cook for about 2½ hours, occasionally skimming the fat and stirring lightly.

REMOVE the lid, and cook over low heat for about 30 minutes to reduce until the sauce lightly coats the back of a spoon.

CHEF JAMIE'S TIPS

My favorite meat for this stew is venison, but you can use beef, lamb, or veal. All are great. Just be sure the meat is lean and trimmed of fat.

This will be lighter than most stews, not thick and heavy. The reason for cutting the vegetables into large pieces is to keep them from losing their shape while they cook for a long time. Don't overstir the stew or the vegetables will break up. And be sure to sear all the meat and vegetables to make the final product tender and sweet.

Onion-Crusted Rabbit with Stewed Greens

MAKES 6 SERVINGS

*R*abbit is so popular in New Orleans that Commander's has its own supplier in Mississippi. This is modern-day Southern cooking, combining time-honored ingredients like stewed greens with more modern additions, such as the onion bits. The cornbread, sauce, greens, and batter can all be done in advance, so you can just heat the greens and panée the rabbit when your guests arrive.

Rabbit:

2 rabbits, 2½ to 3 pounds each, cut into 6 pieces

½ cup Creole mustard

1½ cups buttermilk

2 tablespoons cane vinegar or cider vinegar

Greens:

3 ounces bacon, cut into thin strips

1 small onion, in medium dice

3 large bunches collard or mustard greens, stemmed, cleaned, and diced (see Chef Jamie's Tips)

1 tablespoon vinegar (cane vinegar, if available)

Kosher salt and freshly ground pepper to taste

Batter:

2 cups all-purpose flour

2 tablespoons kosher salt

1 teaspoon crushed red pepper flakes

1 teaspoon freshly ground black pepper

2 heads garlic, cloves peeled and minced

1 large white onion or 2 small onions, in medium dice

Preparation and serving:

2 cups vegetable oil, approximately

Jalapeño Cornbread (page 311)

Worcestershire sauce (preferably homemade, page 305)

IF YOU NEED to butcher a whole rabbit yourself, lay the rabbit on its belly, back facing you. Cut along each side of the backbone using a feathery motion to remove the long thin tenderloins, leaving the flabby belly skin behind. Cut off the legs.

DIVIDE each leg into a drumstick and a thigh. Marinate the rabbit pieces overnight in a mixture of the mustard, buttermilk, and vinegar in a large bowl.

PREPARE the greens. Fry the bacon strips until the fat is rendered, drain the bacon on paper towels, and heat the rendered bacon fat in a large pot. Add the diced onion to the hot fat, and sauté until the onion is translucent, about 3 minutes. Add the greens, or as many of them as will fit, to the pot, and cook briefly until wilted. Add any remaining greens, and stew until tender; the time will depend on the age of the greens. Season with vinegar, salt, and pepper.

MAKE the batter. Place the flour on a rimmed sheet pan, and, using your hands, mix in the salt, red pepper flakes, black pepper, garlic, and onion. One at a time, roll the rabbit pieces and adhering marinade in the flour mixture, being sure to pick up as much of the diced onion as possible.

IN A 10-inch or larger cast-iron skillet, heat enough of the oil to come halfway up the rabbit pieces. Fry the rabbit pieces in the hot oil in two batches, cooking about 10 minutes on each side. The legs will finish cooking first, followed by the tenderloins, then the thighs. The rabbit should be golden brown, so don't let it get dark. Check with a poke of a knife, and look for the juices to run clear. Between the two batches, strain the hot oil and replace with fresh oil if necessary (if the impurities in the oil start smoking and turning black, it's necessary). Remove the rabbit pieces to drain on a rack or paper towels.

PLACE the hot, drained greens on paper towels. Do not dry them, but pat away any excess liquid. Mound the greens on the center of a large serving plate, arrange the rabbit on top of the greens, and sprinkle the crisp bacon over all. Place slices of cornbread alongside the rabbit.

DRIZZLE Worcestershire sauce on the rabbit or use Fig Habañero Barbecue Sauce (page 303) or Homemade Barbecue Sauce (page 304) instead.

 CHEF JAMIE'S TIPS

I like my stewed greens tender. Mature greens might need 20 minutes of cooking, while baby greens might need only 5 to 10 minutes. Let your preference determine the time, and, as always, taste to see if you've gotten there.

Pan-frying is an art. You've mastered it when the meat cooks perfectly without the batter burning. It takes practice. Until you get the hang of it, start the meat in a skillet and finish it in a 325°F oven.

Pheasant Pie

*H*ere in hunting country, this dish is a favorite when there are a couple extra pheasant from the hunt. But whether it's duck, pheasant, or quail from the wild or the market, cook the meat with onions, celery, and turnips, and serve it steaming hot in a flaky pie crust.

3¼ pounds pheasant, quartered, or any game meat

Kosher salt and freshly ground black pepper to taste

Cayenne pepper to taste

3 tablespoons butter

2 medium onions, in medium dice

4 stalks celery, in medium dice

2 medium turnips, in medium dice

1 small head garlic, cloves peeled and minced

⅓ cup flour, plus additional for rolling dough

4 cups cold water

2 cups fresh or frozen peas

2 teaspoons chopped fresh sage or basil

2 teaspoons chopped fresh rosemary

2 teaspoons chopped fresh thyme

3 recipes Pie Dough (page 295), at room temperature

1 egg mixed with 1 tablespoon water

PREHEAT the oven to 375°F. Place a large roasting pan over high heat over two burners on the stove.

PAT the pheasant dry and season on all sides with salt, pepper, and cayenne. Melt the butter in the pan, then add the pheasant pieces. Be careful not to burn the butter. Cook for about 5 minutes, or until the pheasant is brown on one side, then turn and cook for 5 minutes more, or until browned on the second side.

REMOVE the meat and add the onion, celery, turnips, and garlic to the pan. Sauté, stirring occasionally, for about 10 minutes or until the vegetables are lightly browned and almost cooked. Place the meat on top of the vegetables, and roast in the oven until the meat is cooked, about 30 minutes for pheasant or most game, but longer for meats like duck or goose. Remove the pan from the oven, and let cool until the meat can be handled.

REMOVE and discard the skin. Pick the meat off the bones, breaking up any large pieces, and return the meat to the vegetable mixture. With the pan over one or two burners, turn the heat to medium and warm for about 30 seconds. Add the flour, stirring with a wooden spoon, taking care not to burn it. Cook for about 2 minutes. Gradually add the water, while stirring. Bring to a boil, and cook for about 1½ minutes. Check the mixture for consistency; you want the consistency of a light sauce. Cook longer to thicken the mixture, or add water to thin it. If you wish, season with additional salt, pepper, and cayenne. Stir in the peas, sage, rosemary, and thyme. Let cool.

WHILE the mixture cools, divide the pie dough into 4 equal portions (2 will become the pie bottoms, 2 the tops). Lightly dust a work surface with flour, and, using your hands, form each portion of dough into a flat circle. Place on the work surface, and roll, starting at the center and working outward, frequently giving the dough a quarter turn. Try to keep the dough round and about 1/8 inch thick. Place a 9-inch pie pan upside down over the dough. Cut the dough with a 1 1/2-inch overhang and fit each portion into a pie pan. Refrigerate.

WHEN the pie mixture has cooled to room temperature, spoon equal amounts into each pie shell. Top each with a round of pie dough and trim away any excess dough from the top crust. Curl overhanging dough and seal the top and bottom by brushing dough with the egg-water mixture. Brush remaining egg wash over the top dough. Crimp with your fingers, or use a fork. With a knife or fork, poke venting holes in the top crust.

BAKE at 375°F for about 45 minutes, or until golden brown and hot and bubbling in the center. To serve, scoop crust and filling into bowls.

 CHEF JAMIE'S TIPS

Substitute dried herbs, if you wish, by halving the quantities and adding them to the pan when you cook the vegetables.

I love to hunt, so I use this recipe for quail, rabbit, ducks, or squirrel. It works well with leftover turkey, too.

The pies freeze well, so they can be made in advance. From the freezer, bake them at 350°F for 1 hour and 45 minutes.

Skillet-Grilled Squab with Braised Salad and Honey Mashed Turnips

MAKES 4 ENTRÉES

To celebrate the restaurant's one hundredth anniversary, we threw a party for friends, restaurateurs, and "foodies." From beautifully printed menus with photos and history of each dish to a family member at almost every table to a line of cooks in crisp whites parading through with suckling pig to the music in the courtyard, it was a glorious evening. What was our entrée meat? Squab.

4 squab, about 1 pound each, boned (see directions in Chef Jamie's Tips)

Kosher salt and freshly ground pepper to taste

1 tomato, in medium dice

1 onion, in medium dice

1 medium carrot, in medium dice

2 stalks celery, in medium dice

8 cloves garlic, peeled

2 quarts cold water

Flour, for dusting

8 tablespoons (1 stick) butter

3 large turnips, peeled and cut in medium dice

1 1/2 tablespoons honey

3 1/2 ounces cleaned baby greens, such as mustard greens, arugula, watercress, or frisée (see Chef Jamie's Tips)

2 tablespoons olive oil

1 tablespoon vinegar

PREHEAT the oven to 450°F.

RINSE the squab bones and giblets. Remove the legs (drumsticks plus thighs) and season them with salt and pepper. Refrigerate the breasts, legs, and giblets. Place the bones and the wings, tomato, onion, carrot, celery, and garlic in a roasting pan, stir, and roast in the preheated oven for 20 minutes. Stir again, and roast for 20 minutes more, or until the bones and vegetables are brown.

TRANSFER the bones and roasted vegetables to a stockpot with half the cold water. Use the rest of the water to deglaze the roasting pan, scraping up any glaze that might be stuck to the pan. Pour the liquid into the stockpot, bring to a boil, reduce to a simmer, and skim away any fat and impurities from the surface. Simmer for about 2 1/2 hours, and strain. You should have about 2 1/2 cups. (This part can be done a day in advance.)

DUST the seasoned legs and giblets with the flour. Place 2 tablespoons of the butter in a sauté pan over high heat, and melt the butter until it smokes, about 2 1/2 minutes. Do not let it burn. Sauté the legs and giblets until they are browned on one side, about 2 minutes. Turn, reduce the heat, and cook 1 minute more. Remove the meat from the pan, discard any fat and butter, return the legs and giblets, add the 2 1/2 cups of stock that you made, and bring to a boil. Reduce the heat, bring to a slow simmer, skim, and cook for 30 to 40 minutes, or until the leg meat is tender.

MEANWHILE, cover the turnips with cold salted water in a large pot, cover the pot, and place over high heat. Cook until they are fork-tender, about 25 to 30 minutes from start to finish. Drain immediately and place in a mixing bowl. Add 4 tablespoons of the remaining butter, mash with a large fork, add the honey, and season with additional salt and pepper. The turnips should be lumpy.

REMOVE the legs and giblets from the stock and set them aside to cool. Continue simmering the liquid slowly until it reaches a sauce consistency and coats the back of a spoon, about 20 minutes. Pick the meat off the legs and chop the giblets.

WHEN the sauce has reached the proper consistency, strain it into a small pot and whisk in the remaining 2 tablespoons of butter. Set aside.

PLACE a large cast-iron skillet over high heat for about 2 minutes. Season both sides of the breast meat, and cook skin side down for about 3 minutes, or until it is crisp and brown. Turn and cook for $1^{1}/_{2}$ minutes more. The breast meat should be browned but still rare to medium-rare.

SEASON the greens with salt and pepper, add the cooled leg meat and giblets, and toss with the oil and vinegar. Taste and adjust seasoning. Cut the breast on the bias into thin slices.

PLACE a portion of the mashed turnips in the center of each of 4 dinner plates, put some of the greens (with the meat) on top, and place some breast meat, skin side up, around the perimeter, drizzled with some sauce.

CHEF JAMIE'S TIPS

To bone squab (or any small game bird), use scissors to cut down both sides of the backbone and to snip the wings off by the breast. Push your thumb and forefinger between the breast meat and the bone and slowly pull the breast away from the carcass. Pull off the remaining rib cage and hip bones. Use a knife to remove any remaining bones in the breast, if necessary. The breast should be boneless; bones remain in the legs.

Squab should be served rare or medium-rare or not served at all.

The greens you use should be slightly bitter and sturdy enough not to wilt easily. Besides the greens listed, you could use stewed turnip greens from the top of the turnips, so long as you squeeze out all the juice before serving so the juice does not run into your sauce.

At the restaurant, I cut the bottom from a plastic container and use the resulting ring to pack the turnips, greens, and meat. I place the sauce around the outside of the plastic container and then remove the container.

Rack of Venison

*T*he beauty of this dish is that you don't have to make a stock and yet you get a great sauce—just from preparing the dish itself. The dried cherries, the bourbon, the venison drippings cooked on top of the caramelized vegetables all combine to make a sauce with a depth of flavor that belies its ease of preparation. The warm roasted beet salad complements the venison while adding flavor dimensions all its own.

1 rack of venison, 2³/₄ to 3 pounds, frenched (see Chef Jamie's Tips) and silver skin removed, approximately 8 bones
Kosher salt and freshly ground pepper to taste
1 cup dehydrated cherries
1 cup bourbon
4 medium beets, about 2 pounds, washed and wrapped in foil
3 tablespoons butter
1¹/₂ onions, ¹/₂ in small dice, 1 thinly sliced
1 tomato, in small dice
1 rib celery, in small dice

1 carrot, in small dice
20 cloves garlic, peeled and thinly sliced
1 tablespoon chopped fresh rosemary
1 quart water (or veal, chicken, or beef stock)
2 tablespoons vinegar
¹/₄ cup olive oil
¹/₂ tablespoon sugar
1 tablespoon fresh thyme leaves
¹/₄ cup Creole mustard, at room temperature
1 cup coarse bread crumbs, preferably from day-old bread, seasoned with salt and pepper

BRING the venison to room temperature and season it generously on all sides with salt and pepper. Combine the cherries and bourbon in a saucepan and set aside to soak. Preheat the oven to 450°F, and place the foil-wrapped beets in the oven.

PLACE a large roasting pan over two burners on the stovetop, and turn the burners to high heat. Melt 2 tablespoons of the butter in the pan until it's smoking, but do not let it burn. Add the vension, bone side up, and sear it for about 2¹/₂ minutes, or until brown. Turn the meat and sear the other surfaces until brown. Remove the venison. Add the diced onion, tomato, celery, carrot, and half the garlic, and sauté for about 5 minutes or until brown. Add half the rosemary. Place a metal rack over the vegetables in the pan, and place the venison on the rack. Roast in the oven for about 20 minutes, until the meat is medium-rare with an internal temperature of 115°F to 120°F. Remove the pan from the oven and return to the stovetop.

REMOVE the venison and the rack; place on a platter to catch the juices, and keep in a warm place. Heat the roasting pan for about 1 minute over high heat or until the vegetables start to stick to the pan. Add the water, bring to a boil, reduce to a simmer, and cook for about 8 minutes, scraping the bottom of the pan to release any glaze. Purée the liquid.

REMOVE the beets from the oven, and check their doneness with a knife; they should have cooked for about 45 minutes and should be tender. Set them aside to cool until you can handle them.

PLACE the saucepan with the cherries and bourbon over low heat. When warm, remove from the stove, ignite the bourborn, and flame carefully until most of the liquid has evaporated, about 1 minute, depending on how much bourbon has been absorbed. Strain the puréed venison sauce into the saucepan with the cherries, bring to a boil, and skim off any impurities that come to the top. Reduce the heat and simmer for about 5 minutes.

Peel the beets and slice them about one-third inch thick. Place the slices in a bowl, add the sliced onion, remaining garlic, vinegar, olive oil, sugar, thyme, and additional salt and pepper to taste. Mix well. Brush the venison evenly on all sides with the mustard. Add the remaining rosemary to the bread crumbs and coat the venison with the crumbs.

Adjust the sauce consistency by adding more liquid or boiling further. Skim the liquid again, and whisk the remaining butter into the sauce. Portion the chops evenly among the diners. Serve with the beets and place a portion of the sauce over each chop.

CHEF JAMIE'S TIPS

When a rack is frenched, it means that all meat and fat between the ends of the rib bones are trimmed off so that the roasted meat is ready for slicing at the table.

Substitute lamb, if you wish, although you might need 2 racks of lamb for 4 people.

Venison roasts will also vary in size, depending on species, and so cooking time will vary too. As always, be guided by the meat's internal temperature. Boneless loin can be substituted, but again, cooking time will vary. Serve this cut of meat rare to medium-rare; longer cooking can turn the meat gamy, dry, and tough. Removing the chill from the meat before roasting makes for more even cooking. I also like to let the meat rest after cooking to help keep in the juices. If you want, garnish the meat with flat-leaf parsley.

Roast Tarragon Tangerine Chicken with Carrots and Shallots

MAKES 4 SERVINGS

Here's another elegant but simple one-dish meal. Try starting with the chicken breast down so the juices and flavor from the darker meat drip into the white meat, making it even more tender. The aromatic tarragon goes especially well with the tangerines and the carrots. Roasting the chicken and tangerines on top of the carrots will flavor the vegetables with the chicken drippings and the tangerine sugar.

1 whole chicken, 3³/₄ to 4 pounds	1 pound carrots, any size, peeled and cut
1 cup salt	into 2-inch lengths
4 tangerines	8 ounces fresh shallots, peeled
3 tablespoons chopped fresh tarragon	Kosher salt and freshly ground pepper to
15 cloves garlic, peeled and thinly sliced	taste
	1 cup water

REMOVE the giblets and any fat from the chicken cavity and cut into small dice. Wash the bird in cold water. Dissolve the salt in a large bowl in about 3 quarts of cold water, enough water to submerge the chicken. Refrigerate the submerged chicken for 1¹/₂ hours.

WITH a zester or vegetable peeler, remove the outer zest from the tangerines (avoid the bitter white rind underneath). Cut the zest into small strips, and place in a mixing bowl. With a paring knife, remove the skin from the fruit, and section the fruit segments over the bowl of zest so any juice drips into the bowl. Remove any seeds that might have fallen in the bowl. Add the tarragon and garlic and set the bowl aside.

PREHEAT the oven to 375°F.

PLACE a shallow, heavy roasting pan over two stovetop burners over medium heat, add the chicken fat, and cook for 3 to 4 minutes to render the fat, stirring occasionally, until it starts to turn brown. Add the carrots and shallots, turn the heat to high, and add the diced giblets and neck. Cook 5 to 7 minutes, or until the vegetables start to brown, stirring frequently. Turn off the heat.

REMOVE the bird from the salt water, and pat it dry with paper towels. Season lightly with salt and pepper inside and out, and tuck the wings under the backbone.

MOVE the giblet-vegetable mixture into the center of the pan, place the chicken in the pan, breast side down, and spoon one-third of the tangerine mixture on top. Roast for 25 minutes, or until the skin turns golden and the liquids on the bottom of the pan become dark and are almost evaporated.

REMOVE the chicken, stir the vegetables, and return them to the center of the pan. Place the chicken on top, breast side up. Add the remaining citrus mixture to the top of the bird and roast 45 to 60 minutes longer, or until the breast temperature reads 160°F on a meat thermometer (or the legs and thighs read 165°F) and the liquid from the thighs runs clear when tested with a knife. Remove the chicken from the oven, set it on a rack so that it cools evenly, and let it rest while you finish the sauce. Using a slotted spoon, remove the vegetables from the pan, and place them on a platter. Remove the neck, pick off the meat, and place it in the roasting pan.

RETURN the roasting pan to the stove over medium-high heat. Add the 1 cup of water and scrape up any glaze that may adhere to the bottom of the pan. Boil to reduce the liquid by half, adjust salt and pepper if necessary, and transfer the liquid to a sauceboat or pour over the vegetables on a platter. Carve the chicken into serving pieces, and arrange over the vegetables.

The soaking brine will keep the chicken moist, but it can also make it salty, so be **CHEF JAMIE'S TIPS**
aware of this when you season.

Oranges can be used if you have trouble finding tangerines. Add a little honey if the fruit is not sweet. And the tarragon could be changed to thyme, oregano, or sage.

Light Panéed Chicken or Veal and Fettuccine

MAKES 6 SERVINGS

*I*f Commander's Palace has comfort food, this is it. Even though we took it off the menu a long time ago, we still serve a few orders a week to regulars who remember it and to family members who just have to have it every now and then. This updated version has no cream—only olive oil, fresh Parmesan, diced tomatoes, spinach, and garlic. With just a couple of pots and pans, you can relax over a Creole Italian dinner.

¼ cup chopped fresh basil	2 medium eggs
¼ cup chopped fresh thyme	1 cup milk
¼ cup chopped fresh oregano	6 chicken or veal cutlets, 2½ ounces each
¼ cup chopped fresh parsley	1 pound fettuccine
4 cups bread crumbs (from French bread, if possible)	1 cup olive oil
1½ cups freshly grated Parmesan cheese	18 cloves garlic, peeled and minced
Kosher salt and freshly ground pepper to taste	1 pound fresh spinach, cleaned thoroughly and dried
	2 tomatoes, in medium dice (about 3 cups)

COMBINE the herbs, bread crumbs, 1 cup of the grated cheese, the salt, and the pepper in a large mixing bowl. Crack the eggs into another large mixing bowl, beat well, add the milk, and season with salt and pepper.

SEASON the cutlets on both sides with salt and pepper, and place them in the egg wash. One at a time, remove the cutlets, allowing excess egg wash to drain into the bowl, and dip them in the bread crumbs, coating both sides evenly and heavily and smashing down the cutlet with the palm of your hand. (You'll be making the cutlet a little thinner, but even more importantly you'll be helping the crumbs to adhere.) Place the cutlets on a sheet pan.

BRING a large pot of salted water to a boil and add the fettuccine. Cook until just tender and drain. Keep warm while you cook the cutlets.

HEAT ¼ cup of the olive oil in a large skillet over high heat for about 2 minutes, or until the oil is hot enough to bubble when you dip a corner of a cutlet in it. Place 3 cutlets in the skillet, cook for about 30 seconds, reduce the heat to medium-high and cook for an additional 1 minute, or until the cutlets are golden brown and crisp. Cook the second side until crisp, about 1 more minute. Remove with tongs and place the cutlets on a rack or paper towels. Keep them warm. Drain the oil from the pan and wipe the pan clean with a paper towel. Add another ¼ cup of oil, and cook the remaining cutlets.

WIPE the skillet clean again, and add the remaining oil and the garlic over high heat. Lightly toast the garlic for about 30 seconds. Add the cooked pasta to the skillet and heat for about 1 minute, tossing occasionally. Add half the spinach, toss, add the remaining spinach and tomatoes, and cook until hot, about 1 minute. Adjust seasoning. (If necessary, cook the garlic, pasta, spinach, and tomatoes in 2 batches.)

DIVIDE the pasta among 6 plates, and place 1 cutlet on each plate with some of the spinach and tomato. Sprinkle the remaining cheese on top.

 CHEF JAMIE'S TIPS

Be sure the cutlets are thin and even. Sometimes, the cutlets are small and you'll need two for a serving. I like to keep the cooked cutlets warm on a rack in a 250°F oven, so they stay crisp.

Sautéing and panéing are not the same thing. In sautéing, a cook uses only enough fat (usually butter, or oil, or a combination) to coat the bottom of the pan, perhaps a tad more. When panéing, a cook uses enough fat to cover half the item being panéed. So panéing is really halfway between sautéing and frying. But if the heat is too low, the food gets soggy; if the heat is too high, the crust burns before the inside is cooked. Like so many other cooking skills, knowing when the heat is just right takes practice.

Roast Turkey with Oyster Dressing and Giblet Gravy

MAKES 10 SERVINGS

Thanksgiving Day at Commander's sells out months in advance. The place fills up with the same families year after year, and everyone seems to know everyone. There are lots of big New Orleans families with little boys trying to keep their shirts tucked in as they stroll through the kitchen to the patio, staring half in fear and half in amazement at cooks in starched whites and tall hats. Here's what many of them will be eating. To me, oyster dressing means home, family, and all things wonderful. Jamie does a great version based on our family's longstanding recipe.

1 turkey that has not been frozen, about 12 pounds

2 pounds kosher salt

5 ribs celery, in medium dice

3 small onions, in medium dice

3 jalapeños, minced, seeds and stems removed

2 bell peppers, in medium dice

1 medium head garlic, cloves peeled and minced

3 bay leaves

5 tablespoons poultry seasoning

Kosher salt and freshly ground pepper to taste

9 tablespoons (1 stick plus 1 tablespoon) butter

3 cups shucked oysters in their liquor

16 cups crispy French bread cut into 1-inch cubes

4 medium eggs

2 cups chopped fresh parsley

2 green onions, thinly sliced

1½ tablespoons chopped fresh rosemary

½ cup Dark Roux (page 300)

WASH the bird's neck and giblets thoroughly in cold water and set aside. Place the turkey in a large deep pot, and sprinkle the salt in the cavity and on all surfaces of the bird, rubbing it into the skin. Cover the bird with cold water, and stir to dissolve the salt and soak in. Refrigerate overnight, up to 12 hours.

PLACE the neck and giblets in a large saucepot. Add half the celery, half the onions, half the jalapeños, half the bell peppers, and half the garlic. Add about 3 quarts of cold water and the bay leaves, and season with salt and pepper. Bring to a boil and skim away any foam that comes to the top. Stir in 3 tablespoons of the poultry seasoning. Reduce the heat and simmer, skimming occasionally, for about 2 hours or until the stock has a good poultry flavor and smells good. Remove the neck, and pick off the meat and dice it. Remove the giblets, including the liver, dice, and refrigerate for later use.

PREHEAT the oven to 350°F. Use 1 tablespoon of the butter to grease a piece of foil.

PLACE 4 tablespoons of the butter in a large pot, and melt over high heat until the butter starts to smoke. Add the remaining celery, onions, jalapeños, bell peppers, garlic, and poultry seasoning. Sauté for 15 minutes over medium heat, or until the vegetables turn brown and become tender. Add the oysters and any liquid they might be stored in, and cook 4 to 5 minutes, or until the oyster edges curl. Turn off the heat, add half the bread, and stir, soaking up any liquid. Add 1 cup of unstrained stock, and stir. Add the remaining bread and stir. Add the eggs quickly, stirring constantly to be sure the eggs don't cook when they hit the hot vegetables, oysters, and liquid. Season with salt and pepper, and add the parsley, $1/2$ tablespoon of the rosemary, and green onions. The stuffing should be moist but pliable, damp but not wet. If it's too wet, add more bread; if it's too dry, add more liquid.

REMOVE the turkey from its brine, and rinse under cold running water, inside and out, until there is no sign of salt. Using one hand, separate the breast skin from the meat and place 4 tablespoons of butter, cut into small pieces, between the skin and the breast meat. Try not to tear the skin. Pat the skin dry with a towel, and season the bird inside and out with salt, pepper, and $1/2$ tablespoon of the remaining rosemary.

PLACE the bird on a rack in a roasting pan. Tuck each wing tip under the turkey. Stuff the bird in the neck area first, pulling out the skin and packing tightly. Then pull the skin around the stuffing and tuck it under the bird. Stuff the main cavity and tie the legs at the ankles with butcher's twine. Cover the main cavity and breast with buttered foil, leaving the legs, thighs, and wings exposed. This will protect the breast and keep the stuffing from burning. Add one quart of stock and roast for 1 hour, basting the exposed portions of the turkey. Cook for an additional hour, basting every 20 minutes. Remove the foil, turn the heat up to 375°F, and roast 1 hour more, or until the center of the stuffing reads 160°F on an instant-read thermometer. Breast skin should be golden brown.

REMOVE the bird from the oven, and place it on the buttered platter, covered loosely with foil. Allow it to rest at least 20 minutes.

STRAIN the pan drippings into a saucepot, and skim away any excess fat. Place the roasting pan over two burners on the stove, both on high heat. Add 3 cups of stock to the pan, and scrape any glaze off the bottom with a wooden spoon. When the liquid comes to a boil, remove and strain it into the saucepot containing the drippings.

(continued)

PLACE the saucepot on the stove over high heat and bring to a boil. Skim off any impurities that rise to the top. Whisk in the roux and return to a boil. Add the giblet meat, the remaining $1/2$ tablespoon of the rosemary, and adjust seasoning. Adjust the consistency of the gravy by adding more liquid or reducing if too thin. Keep hot while turkey is being carved, and serve in a gravy boat to accompany the turkey slices and dressing.

CHEF JAMIE'S TIPS Be sure the turkey will fit into the pan and your oven. I think 12 pounds is a good weight because those young birds are more tender and moist. When buying a bird, remember that the weight on the package includes the neck and giblets plus lost water weight. This is important for your yield and cooking time. A bird that has never been frozen will be much juicier.

A lot can be done the day before—soaking the turkey in salt water, making the stock, and cutting the bread.

When seasoning this bird and making the stuffing and gravy, remember that the bird may have become salty because of the brine solution. Also, oysters can be salty.

I like stuffing a lot, so this recipe might yield extra. Cook any stuffing that doesn't fit in the bird in a buttered glass or earthenware dish next to the bird. Cover for two-thirds of the cooking time, then remove cover and let brown for the remaining cooking time.

If you'd rather cook all the stuffing outside the bird, remember to reduce the turkey's cooking time. The internal temperature of the meat should be about 165°F and the juices where the thigh meets the body should run clear.

Lagniappe

CASSOULET

It's 1950, and the Brennans are starting to get a food reputation at their restaurant on Bourbon Street. So they decide they had better start educating themselves about food, starting with the French classics. They've read and heard a lot about cassoulet, the classic French dish from the Languedoc region, so they gather recipes from all their favorite French cookbooks and set out to make cassoulet.

The recipes were in French and used lots of fancy-sounding ingredients and techniques. When Ella and longtime chef Paul Blangé finally deciphered the instructions and put the ingredients out on a table, they started laughing uproariously. Why had they been so intimidated, they asked themselves. "This is nothing more than red beans and rice made with white beans." As they taught themselves more and more about cooking, they would laugh at their innocence many times as they rediscovered what they already knew time and time again.

Duck and Sausage Cassoulet

This is what we call a fancy comfort food. It's really good on a cold, wet night, when the steaming cassoulet will warm your soul. This recipe uses duck and a couple of pork products, but we also make it with rabbit, lamb, or pheasant, and the required white beans. We like to serve it in cute little copper pots from Italy.

1½ pounds dried white beans (see Chef Jamie's Tips)

3 tablespoons duck fat or butter

2 pounds fresh sausage links (about ten 4-inch links), cut in half

1 pound ham hock, split, or fresh pork

2 medium heads garlic, cloves peeled and minced

2 large onions, in large dice

2 quarts water

Kosher salt and freshly ground pepper to taste

4 bay leaves

½ teaspoon freshly grated nutmeg

4 whole duck legs or confit of 1 duck (page 202)

6 sprigs fresh thyme

WASH the beans thoroughly in cold water, looking for small stones or other debris; drain and set them aside.

PLACE a large heavy pot over high heat, melt the fat or butter, and add the sausage, ham hocks, and garlic. Cook for about 8 minutes, turning the sausage so that it's completely brown and the garlic is toasted. Keep a close eye on it and stir. Remove from the pan and set aside.

SAUTÉ the onion in the pot until it begins to get tender, about 5 minutes. Add the beans and cook for 3 minutes, stirring. Add the water, season with salt and pepper, add the bay leaves and nutmeg, and bring to a boil. Boil for 10 minutes, then reduce the heat and simmer for about 1 to 1¼ hours, or until the beans are tender. Don't overcook the beans or break them up by stirring. Don't let them burn on the bottom of the pot.

PREHEAT the oven to 350°F.

USING a slotted spoon, place about half the beans in a large, wide-mouthed earthenware, cast-iron, or cassoulet bowl. Layer the sausage on top, then the pork, then the duck legs, each cut into a drumstick and thigh. (If you're using whole duck confit, cut each breast in half.) Place the remaining beans on top of the duck, reserving all leftover bean liquid. Place the thyme on top, slightly submerging it, and top off with any remaining bean liquid or, if needed, water, so that the liquid just reaches the top of the beans.

BAKE uncovered for 1 hour, or until the cassoulet comes to a simmer and a crust starts to form. Reduce the heat to 250°F and cook for about 6 hours, checking every hour to make sure the cassoulet is barely simmering. Whenever a crust has formed, gently push it down with the back of a spoon, allowing new crust to form on top. As necessary, add enough bean liquid or water to moisten the beans. After 6 hours, remove the cassoulet from the oven, and let it rest for 20 to 25 minutes. If you've used ham hocks, remove the meat and discard the bones. Serve from the pot.

CHEF JAMIE'S TIPS

One rule about cassoulet: You must use a white bean. Great Northern or navy beans are the easiest to find.

I've used other cuts of meat, such as lamb and game sausage. My favorite is duck or goose confit. I've also seen recipes with pork rind. I believe that a good portion of pork is essential for a cassoulet.

When using confit, be sure to remove the small bones, if any, such as ribs and breast bones.

I almost always make this a 2-day production. I cook it the first day and let it get better in the refrigerator overnight. After it comes out of the oven, let it cool, then cover and refrigerate. The next day, remove from the refrigerator, let sit for 1 hour, remove the cover, and reheat for 1 hour in a preheated 350° F oven. Reduce the oven temperature to 250° F, break any crust that has formed, and heat to a simmer.

Crispy Roast Duck with Roasted Vegetables and Orange Brandy Sauce

MAKES 4 SERVINGS

La Tour d'Argent in Paris has one of the world's oldest and most beautiful duck presses. It also has a view of the Seine. The ambiance and the elaborate duck preparation are hard to beat. But if you don't happen to be in Paris and you don't have time to hang your ducks for two weeks as we do, then this recipe is one heck of a good substitute.

1 Long Island duck, about 5 pounds

1 quart cold water

Kosher salt and freshly ground pepper to taste

2 large carrots, peeled and cut in half crosswise

2 medium turnips, peeled and halved

4 large new potatoes, halved

8 shiitake mushrooms, trimmed of their stems

12 cloves garlic, peeled

2 small onions, peeled and halved, or 12 pearl onions

Juice of 1 large orange

2 tablespoons chopped fresh rosemary

1/4 cup brandy

THOROUGHLY rinse the duck giblets, including liver and neck, place in a large pot with 1 quart of cold water over high heat, season lightly with salt and pepper, bring to a boil, and simmer for 20 minutes.

TRIM excess fat from the duck, especially around the neck and inside the cavity, and prick with the tines of a kitchen fork just deeply enough to penetrate the skin and fat, especially where the fat is concentrated. Make a one-inch incision under each leg bone where it meets the backbone. (You'll see a lot of fat at this spot.)

PLACE the duck, carrots, turnips, potatoes, mushrooms, garlic, and onions in the pot. Bring to a simmer, cover, and continue simmering for about 40 minutes, or until the vegetables are cooked but still firm and the duck seems cooked but not overcooked. Gently remove the duck and the vegetables, set aside, and let cool for about 30 minutes. Remove the giblets, and set aside. Transfer the cooking liquid to a bowl and refrigerate.

PREHEAT the oven to 425°F. Brush the duck with some of the orange juice, and season with salt, pepper, and half the chopped rosemary.

PLACE the giblets and neck in the center of a roasting pan and, using them as a rack, place the duck on top so that it does not touch the bottom of the pan. Gently arrange the vegetables around the duck, and place the pan in the oven. Roast until the skin is very crisp, about 45 to 50 minutes, or until the internal temperature of the duck reads 165°F on an instant-read meat thermometer, checking periodically to make sure the duck is not burning.

WHEN finished, place the duck in the center of a serving platter and place the vegetables neatly around the duck. Pick the meat from the neck, dice the giblets, and pour off the fat remaining in pan. Remove the cooking liquid from the refrigerator and discard any fat that has floated to the surface.

PLACE the roasting pan over two burners on top of the stove over high heat. Add the remaining rosemary and the brandy, being careful of a possible flareup. Using a wooden spoon, scrape off any glaze that may be on the bottom of the pan. Add the cooking liquid and the remaining orange juice, bring to a boil, then simmer to reduce for about 10 minutes, until the liquid has reached a saucelike consistency.

STRAIN the sauce into a small pot, add the reserved neck and innards meat, and season with salt and pepper.

CARVE the duck, and serve the sauce in a separate bowl on the side, not poured over the crispy duck skin.

CHEF JAMIE'S TIPS

At Commander's Palace, we use fresh Muscovy ducks. You can use any domestic duck for this recipe (about half of them are Long Island ducks). Fresh ducks can be hard to find, but don't let a frozen bird stop you. I always use a Grade A duck. The blanching of the duck and vegetables can be done up to a day in advance.

Chilling the cooking liquid lets unwanted fat rise to the top. That's why a wide bowl works so well; the liquid cools fast and there is a large surface.

Vegetables should be brown and very tender. Be careful not to break them up.

Lagniappe

MENTORING

We believe in mentoring—big-time. We take young managers under our wings and spend lots of time discussing the ins and outs, ups and downs of the business with them. We give them books about business, food, and just plain life. And then we talk, one on one. We start by sharing something we've all learned from my mom. She says to young managers, "I want you to know that I am going to come to work each day and try to earn your trust and respect. And I want you to try to earn mine. But I don't feel you should automatically give that to me."

She works with them on their careers and their personal lives, wherever they want to be mentored. She always says that she had the best mentor, her brother Owen Brennan, who let her "follow him around like a puppy." She adored him. He could be brusque, though. One day, when he was not happy with the job she had done on the inventory and the resulting food cost, he found her in the ladies' room applying lipstick. He grabbed the lipstick from her hand and wrote on the mirror: 40%. That was the food cost he wanted. Then he stormed out.

While we use less dramatic techniques, we get just as impressive results.

Skillet–Grilled Squab with Braised Salad and Honey Mashed Turnips

Jumbo Lump Crabcakes with Sweet Corn and Jalapeño

Hickory–Grilled Pompano with Citrus Salsa and Corn–Fried Oysters

Seafood Jambalaya

Ponchatoula Strawberry Shortcake

The Chef's

Table

he Chef's Table is the center of our culinary universe. By night, it belongs to our guests. By day, it belongs to our staff.

It seats only four, it's in the middle of the kitchen, and it's often booked months in advance. For dinner, it's the kitchen table, and what a show our guests get. The Chef's Table gives you more than a front-row seat—it puts you in the middle, really, of all the action. Are you a real foodie? If so, settle in to the banquette Chef's Table and let us blow your mind with a night of true culinary theater. It's noisy, interactive, and wildly indulgent.

Warning: The experience is *not* for everyone.

That's right. This is *not* the table to request for a romantic dinner for two or a private, serious business dinner. We want to involve and enthrall you with the culinary performance happening all around you. The pace is fast! There's lots of work to be done—and quickly! This place has a pulse! You're in the midst of it all, yet you're removed and comfortable. It's like watching Mardi Gras from a Bourbon Street balcony—you're close enough to the chaos to have a ball but removed enough to feel pampered.

Oh, how they pamper you!

Chef Jamie Shannon serves a "tasting menu" for you that night. There will be lots of small tastes paired with glorious wines, all ending with what we call the "dessert bomb"—an array of all our desserts, everything spread out to fill the entire tabletop.

"This is where we let the horses become slightly unbridled," brags Ella Brennan about the food-passionate team in Commander's Kitchen. Discovering, improving, and creating the food that will set the coming standards for the New Orleans food scene is a religion at Commander's Palace. The keepers of the faith are there to tempt you to sin a little during your evening in the kitchen. (Now that's my kind of religion!)

So for that night, you and your guests are at the center of all the action. Even the other customers parading by on the way to their table wear an expression that seems to ask, "Wow, who's so important that they get *that* table—and the chef is serving them?"

But before that table becomes the center of *your* world, it's the center of *ours*. All day long we meet there to talk about food and service, to share the latest improvement of our service system, to see pictures of our manager's new baby, to taste a wine, to hear about Lally's latest trip, and, of course, to keep abreast of local politics and local "goings on." That table is like a magnet—it pulls us all in. For us, it's better than e-mail.

The recipes in this chapter are show-off dishes. In some cases, it's the ingredients themselves, simply prepared. In other cases, it is more technique. But in all cases, these dishes are a wow. The Salt-Crusted Whole Baked Redfish is a knock-your-socks-off presentation, but it's easy to prepare and the fish will literally melt in your mouth. Over and over, the Creole Cream Cheese Ice Cream has been declared the best ice cream ever.

Shrimp and Tasso Henican

MAKES 8 APPETIZER SERVINGS

This is what Commander's calls a new classic. At first it went on the menu occasionally, but guests quickly insisted that it be there all the time. And why not? Pickled okra, five different peppers, jumbo shrimp, and Louisiana hot sauce have long been part of the Creole cook's pantry. But never have I seen them combined with such perfection. Want to knock the socks off your guests? Start your meal with this dish. It is named after a long-time dear family friend, Joe Henican.

24 jumbo shrimp, peeled and deveined

2 ounces tasso (see Note), cut into twenty-four 1-inch strips

$^1/_2$ cup all-purpose flour

Creole Seafood Seasoning (page 294) or any Creole seasoning mix

$^1/_2$ cup vegetable oil

$^3/_4$ cup Crystal Hot Sauce Beurre Blanc (page 299)

$^3/_4$ cup Five-Pepper Jelly (recipe next page) or a good-quality prepared pepper jelly

12 pieces pickled okra, cut in half top to bottom

CUT a quarter-inch-deep incision down the back of each shrimp where it has been deveined, and place a tasso strip in each incision. Secure with a tooth-pick. Combine the flour with the Creole seasoning and lightly dredge each shrimp.

HEAT the oil in a large skillet over medium heat and fry the shrimp in the hot oil for about 30 seconds on each side. Shrimp should be firm with a red-brown color. Remove the shrimp and drain briefly on a paper towel. Toss the shrimp with the Crystal Hot Sauce beurre blanc in a bowl, coat thoroughly, and remove the toothpicks.

PLACE a portion of five-pepper jelly on each of 8 appetizer plates, and arrange 3 shrimp on each plate, alternating with 3 pieces of pickled okra.

NOTE: Tasso is a seasoning ham widely used in New Orleans but hard to find elsewhere. You could order it by mail, or you could substitute 1 ounce of ham cut in 1-inch strips and tossed with 1 part cayenne and 3 parts paprika.

Five-Pepper Jelly

MAKES 2 CUPS

1½ cups light corn syrup
1¼ cups white vinegar
½ teaspoon red pepper flakes
Kosher salt and freshly ground black
    pepper to taste

1 each large red, yellow, and green bell
    pepper, seeded, membranes trimmed,
    and finely diced
4 jalapeño peppers, seeds and membranes
    removed, finely diced

PLACE the corn syrup, vinegar, red pepper flakes, salt, and black pepper in a small saucepan. Simmer to reduce by two thirds, until mixture is thickened. It will get even thicker as it cools, but the peppers will thin it again when they are added.

BRIEFLY place the peppers in a hot dry skillet and sauté until tender and their color is brightened, about 30 seconds. Using a slotted spoon, remove the peppers from the pan and add them to the corn syrup mixture.

USE as directed in the previous recipe. Five-pepper jelly also goes well on toast and as a glaze for roast chicken.

NOTE: This recipe can be made ahead and stored in the refrigerator. A good store-bought version is also available, by mail if necessary.

Lagniappe

COMMANDER'S KITCHEN

"Follow me. Yes, right this way."

"Through the kitchen?"

"Yes, sir. Come on in. This is the way to the bar and your table."

First-time customers always react the same way, and we never tire of seeing the amazed looks on their faces as they follow a team member into the middle of the kitchen where waiters and cooks whiz by. We know of no other restaurant where guests have to go through the kitchen to get to their table.

Ella, Dottie, Adelaide, Dick, and John made a lot of changes when they bought Commander's. One of the first decisions was to place the bar right outside the kitchen. They just thought that was jazzy and fun—very New Orleans. I'm amazed that more than 25 years later, nobody has copied that idea.

Jumbo Lump Crabcakes with Sweet Corn and Jalapeño

MAKES 4 ENTRÉES OR
8 APPETIZERS

I know what you're thinking: Another crabcake. Well, all crabcakes are *not* alike. When this dish goes on the Commander's menu, more than half our patrons will order it. They probably feel as my mother does: "True jumbo lump crabmeat is the caviar of Louisiana." We want to highlight the crabmeat, not mask it with heavy binders or frying, so this has no bread crumbs and only a small amount of binder. And the cakes are *not* fried, making them incredibly light. As for the accompaniment, crab and corn are a classic Creole combination.

Crabcakes:

1 pound jumbo lump crabmeat, picked over for bits of shell and cartilage (other crabmeat can be substituted)

1 small red onion, in small dice

½ large red bell pepper, in small dice

⅔ cup mayonnaise (homemade will be better), with Tabasco and freshly ground black pepper added to taste

⅓ cup Creole mustard or other coarse mustard

2 teaspoons capers, drained and coarsely chopped

½ medium hard-cooked egg, diced small

1 teaspoon prepared horseradish

Kosher salt and freshly ground pepper to taste

1 teaspoon Creole Seafood Seasoning (page 294) or any Creole seasoning mix, or to taste

2 tablespoons butter

Corn accompaniment:

2 tablespoons butter

3 cups freshly shucked corn kernels, about 6 ears

2 jalapeño peppers, seeds and membranes removed, in ⅛-inch dice

Kosher salt and freshly ground pepper to taste

1 tablespoon minced fresh thyme

For serving:

1 green onion, finely sliced

Fresh thyme sprigs (optional garnish)

PLACE the crabmeat in a bowl, breaking it up as little as possible. In a separate bowl, combine the onion, bell pepper, mayonnaise, mustard, capers, egg, horseradish, salt, pepper, and seafood seasoning. Mix well, add the crabmeat, and fold together, again taking care not to break up the crabmeat.

SHAPE the crabcakes. If you wish, you can roughly shape them by hand before placing the mixture in metal rings or round cookie cutters, each about 2½ inches in diameter. Or you can place the rings on a flat surface, put 2½ to 3 ounces of the mixture in each ring, and press lightly on each cake.

PREHEAT a nonstick pan or a seasoned cast-iron skillet over medium heat. Add 1 tablespoon of the butter, but don't let it smoke. Using your finger and a small spatula, guide about four of the rings into the skillet. Cook the crabcakes for 1½ minutes, or until golden brown. Turn them over, using the spatula, and cook again for 1½ minutes or until golden brown. Using the spatula, move the cakes to a sheet pan, and remove the rings. Repeat until the entire mixture is used. About halfway through, discard the butter and use a second tablespoonful.

TO MAKE the corn accompaniment: Place a sauté pan over medium heat, and add ½ tablespoon of butter. Be careful not to let the butter burn. Place the corn and jalapeño in the pan, and stir constantly, seasoning with salt and pepper. When the corn is hot (1½ to 2 minutes), stir in the remaining 1½ tablespoons of butter and add the minced thyme. Cook until all the butter has melted. Season to taste.

SERVE one crabcake for an appetizer portion, two for an entrée. Spoon some of the corn mixture over the top of each cake, sprinkle with the green onions, and garnish, if desired, with thyme sprigs.

CHEF JAMIE'S TIPS

This dish is a great example of how I try to extract the flavor from the jalapeño, not just get the hotness from it. By removing the seeds and the membrane from the pepper, and by cutting it into small dice, the heat is so greatly reduced that I can use twice as much jalapeño and it won't be incredibly hot. You'll just get the good flavor of the pepper.

Remember: The crabmeat is already cooked, so the crabcakes don't need much cooking. We just put a sear or crust on both sides and heat it through just enough to warm. You know that they are ready when you start to see a sear around the ring and they start to bubble a little. And be careful; it's easy to burn your fingers when you're flipping the cakes.

Panéed Fish with Roasted Artichokes and Wild Mushrooms

MAKES 4 SERVINGS

Chef Jamie knew he was on to something when he first told Lally and me about this dish. We went gaga, and now it's a new favorite at Commander's. Local friend and acclaimed food writer Gene Bourg ate this and said, "Jamie does the most wonderful things with fish." He's so right. Roasting the artichokes summons their full earthy flavor. The lightly roasted oysters and quickly panéed fish are surrounded by a very light and frothy Pernod sauce. Keeping that sauce frothy is critical to adding flavor, not heaviness, to this dish.

Juice of 1 lemon

1 cup olive oil

Kosher salt and freshly ground pepper to taste

4 artichokes, quartered (if large, cut into eighths) and hairy chokes removed (see Note)

1/4 pound wild mushrooms, such as shiitakes or morels, cleaned and coarsely chopped

8 large cloves garlic, peeled and thinly sliced

1 pint shucked oysters with their liquor

1/4 cup Pernod or licorice-flavored liqueur

3/4 cup cleaned and chopped fresh parsley

1 cup heavy cream

1 cup dried bread crumbs

2 tablespoons chopped fresh oregano

2 tablespoons chopped fresh basil

1/4 cup grated Parmesan cheese

2 medium eggs

1/2 cup water

3/4 to 1 pound thin fish fillets, cut into 8 squares (see Chef Jamie's Tips)

PREHEAT the oven to 400°F.

COMBINE the lemon juice, 2 tablespoons of the olive oil, salt, and pepper in a medium, ovenproof saucepan. Toss the prepared artichokes in this mixture until coated. Place in the pan in one layer and roast in the preheated oven for 40 minutes, until the artichokes are golden brown and tender. Stir occasionally. Add the mushrooms and garlic, and roast for 20 minutes more, or until the garlic is golden. Add the undrained oysters, and cook until their edges curl, about 3 to 5 minutes.

REMOVE the saucepan from the oven, remove two-thirds of the mixture (an even amount of each ingredient), and keep warm. Place the pan with the remaining artichoke mixture on the stovetop over high heat, deglaze with the Pernod to release any flavorful bits clinging to the bottom, stir, and cook for a few seconds. Add half the parsley and all the cream and bring to a boil.

PURÉE the mixture in a blender or food processor, and strain it through a fine-mesh sieve. Adjust the seasoning. Adjust the consistency, either by reducing the mixture over a high flame or by adding cream. Set the sauce aside and keep warm.

THOROUGHLY combine the bread crumbs, remaining parsley, oregano, basil, and cheese in a large bowl.

WHISK the eggs and the water in another large bowl, to combine into an egg wash. Piece by piece, season the fish with salt and pepper, dip in the egg wash, then dip in the breading mixture. Shake off any excess.

PLACE a skillet with the remaining olive oil on the stove over medium heat. When the oil is hot but not smoking, place half the fish skin side up in the pan, cook until golden brown (about 1½ minutes, depending on the thickness of the fish), gently flip the fish, and cook for another 1½ minutes, or until done. Remove the fish to drain on a paper towel. Repeat with the remaining fish pieces.

PLACE an even amount of artichoke mixture in the center of each of 4 dinner plates. Arrange 2 pieces of fish on top and drizzle sauce around the edge of the artichoke mixture.

NOTE: The artichokes should be prepared so that they'll be fully edible after cooking. To prepare them, trim off the stems, pick off the outer two layers of leaves, use a sharp knife to cut off the tops where the inner leaves turn from yellow to green, and trim all green from the bottoms so they are completely yellow. Then quarter the artichokes and remove the hairy chokes from inside. (If you're using baby artichokes, you don't have to remove the inner choke.)

CHEF JAMIE'S TIPS

Fish should be a thin white meat, such as small redfish, snapper, trout, flounder, bass, etc. Sauce should be frothy and light with a green tinge and the consistency of a light milkshake.

Use one hand for dipping the fish in egg wash and keep the other hand dry for breading. It will make the breading cleaner and will keep the crumbs dry to prevent lumping and uneven breading.

Preparing the artichokes might take a little practice.

Shoestring Potato–Crusted Lyonnaise Fish

MAKES 6 SERVINGS

We put this dish on the Commander's menu as a special and it just took off. Now it's what we call a new classic. But it shouldn't have been a surprise, considering how moist the fish turns out and New Orleanians' love affair with shoestring potatoes. The trick to moist fish and a crispy potato crust is simple—the potatoes do it. The heat from the water in the potatoes steams the fish while it crisps the potatoes. The dramatic texture contrast and the moist fish, which has retained all its juices, make this a scene-stealer. For a lighter version, skip the beurre blanc and serve with sliced Creole or vine-ripened tomatoes or over greens.

4 large russet potatoes

6 fish fillets (speckled trout, snapper, catfish, or flounder), each 5 to 6 ounces, of even thickness, and free of bones

Kosher salt and freshly ground pepper to taste

1 cup flour, seasoned with salt and pepper

$2/3$ cup milk

2 medium eggs, beaten

1 cup white wine

2 lemons, peeled, white pith removed, and quartered

5 cloves garlic, peeled

6 whole black peppercorns

$1/2$ pound (2 sticks) butter, at room temperature

$1/4$ cup vegetable oil

$1/4$ cup toasted capers (see Note)

1 large onion, sliced, then caramelized (see Note)

PEEL the potatoes and cut them into a fine shoestring size (see Chef Jamie's Tips), with each piece about 2 inches long, $1/8$ inch wide, and $1/16$ inch thick. Place the potatoes in a bowl of cold water and rinse until the water runs clear.

SEASON the fish fillets with salt and pepper and dust in seasoned flour, shaking away any excess flour. Combine the milk, eggs, and additional salt and pepper, and place the fish in the egg wash.

REMOVE the potatoes from the water, and drain them, using a clean dish towel to squeeze out any excess water. Place a thin layer of potatoes, enough to coat one side of all the fillets, on a work surface. Place the fish on top of the potatoes, then place a layer of potatoes on top of the fish, covering it completely.

TO MAKE the sauce, put the wine, lemons, garlic, and peppercorns in a small saucepan over high heat, bring to a boil, and reduce the heat to a high simmer. Use a whisk to break up the lemon sections. Cook for 7 to 9 minutes, or until the liquid starts to thicken. Reduce the heat to low and whisk in the butter, about 4 tablespoons at a time. Make sure the sauce doesn't separate, which will happen if the heat is too high. Whisk constantly, watching to keep a very warm temperature. Continue adding butter until it has all been incorporated, waiting to add more butter after the previous addition has been incorporated. Season with salt, strain, and keep the sauce warm.

HEAT 2 tablespoons of the oil over high heat in a large nonstick skillet for 2 to 3 minutes, or until it just begins to smoke. With a spatula, gently place 3 fish fillets in the pan, and reduce the heat to medium high. The fish might stick at first, but don't move it; as the potatoes cook, their starch will turn to sugar and the fish will come free.

USING the spatula, push any loose potato pieces up against the fish, but break away pieces that have turned very dark and crisp without adhering. Reduce the heat if the potato starts to burn. Cook for 5 to 6 minutes, or until the crust is golden and crisp. Gently turn the fish pieces over, reshaping with the spatula as necessary. Cook 4 to 5 minutes more, or until golden and crisp. Flip again, and recrisp the first side for about 30 seconds. Remove, adjust seasoning, and keep warm on a rack. Wipe the pan with a paper towel, and repeat with the second batch of fish fillets.

To serve, pool about 2½ tablespoons of sauce on a warm plate, place a fish fillet on top, and sprinkle the capers and onions around the plate.

NOTE: Toasted capers have been cooked in a little hot oil over high heat until they become crisp. Caramelized onions are chopped onions that have been cooked in a little butter over high heat until their natural sugars cause them to brown; they should drain on a paper towel when they're crisp. If you wish, prepare both in the same pan, using butter.

CHEF JAMIE'S TIPS

Use a box grater to cut the potatoes, holding the potato the long way so you get the longest pieces. If you have a mandoline, that works well, too. A mandoline is a hand-operated machine that can be fitted with different blades for different uses and cuts. At Commander's, we use both French (metal) and Japanese (plastic) mandolines in the kitchen.

When making lemon butter sauce, be sure the heat isn't too high when adding butter or the sauce can break. Adjust the heat as you add the butter, if needed. If the sauce becomes too thick, that means it's not hot enough, so add a little more heat.

Duck Confit and Duck Crackling

MAKES ABOUT 1½ POUNDS OF MEAT

*G*reat cooking techniques are at the core of Creole cooking, and confit is a classic. A confit is meat or game, slow-cooked and preserved in its own fat, and in this recipe, it's a method that intensifies the duck's flavor. We use it in our mixed grill dish, in salads, on our *garde manger,* or butcher's, plate, and in cassoulet.

1 duck, 4½ to 5 pounds
2 tablespoons chopped fresh rosemary
2 tablespoons kosher salt
2 tablespoons freshly ground black pepper
2 bay leaves

20 cloves garlic, peeled
4 to 5 cups duck fat (render the fat from
    the skin and add olive oil for the rest)

PREHEAT the oven to 350°F.

REMOVE and reserve the skin from the duck by slicing down the center of the breast and working your way down the breast meat, past the wing and leg, until you reach the center of the duck's backbone. Continue cutting on the other side of the backbone, then remove the skin. Remove any fat around both cavities of the duck. Remove the entire leg by cutting where the thigh meets the breast and pulling back. Repeat with the second leg. Remove the breast meat from the carcass, leaving the wing bone attached. Remove the middle and the tip of each wing. Remove the skin from both legs and remove any skin remaining on the breast and wing pieces and on the duck carcass.

PLACE the carcass, innards, and wing tips in a bag and freeze for future use, such as stocks (or, at least in these parts, for crab bait).

SEASON the meat with half the rosemary and all the salt and pepper, then place in an earthenware container, cover with plastic, and refrigerate overnight.

TO MAKE the cracklings, cut the skin and fat into ½- by 3-inch strips, place all the pieces in a baking pan, and bake for 2½ to 3 hours, stirring occasionally, until very crisp and golden brown. Remove the cracklings with a slotted spoon and drain on paper towels; season with salt while still hot. Strain the fat through cheesecloth or a fine sieve, and refrigerate.

THE NEXT DAY, brush as much seasoning off the duck as possible with a clean towel. Some of the salt will have dissolved and cured the meat.

REMOVE the duck fat from the refrigerator, melt it in a pot, and top it off with as much olive oil as needed to give you a total of 5 cups. Heat the fat to 185°F on a deep-fry thermometer. Add the duck meat, and pack it tightly so the fat totally covers the meat. Add the bay leaves, remaining rosemary, and garlic. Be sure everything is submerged; if it's not, top it off with a little more olive oil. Season with pepper and cook at 185°F (below a simmer) for about 2½ hours or until fork-tender. When finished, transfer to an earthenware container, with the meat still submerged in the fat. Let cool in the refrigerator. The duck will taste best in a week; it will keep for up to a month.

WHEN the cracklings have completely cooled, store at room temperature in a plastic bag for a week to 10 days.

CHEF JAMIE'S TIPS

If you have a source for duck fat, use it instead of skinning the duck. The keys to great confit are: don't overseason, leave the initial seasoning on for about 12 to 18 hours, never let the fat boil, and make sure to keep the meat totally submerged in fat.

Eat the crackling as a snack. I use it in place of croutons to make a confit salad.

In the kitchen, we use confit for game pies, salads, cassoulets, hors d'oeuvres, cooking legumes, and various side dishes. I like confit on French bread accompanied by a glass of wine.

Duck Confit and Arugula Goat Cheese Salad

MAKES 6 ENTRÉES OR
12 APPETIZERS

*T*his makes an exciting warm or cold salad. We use confit (a meat cooked and preserved in its own fat) on our *garde manger* plate (or butcher's plate), on the tasting menu, and often at the kitchen Chef's Table. Confit is so rich that the greens and vinegar in the salad cut the fat somewhat, drawing even more of the distinctive duck flavor out of the confit.

1 pound arugula (or specialty green of your choice, such as frisée, watercress, spinach)

Confit of 1 duck (the confit segment of the recipe on page 202)

$\frac{1}{3}$ cup balsamic vinegar, or to taste

1 large onion, cut in half and thinly sliced

3 roasted bell peppers, thinly sliced (store-bought, or page 306)

3 cups croutons or duck crackling (page 202)

12 ounces goat cheese, crumbled

Kosher salt and freshly ground pepper to taste

CLEAN the greens thoroughly, rinsing them three times. Spin dry and set aside.

PICK the confit off the bone, break the meat into bite-sized pieces, and place it in a large stainless-steel bowl. Add the vinegar, place over low heat, and stir. A few seconds of heat is all you need; you're not cooking the meat, just warming up the congealed duck fat that coats it. If desired, add more fat or vinegar to taste.

REMOVE the bowl from the heat and toss in the onion, peppers, croutons, greens, and goat cheese, and season. Serve slightly warm.

CHEF JAMIE'S TIPS This salad is very popular at the Chef's Table. We have many versions of it, using seared foie gras, smoked quail, smoked duck breast, even sunny-side-up quail eggs.

Lagniappe

FOODIES

Back in the mid-'70s, we hired a very bright ad executive named Betty Hoffman. So many business meetings lapsed into food meetings that she finally said, "Y'all are just a bunch of foodies. I can't get you to talk about anything but food."

So we started using the word to describe each other, certain customers, and even people we were considering hiring. In the late 1990s, the food media began using the word to describe such people. We don't know whether Betty invented the term, but my mother, Ella Brennan, says she had never heard the word until Betty accused her of being a hopeless foodie.

Are you a foodie? To me, a foodie: (1) is a food fanatic; (2) is a person unreasonably interested in all things food-related; (3) knows the CIA is into recipes, not secrets; (4) does at least a fair Julia Child imitation; (5) knows that "86" means more than 43 times 2; (6) reads cookbooks like novels; (7) knows Pinot Noir is not a daiquiri flavor. In 1999, we named our new meals market in New Orleans Foodies Kitchen. What else?

Salt-Crusted Whole Baked Redfish

MAKES 4 SERVINGS

This dish is a showstopper. When I know that it will be served to customers at our Chef's Table, I try to be around for the presentation. Out walks this smiling 6-foot-3 Irishman, Chef Jamie, in his crisp whites, carrying an oversize oval copper pan with what looks like a mound of baked salt. Then Jamie cracks the salt crust to reveal a fish so moist and fresh that you'll swear you can taste the sea. The feigned nonchalance of even the most serious foodies is overcome. When you present this dish at home, only you'll know how simple it is to prepare.

One 6-pound redfish, gutted, rinsed, and
    gills (but not scales) removed
    (snapper makes a good substitute, as
    does bluefish, rockfish, or salmon)
8 pounds kosher salt

1/2 cup extra-virgin olive oil
2 lemons, halved
4 sprigs fresh rosemary or other fresh
    herb
Freshly ground black pepper to taste

PREHEAT the oven to 450°F.

PAT the fish dry with a towel. Place a 1/4-inch-thick layer of salt on a sheet pan large enough to keep the fish from hanging over the edges. Place the fish on top of the salt, and, using your hands and the remaining salt, mound the salt so that it completely covers the fish.

PLACE the fish in the oven for 1 hour (or for 10 minutes per pound), or until an instant-read thermometer inserted into the thickest part of the fish registers an internal temperature of 130°F.

IN A saucepan over low heat, bring the olive oil to 185°F and add the lemon halves, rosemary, pepper, and a touch of salt from the crust of the fish. Remove from the heat and let steep.

BRUSH off the excess salt from the fish. You should have a hard, white crust that encases the entire fish. Crack off the top part of the crust. With a fork, poke into the skin near the dorsal fin at the top of the fish, and run a tine of the fork under the skin up the back of the fish to the head, then in the opposite direction to the tail. Still using the fork, peel the skin back from the length of the fish, being careful not to let the fish flesh touch the salt. Using two large spoons, remove the top fillet and neatly place it on a serving platter. Remove the backbone by lifting it from the tail toward the head. Before removing the bottom fillet, push all of the small fin bones off to the side. Remove the bottom fillet in the largest pieces possible, removing any bones that you see.

WITH one of the spoons, take up any liquid remaining in the pan and spoon it over the fish. It's loaded with flavor.

SERVE with a touch of the rosemary-infused olive oil. Garnish with a sprig of rosemary and a lemon half.

Trust me, even though this dish calls for 8 pounds of salt, it will not taste salty. The salt crust acts to seal in the natural flavors and juices of the fish. I also like to serve a piece of the salt crust with the fish for seasoning and as a garnish. In the summer, I like to garnish this dish with Creole or vine-ripened tomatoes; in the winter, I'll garnish with Creole Roasted Ratatouille (page 255).

CHEF JAMIE'S TIPS

Hickory-Grilled Pompano with Citrus Salsa and Corn-Fried Oysters

MAKES 6 SERVINGS

*P*ompano is often considered America's finest fish, and it's an overwhelming New Orleans favorite. Pompano, found only in the South Atlantic and Gulf Region, has a mild, delicate flavor that should not be overwhelmed with other ingredients. We have come to love Chef Jamie's Citrus Salsa as the perfect complement to pompano. The lightly fried oysters complete the dish.

Salsa:

1 medium lemon, zest removed and minced

1 medium lime

1 medium navel orange

1 medium ruby red grapefruit

1 satsuma (a variety of citrus; tangerine can be substituted)

3/4 cup light corn syrup

1/2 cup cane vinegar or white distilled vinegar

2 jalapeño peppers, seeds and membrane removed, cut in small dice

Kosher salt and freshly ground pepper to taste

1 red, 1 yellow, and 1 green bell pepper, roasted (roast your own, as on page 306, or use good-quality store-bought roasted peppers)

1/2 large red onion, in very small dice

1/2 bunch green onions, sliced thin on the bias

2 tablespoons chopped fresh cilantro

Fish and oysters:

6 pompano fillets, 4 to 5 ounces each, skin on

Creole Seafood Seasoning (page 294) to taste

3 cups canola oil

1/2 cup masa flour (fine-ground corn flour)

1/3 cup all-purpose flour

1/2 cup cornmeal

Creole seasoning to taste

24 large oysters

Fresh cilantro leaves (optional garnish)

SECTION the citrus fruits by slicing off the rinds with a sharp paring knife and removing any pieces of bitter white pith. Slice on either side of each dividing membrane to free the citrus segments. Set them aside. Squeeze the juice from the membranes that remain after sectioning into a small bowl. Strain. Add to this the juice that has accumulated underneath the citrus segments. You should have about 1/2 cup.

COMBINE the citrus juice, corn syrup, and vinegar in a medium saucepan. Cook over medium heat, reducing the liquid by three-quarters, or until it coats the back of a spoon. Remove from the heat. This reduced mixture, or gastrique, will be the base of the salsa. Add the minced lemon zest and jalapeño, season lightly with the salt and pepper, and set aside to cool. Roast the bell peppers, cut into medium dice, and set aside.

PREPARE a fire in an outdoor grill. After the charcoal has caught, add either hickory wood or chips. If you are using hickory chips, soak them in water while the fire catches, then drain them and scatter over the coals, which should be glowing red, not flaming.

DUST the pompano with Creole seafood seasoning, and place the fillets, skin side up, on the grill for 2 to 4 minutes. (Move them halfway through the cooking to give them crosshatch grill marks.) Turn the fish skin side down to finish cooking. The actual time depends on several variables, so you may need to adjust it. The fillets should be firm to the touch. Keep the fish warm in a low oven while frying the oysters.

HEAT the canola oil to 350°F in a deep skillet or deep-fryer. Combine the masa flour, all-purpose flour, cornmeal, and Creole seasoning. Dust the oysters in the mixture, shake off the excess, and fry in small batches for 45 to 60 seconds, until the edges curl and turn golden brown. Drain on paper towels. Keep the cooked oysters warm in a low oven while you fry the remaining oysters.

MAKE the salsa: Combine the reduced citrus liquid, the citrus segments, roasted peppers, red onion, and green onion in a large bowl. Stir in the chopped cilantro, and season the salsa to taste with salt and pepper.

PLACE a pompano fillet in the center of each dinner plate. Spoon a portion of the salsa over the top, place 4 fried oysters around the pompano, and garnish, if desired, with fresh cilantro leaves.

 CHEF JAMIE'S TIPS

I usually use a sweetish variety of lemon called Meyer lemons, although any lemon will work fine. Alternatives to pompano could be tuna, bluefish, or amberjack.

Quail with Crawfish Stuffing

MAKES 8 SERVINGS

Chef Jamie says quail is so common in Louisiana that we have lots of quail farms and quail ranges around here. Groups of guys will take their dogs into the fields, shoot quail, and retire to the lodge to share stories and drinks before a game dinner. Women tell their own stories of men returning from their great hunts with the dogs as clean as when they left. Hmmm. This dish is one of our top three sellers, served for both brunch and dinner. All the bones are removed except for the legs and then the quail are stuffed with a crawfish stuffing.

16 quail, each 5 to 5½ ounces
2 medium carrots, peeled and coarsely chopped
3 ribs celery, coarsely chopped
2 small onions, peeled and coarsely chopped
30 cloves garlic, peeled and coarsely chopped
2 medium tomatoes, coarsely chopped
2½ cups port wine
2 bay leaves
Kosher salt and freshly ground pepper to taste

2 pounds ground pork
Creole Seafood Seasoning (page 294) or Creole Meat Seasoning (page 293), to taste
2 medium eggs
½ cup fine dried bread crumbs
½ cup heavy cream
½ cup ice water
1 cup packed or 6 ounces crawfish tails, cooked (you can use shrimp instead)
¼ cup sugar
4 tablespoons (½ stick) butter

PREHEAT the oven to 450°F.

REMOVE all the bones but the leg bones from each quail. Hold a breast in the palm of one hand with the legs facing you and, with large scissors, cut to one side of the backbone. Turn the bird around and cut the other side of the backbone so it detaches. Then cut off the wings. Burrow your thumb and index finger into the cavity of the quail, pinch the breastbone, and pull it out, which should bring the hip bones with it. Finally, remove the wishbone.

NEXT, make a quail stock. Rinse and drain the bones and place in a large roasting pan with the carrots, celery, two-thirds of the onion, two-thirds of the garlic, and the tomatoes. Roast for about 1 hour, stirring occasionally, until the vegetables have caramelized and turned a golden brown. Place the roasting pan over two stove burners, and, over high heat, deglaze with ½ cup of the wine, scraping any glaze from the bottom of the pan. Pour in enough cold water to just cover the bones; add the bay leaves, and a bit of salt and pepper. Bring to a boil, skim away any foam that might float to the top, reduce to a low simmer, and cook for about 2 hours, skimming occasionally. The stock should have a golden brown color and a good quail flavor.

STRAIN the stock into a medium saucepan, bring it to a boil, and simmer, reducing to about 2 cups or until the sauce thickens a bit and coats the back of a spoon (about 40 minutes, depending on how you simmer).

WHILE the stock is simmering, make the quail stuffing. Place the ground pork, remaining onion and garlic, about ¼ cup of the Creole seasoning (or to taste), eggs, and bread crumbs in the workbowl of a food processor, and pulse until the ingredients are well combined. Combine the heavy cream and the ice water in a measuring cup with a pour spout, and slowly add the mixture to the workbowl, pulsing as you add the ingredients. Place in a mixing bowl. Fold in the crawfish or shrimp, and refrigerate.

BRING the remaining wine and the sugar to a boil in a small saucepan, and reduce slowly to ¼ cup, simmering over medium heat until the mixture starts to thicken and small bubbles appear, about 20 to 30 minutes. Be careful not to burn. Add the 2 cups of quail stock, bring to a boil, then simmer for 20 minutes or until the mixture reaches a saucelike consistency and small bubbles appear. Whisk in 1 tablespoon of the butter, and season, if needed. Keep warm.

PREHEAT the oven to 400°F. Melt the remaining 3 tablespoons of butter in a small saucepan, and brush some of the melted butter on the bottom of a large roasting pan.

WHILE the sauce is reducing, remove the quail and stuffing from the refrigerator. Lay the quail skin side down on your work surface, and sprinkle additional Creole seasoning over the birds. Roll the stuffing into 3-ounce balls and place one ball in the center of each quail. Wrap the quail around the stuffing, gently re-creating the original bird shape as best you can. Place each quail in the pan with its legs in the air. The quail should not touch each other or the sides of the pan. Brush the remaining melted butter over each bird, and season with additional Creole seasoning.

ROAST the quail for 35 to 40 minutes, or until done. The birds should be golden brown and the ground pork needs to be fully cooked. The center of the stuffing ball should read 160°F to 165°F on an instant-read thermometer. Remove from the oven and let rest for 5 minutes.

IN COMMANDER'S kitchen, we serve our quail with a sauté of fresh corn, but it will go well with any of your favorite side dishes—especially after it's been napped with sauce.

(continued)

CHEF JAMIE'S TIPS This makes a great alternative to a holiday turkey dinner. Quail sizes, and therefore cooking time, vary, and occasionally you might find birds large enough that
one bird would make a single serving.

Another way to make this would be to buy the quail already boned, which means
they'll have only the wing and leg bones, and to make an easier stock. Cut off the wings
and roast them with the vegetables, as directed, but add chicken stock instead of water.

*E*veryone at Commander's wants our menu to evolve, but we all have a dish or two that we'll fight to keep just as it is. This is one of mine. No food architecture, no plate-painting—just a great dish. There was a time when a top restaurant wouldn't serve grits. But the Commander's team decided long ago that some of the greatest food in the world was right under our noses. Like grits. Cooked to the perfect texture and molded with pungent goat cheese from nearby Chicory Farms, well, you might find a fancier complement to veal tenderloin, but you won't find a better one.

Mushroom sauce:

1 tablespoon clarified butter

6 medium cloves garlic, minced

2 shallots, chopped medium

3/4 ounce dried morels, reconstituted, or 3 ounces fresh

6 cups Veal Stock (page 73), reduced to lightly coat back of spoon

1 tablespoon whole butter

Goat cheese–thyme grits:

1 quart milk, any kind

2 tablespoons butter

Kosher salt and freshly ground pepper to taste

1 cup white grits

1 tablespoon chopped fresh thyme

6 ounces fresh soft goat cheese

Veal:

1/4 cup clarified butter

12 medallions of veal, each about 2 ounces and 1 inch thick, cut from the tenderloin

Kosher salt and freshly ground pepper to taste

6 cups mushrooms, any type, sliced

3 medium leeks, trimmed of green parts and roots, split from top to bottom, washed, and cut in strips or shreds

1/2 cup brandy

1 tablespoon unsalted butter

Optional garnish:

6 sprigs fresh thyme

TO MAKE the sauce: Melt the clarified butter in a large saucepan over medium heat, and sauté the garlic, shallots, and morels until they begin to release their liquid. Add the veal stock, raise the heat to high, skim, simmer, and reduce the liquid by half. When the reduction is completed, finish the sauce by whisking in the butter.

(continued)

TO MAKE the grits: Heat the milk, 1 tablespoon of the butter, and a bit of salt and pepper in a medium saucepan, and bring to a simmer. Stir in the grits and cook, stirring, for about 3 to 5 minutes, or until tender. Taste and adjust seasoning. Stir in the remaining butter, the thyme, and the cheese. Keep the pot in a warm place, covered with plastic wrap, until you're ready to assemble the dish.

TO COOK the veal and prepare the mushroom mix: Place half the clarified butter in a 10-inch sauté pan over medium heat. Season the veal medallions on both sides with salt and pepper. Place 6 medallions in the pan, cook about 2 minutes per side until medium-rare, set aside, and keep warm. Repeat with the remaining 6 medallions. Add the mushrooms to the same pan, and sauté for 1 minute, stirring occasionally. Add the leeks and cook about 2 minutes, so that they still have some bite to them. Adjust seasoning.

DISCARD any remaining fats and make certain that the fond is golden brown. (A fond is the residual sugar from the meat that has caramelized. It adds great flavors to a sauce when removed from the bottom of the pan through deglazing.) Deglaze the pan with brandy. When the mushroom-leek mixture (the ragout) is the consistency of a thick sauce, whisk in the butter. Remove from the heat, and adjust seasoning.

TO ASSEMBLE, mound a portion of the grits on each dinner plate. Make a well in the center, and fill with a portion of the mushroom-leek ragout. Top each portion with two of the veal medallions. Drizzle the sauce on top, and garnish, if desired, with a sprig of fresh thyme.

CHEF JAMIE'S TIPS This recipe is written for the quick grits sold in most groceries. I prefer using stone-ground grits, which can be difficult to find but yield much more flavor. They also need a lot more cooking. All grits can stick, so be careful not to burn them.
Veal tenders cook very quickly, so be careful not to overcook them.

*Y*ou have never eaten anything better. Period. This is the richest, creamiest, most worthwhile blast of calories and cholesterol you have ever consumed. My skinny, glamorous Aunt Dottie has the right take on this. She says that her way to stay thin is to make her calories worthwhile. In other words, don't waste calories on bad desserts or junk food. Well, this is worth it, and then some.

1 cup heavy cream	8 medium egg yolks
¹/₂ cup whole milk	²/₃ cup Creole Cream Cheese (page 309)
²/₃ cup sugar	¹/₃ cup sour cream

COMBINE the cream and milk in a large pot over medium heat, whisk in the sugar, bring the mixture to a boil, and remove from the heat.

PLACE the egg yolks in a large mixing bowl, and whisk in the cream-and-milk mixture. Return the entire mixture to the pot, and place it over medium heat. Stirring constantly with a wooden spoon, cook the custard until it coats the back of the spoon, about 2 minutes. Do not let the custard boil or it will curdle. Strain through a fine sieve into a bowl, and refrigerate until chilled. Fold in the Creole cream cheese and sour cream. Freeze in an ice-cream maker according to the manufacturer's directions.

The whisking is extremely important to keep the eggs from curdling when you temper them by adding the hot milk.

CHEF JAMIE'S TIPS

The slow cooking of the custard is a mark of Creole cooking.

Store-bought sour cream may be substituted for the Creole cream cheese, but it will taste different.

Lagniappe

Eye contact is critical to Commander's fine service. It refers to how quickly a guest can catch the eye of someone on the service staff. Years ago, we determined that the best thing we could do to speed up eye contact was to make sure that the service team was always in the dining room with the guests— not off in the kitchen or at the bar, fetching food and drinks.

So we added another layer of staff called runners. A runner's job is to wait in the kitchen for the finished food. The instant it's ready, a runner takes it to the appropriate dining room, where the service team is waiting to serve it. Not only does that system get the food to a table while it's still hot, but it keeps the service team close to the guests—ready and available for eye contact and any other manner of service. Of course, this costs more, but it works so well that we have encountered this system in more than a few restaurants across the country since we began it in 1980.

At the beginning of the evening, the runners seat guests and act as ambassadors for the restaurant. It's a great way for a new team member to get to know the restaurant, and vice versa. Many of our finest waiters started as runners.

9

Krewe Meals

rewe meal, Family meal, Help meal—it has had various names over the years, but the idea has never changed. In New Orleans, the term "Krewe" refers to a carnival organization—one of the groups that put on Mardi Gras parades, support charitable causes, and generally do so with much humor and feigned pomposity. With a little bit of punning, we've turned a local term into a Commander's Palace term.

The restaurant business demands long hours that can be stressful. Weekends, nights, and holidays—when people are at play, we serve them. Now, most of us would never think of trading 12 hours in a restaurant for 8 hours at a desk. Making people happy is a satisfying, positive goal for a work-day. But we need a break, too! And we take it at Krewe meal.

Twice a day, we stop everything and sit down to a meal together, followed by a pre-service meeting. The idea is to share a meal together, relax, and visit with each other before the next "show." Two shows daily, 362 days a year. Stressed-out, hungry people are not gracious, warm, and welcoming. By the time the guests arrive, all of us are well fed, prepared, and looking forward to serving you.

Naturally, the food we serve at these meals is important. While menu items sometimes make it into the Krewe meal lineup, more often than not, Krewe meal showcases a lusty, satisfying, "stick to your ribs" brand of home cooking. Everyone loves Krewe meal. Dottie and Ella Brennan live next door to Commander's. If they are home instead of working that night, they come over or call to see what's for Krewe meal. If it's Red Beans and Rice with an-douille, Ella asks the staff to hold her a plate. If it's Stewed Hen with Buttermilk-Herb Dumplings, Dottie is sure to be sharing a meal with team members oooohing over how the hen is so tender that it's "falling off the bone," just like her mother used to make.

I'm often asked of our team members, "Where do you get these people?" Or, "The people at Commander's are so nice—what are you doing to them?" Well, it's true, and it's noticeable. Our team is made up of a brand of people with a genuine and infectious warmth. The key is to hire only good-natured people. In other words, they came that way. People with chips on their shoul-ders or "snobby" attitudes don't usually make it to a second interview. So the credit for our team members' sincere desire to please our guests rests with the team members themselves. But once, a gentleman who said he had never had better service from such a happy group of people asked me, "What are you feeding these people?" Hmmmm.

Why is it traditional to serve red beans and rice on Monday? The reasons run from the practical (a good way to use Sunday's ham bone) to the probable (two starches served together do a fine job of soaking up the weekend's excesses). There are several "musts" with this dish. One is soaking the beans, which my Aunt Adelaide insisted should be for 24 hours. Another is that the marrow from the bone must be allowed to cook with the beans to help make the beans smooth and creamy. Finally, the beans, flavored with the ham bone and thyme and garlic and onion, must be ladled over a heaping plate of steaming white rice.

1 pound dried red kidney beans

1 pound smoked sausage, sliced ¼ inch thick

1 tablespoon butter

2 medium onions, in medium dice

5 ribs celery, in medium dice

2 bell peppers, in medium dice

15 cloves garlic, peeled and minced

¼ teaspoon cayenne pepper, or to taste

1½ tablespoons Creole Meat Seasoning (page 293) or seasoning of your choice, or to taste

8 cups cold water

1 pound smoked ham hock

3 bay leaves

Kosher salt and freshly ground black pepper to taste

Boiled Rice (page 252)

Hot sauce, chopped green onions, French bread (optional accompaniments)

RINSE and pick through the beans thoroughly, and soak them for 6 hours or overnight. Soaking speeds the cooking process and helps the beans to break down.

COOK the sausage in the butter over medium heat in a large, heavy pot for 3 to 5 minutes, or until brown. (The small amount of butter will keep the sausage from sticking before the fat renders out.) Add the onions, celery, peppers, and garlic, and sauté until tender. Add the cayenne and Creole seasoning, and stir. Add the water, ham hock, and bay leaves. Bring to a boil, stirring occasionally. Reduce to a simmer, and cook for 1½ hours, or until the beans are tender. Be careful not to scorch the beans—add more water while cooking if necessary. Season to taste with salt, black pepper, and cayenne.

SERVE the beans with boiled rice, and, if desired, with hot sauce, chopped green onions, and French bread on the side.

(continued)

This recipe calls for smoked sausage and ham hocks, but you can use just about any type of meat you want: smoked turkey necks, drumsticks, tasso, seasoned meat, pigs' tails, salt pork, or your favorite sausage—you name it. (Pickled pork is my favorite.) I like my beans meaty so I can serve this as a complete meal. It's a good idea to render the fat out of whatever meat you use with the vegetables. That way, you can use the flavored fat to sauté them.

Lagniappe

JAMBALAYA

Only in New Orleans, while researching the derivation of jambalaya and gumbo, could I encounter dueling newspaper editorials on the subject. Imagine the major newspaper in any other city devoting valuable space to the argument of whether jambalaya is of French or Spanish origin.

"There is no need to make the difficult stretch to Spanish when the French heritage of jambalaya is obvious," said one writer, quite authoritatively.

Various pronunciations of jambalaia, jabalaia, jambaraia *are all said to mean stew of rice and fowl. Others say "alaya" is from an African language and means "rice." And yet the similarities with paella, minus the saffron, seem obvious.* Jambon *is French for "ham" and was a common ingredient in early versions.*

But the fact that we are still publicly arguing about it is what I love. To the dismay of some, it seems to me that the jambalaya we eat today has multiple ancestors, but I hope the battle over just that wages on.

Seafood Jambalaya

MAKES 8 LARGE SERVINGS

*J*ambalaya rivals gumbo as Louisiana's quintessential Creole dish. All you need is a tangy green salad, some garlic bread, and a feisty Sauvignon Blanc. It's a great party dish that you can prepare ahead so you can enjoy the party yourself. (Now *that's* New Orleans.)

2 tablespoons butter

1 pound andouille sausage, in ¼-inch slices

1 large bell pepper, any color, in large dice

1 large onion, in large dice

3 ribs celery, in large dice

1 small head garlic, cloves peeled and minced

Creole Seafood Seasoning (page 294) or any Creole seasoning, to taste

Kosher salt and freshly ground black pepper to taste

2 large tomatoes, cored, peeled, seeded, and chopped

1 pound medium shrimp, peeled

½ pound fish fillets, diced (trout, catfish, redfish, bass, and bluefish would work well)

2 bay leaves

3 cups long-grain rice, rinsed 3 times

6 cups water

1 pint shucked oysters, with their liquor

2 bunches green onions, thinly sliced

¼ teaspoon hot sauce, or to taste

COMBINE the butter and sausage in a Dutch oven or heavy-gauge pot over high heat, and sauté for about 6 minutes, stirring occasionally. Add the bell pepper, onion, celery, and garlic, and season with Creole seasoning, salt, and black pepper. Sauté, still over high heat, for about 8 minutes, or until the natural sugars in the vegetables have browned and caramelized.

ADD the tomatoes, shrimp, fish, and bay leaves, and stir. Add the rice, stir gently, and add the water. Gently move the spoon across the bottom of the pot, making sure that the rice is not sticking. Bring to a boil, then reduce the heat, cover, and simmer for about 15 minutes or until the rice has absorbed most of the liquid. Turn off the heat, then fold in the oysters, cover, and let sit for about 8 minutes, during which time the jambalaya will continue cooking from residual heat.

TO SERVE, transfer to a serving bowl, and mix in the green onions. Season with hot sauce.

Jambalaya is a very versatile dish, so different combinations of other ingredients will work well in this recipe. If you'd rather use chicken instead of fish, or if you'd prefer to omit the oysters, go ahead. **CHEF JAMIE'S TIPS**

After adding the rice, the less stirring you do the better. You don't want to pull out excessive starch from the grain. This is not risotto. While simmering, be sure the rice is not sticking to the bottom. If it is, you might need to add a little water or reduce the heat.

If no andouille is available, another smoked sausage may be substituted.

Buttermilk
Fried Chicken

MAKES 6 TO 8 SERVINGS

*H*ere's one of those recipes that are great the first day and even better the second. This pan-fried recipe makes crispy, rich chicken right away. And by Day 2, it has had even more time to absorb the buttermilk, spices, and hot sauce. This Krewe meal favorite is great for picnics. At home, Chef Jamie uses hydrogenated vegetable shortening to avoid the smell of oil. The critical equipment is the heavy-gauge black iron skillet, seasoned from years of use, that you probably inherited. I don't know anyone who has bought a black iron skillet.

2 chickens, about 3 pounds each (see Note), each cut into 10 serving pieces (with each breast half cut in half)

Kosher salt and freshly ground black pepper to taste

4 cups buttermilk

1½ tablespoons hot sauce, or to taste

4 cups all-purpose flour

3 tablespoons dried thyme

3 tablespoons dried sage

3 tablespoons coarse black pepper

1 tablespoon cayenne pepper, or to taste

3 tablespoons kosher salt, or to taste

6 cups vegetable shortening

SEASON the chicken pieces with salt and pepper, add the buttermilk and hot sauce, stir, and refrigerate for 4 hours, or overnight.

PLACE the flour, thyme, sage, black pepper, cayenne pepper, and salt in a large bowl. Taste it. The mixture should have a good peppery-herb flavor and be slightly salty. This is important, because you want the seasoning cooked in, not added at the end.

REMOVE the chicken from the refrigerator, coat one piece at a time with the flour mixture, and place the coated pieces on a sheet pan. (The best way is to pick up a chicken piece with your left hand, let the excess liquid drain, place the chicken piece in the flour mixture, switch to your right hand to coat the chicken, shake off any excess flour, and place the piece on a sheet pan.) Repeat until all the chicken is coated.

USING a large, well-seasoned cast-iron skillet and a deep-fry thermometer, bring half the shortening to 350°F over high heat. Cook the chicken pieces in three batches to avoid crowding the pan. Place the first batch into the hot shortening, making sure that the oil keeps bubbling, even as the temperature falls a bit, and that the chicken pieces are not touching. Fry for about 5 to 6 minutes, or until the pieces are an even golden brown on one side. Turn the pieces, and cook for 7 to 8 minutes more, or until done. Place the cooked chicken on a wire rack with a sheet pan underneath, and repeat with the second batch of chicken. After the second batch, discard the hot fat into a safe container, wipe the pan with a paper towel, add the remaining shortening, and cook the third batch.

NOTE: Buy the smallest possible chickens, which may be heavier than 3 pounds. If they are, adjust the cooking time accordingly.

 CHEF JAMIE'S TIPS

I like the smaller (3-pound) chickens. They cook much more evenly and you need not worry that the pieces are too thick. Cut each piece of the split breast in half so that the pieces are the same size as the other cuts and cook evenly.

I like to soak the chicken in buttermilk with hot sauce. They add flavor and tenderize the meat.

By using only enough fat to come halfway up the chicken, you can fry evenly and achieve the right texture and color. Be sure to keep the oil temperature at about 250°F to 300°F during frying. You can test for doneness by inserting a paring knife into the thickest part of the largest piece. If the juices run clear, the chicken is done. If the chicken is not fully cooked but has the desired color, place the pieces on a rack and finish cooking in a 250°F oven. Turn the chicken with tongs; a fork will puncture the meat and release the juices.

A faster way to cook the chicken is to have two pans going at the same time. Keep the cooked chicken warm in a 250°F oven with the door ajar while you cook the later batches. The chicken will stay crispy and hot until it's ready for serving.

Chicken Étouffée

hef Jamie says he's never seen chicken done this way, cooked down until it's "falling off the bone" with a dark roux, other than in New Orleans. It seems as basic as bread pudding and red beans and rice to me. The line for Krewe meal is long when this is on the menu.

1 chicken, about 3½ pounds, quartered
Kosher salt and freshly ground pepper to
     taste
½ cup all-purpose flour
½ cup vegetable oil
2 medium onions, in large dice
2 medium bell peppers, in large dice

2 jalapeño peppers, seeded, stemmed,
     and minced
15 cloves garlic, peeled and thinly sliced
2 teaspoons dried thyme
2 teaspoons dried sage
3 cups water
Hot sauce to taste
2 recipes Boiled Rice (page 252)

SEASON the chicken pieces with salt and pepper and dust them with some of the flour.

PLACE the oil in a large, heavy-gauge stockpot and bring it to the smoking point over high heat. Add the chicken, and cook for 7 to 10 minutes, or until the pieces are brown on one side. Turn the pieces and repeat on the other side. Remove the chicken from the pot.

RETURN the oil to the smoking point, add the onions, peppers, and garlic to the pot, and stir. Cover and let cook about 12 minutes, stirring occasionally and taking care not to let the vegetables burn. Add the remaining flour and sauté for 5 minutes, scraping the bottom and sides of the pot with a wooden spoon. Be careful not to burn the mixture, but allow it to turn dark brown, take on a nutty aroma, and dry out. Add the thyme and sage, adjust the salt and pepper, and gradually add the water, stirring constantly to prevent lumps and burning. When everything is well mixed, return the chicken to the pot, bring to a boil, and reduce to a simmer.

Cook for 20 to 25 minutes, or until the chicken is tender and almost falling off the bones. Stir occasionally. Remove the chicken and adjust the sauce consistency to your liking by either reducing or adding a bit of water. Skim off any excess fat, if needed. Adjust seasoning with hot sauce, salt, and pepper. Serve with boiled rice.

When you cook the vegetables with the flour and the oil, you're making what we call a vegetable dark roux. Keep an eye on your roux and sauce. Be careful not to either burn or over-reduce the sauce. Skim as needed. Try to keep the pieces intact for serving.

Stewed Hen with Buttermilk-Herb Dumplings

MAKES 8 SERVINGS, WITH ABOUT 65 DUMPLINGS

*T*his is one of our favorite recipes for Krewe meal. We make a lot, using perhaps 5 hens to feed our crew, and although that's far more than you'll ever need, it works the same way at home. You cook this down with carrots and other vegetables to produce tender, juicy meat that's falling off the bone.

Hen:

1 stewing fowl, 4 to 5 pounds, cut into 10 pieces (2 drumsticks, 2 thighs, 2 wings, and 4 breast pieces)

Creole Meat Seasoning (page 293) to taste

Flour, for dusting

8 tablespoons (1 stick) butter

4 medium carrots, in ¼-inch slices

4 medium turnips, in large dice

3 medium onions, in large dice

8 stalks celery, in large dice

2 bell peppers, any color, in large dice

15 cloves garlic, peeled and minced

4 quarts cold water

1 teaspoon dried thyme

1 teaspoon dried marjoram or sage

4 bay leaves

Kosher salt and freshly ground pepper to taste

2 bunches green onions, sliced

½ bunch fresh parsley, chopped

Dumplings:

1½ cups all-purpose flour, plus additional for dusting and rolling

¾ teaspoon baking powder

Kosher salt and freshly ground pepper to taste

1 tablespoon chopped fresh thyme

1 tablespoon chopped fresh basil

2 tablespoons fat reserved from cooking the hen

½ cup buttermilk

RINSE the hen pieces and pat dry. Season each piece with Creole seasoning, and dust with flour. Melt the butter in a large pot (at least 8 quarts) over medium heat, taking care not to burn the butter. Brown half the hen pieces on one side, shaking the pot and adjusting the heat to avoid burning the butter. Turn the pieces and brown the second side. The total browning time should be 10 to 12 minutes.

REMOVE and repeat with the remaining hen pieces. When they are browned, add the carrots, turnips, onions, celery, peppers, and garlic, and sauté the vegetables for 8 to 10 minutes, or until the onions are cooked. Return the first batch of browned hen pieces to the pot.

ADD the water, stir with a wooden spoon, and add the thyme, marjoram, and bay leaves. Bring to rolling boil, then reduce heat to a simmer. As it simmers, spoon off fat from the surface of the stew. Save 2 tablespoons of the fat for making the dumplings, and discard the rest.

AFTER the stew has simmered for about 2 hours, the meat should be falling from the bones. Season with salt and pepper, add the green onions and parsley, and remove the bones.

MAKE the dumplings shortly before the stew has finished cooking. Combine all but 2 tablespoons of the flour with the baking powder, salt, pepper, thyme, and basil in a mixing bowl, and form a well in the ingredients. Add and incorporate the chicken fat and buttermilk. The dough should be sticky.

DUST the work surface and the dough with the remaining 2 tablespoons of flour. Pat the dough into a ¼-inch-thick rectangle, about 5 by 10 inches, and cut into ¾-inch squares with a floured knife. Add about 10 dumplings at a time to the stew. Continue adding dumplings at one-minute intervals. Cook dumplings uncovered for 10 to 12 minutes.

Stewing a hen brings out its flavor. The size and age of the bird will determine its actual cooking time, so focus on when the meat falls from the bones.

 CHEF JAMIE'S TIPS

Creole Stuffed Peppers

MAKES 6 GENEROUS SERVINGS

I love the sight of a stuffed pepper. It must trigger some taste memory of childhood comfort food. Maybe these Creole Stuffed Peppers were how Mom got us to eat vegetables early on. They can be a meal in themselves. You get your vegetable, starch, and meat, all in one go-go pepper. Try it with dirty rice or homemade sausage.

3 pounds ground-meat mix (1 pound pork, 1 pound beef, 1 pound veal)
Boiled Rice (page 252), chilled
3 medium onions, in medium dice
1 medium head garlic, cloves peeled and thinly sliced
1 bunch green onions, thinly sliced
1 teaspoon cayenne pepper, or to taste
Kosher salt and freshly ground black pepper to taste
2 tablespoons olive oil

12 large green bell peppers, cored and seeded, tops removed (edible portion of tops cut in large dice)
4 stalks celery, in medium dice
8 medium Creole or vine-ripened tomatoes, peeled, seeded, and cut in medium dice, or two 28-ounce cans tomatoes, drained and diced
3 bay leaves

PLACE the ground meat in a large bowl, add the rice, half the onions, half the garlic, half the green onions, and the cayenne, and season with salt and pepper. Mix thoroughly with your hands until the mixture feels sticky. Refrigerate.

PLACE a large, deep roasting pan over high heat across two burners. Add the oil, and heat for about 2 minutes. Add the remaining onion and garlic and the diced pepper tops, and sauté, stirring occasionally, for 5 to 7 minutes, or until the garlic and onion start to brown. Add the celery, and cook for 4 to 5 minutes, stirring as needed to keep the celery from burning. Add the tomatoes and bay leaves. Season and simmer for 10 minutes or until the sauce starts to reduce. Turn off the heat.

PREHEAT the oven to 350°F.

WHILE the sauce is simmering, stuff each pepper with about 5 to 6 ounces of the meat-rice mixture. Stand the stuffed peppers in the pan with the simmered sauce, cover, and bake for 45 minutes. Remove the cover, and bake for 45 to 60 minutes more, or until the peppers are tender and the meat is completely cooked (to an internal temperature of about 165°F). When done, the peppers should have a deep color and be golden brown on top. Remove with a slotted spoon and place on a serving platter.

Krewe Meals

230

IF THE SAUCE is too thin, reduce it by placing it back on the stove. Adjust seasoning, spoon the sauce over the peppers, sprinkle the peppers with the remaining green onions, and serve.

 CHEF JAMIE'S TIPS

Use any lean meat mixture you like, though I suggest that at least one-third be pork to take advantage of pork's good binding qualities. Fresh ground sausage works very well.

When you're buying peppers, select those that seem able to stand up on their own. (Otherwise, you'll need to trim a thin slice from the bottoms to make them level.) Two peppers per serving might be too much for some diners.

Use a tall roasting pan. The cooking liquid will rise as juices render from the meat.

Honey Mustard Ham with Black-Eyed Peas and Cabbage

MAKES 8 SERVINGS, PLUS SOME HAM
FOR SANDWICHES AND SOUP

*I*t's just not New Year's Day without black-eyed peas and cabbage for good luck and good fortune. But this dish is also a classic New Orleans Irish Channel Sunday supper. It's made with a bone-in ham. Save the ham bone, with the marrow, as a critical ingredient for cooking red beans.

1 smoked bone-in ham, 10 to 11 pounds (see Chef Jamie's Tips)

2 medium onions, in medium dice

3 stalks celery, in medium dice

2 bell peppers, any color, in medium dice

1 small head garlic, cloves peeled and minced

1 pound dried black-eyed peas, rinsed and picked through to remove any debris

2 quarts water

3 bay leaves

1 tablespoon whole cloves

1/2 cup honey

1 cup Creole mustard or coarse German-style mustard

1 large head cabbage, cut into 8 even pieces, or 2 small heads, each cut in quarters

Kosher salt and freshly ground pepper to taste

TRIM but do not discard any excess fat from the top of the ham and around the shank. Place a large roasting pan over two burners of the stove over high heat. Put the trimmings in the pan, and render the fat for 2 to 3 minutes, stirring. Add the onions, celery, peppers, and garlic, and sauté, stirring occasionally, for about 10 minutes or until lightly browned and tender. Add the peas and sauté for about 2 minutes, stirring. Add the water and bay leaves, bring to a boil, and cook for 10 minutes.

MEANWHILE, lightly score the top of the ham fat to create a diamond pattern. Each diamond should have about 1½ inches between the parallel edges. Insert a clove at each corner. Combine the honey and mustard, and brush a small, even coat on the surface of the ham, using about a quarter of the mixture.

PREHEAT the oven to 350°F.

PLACE the ham on top of the peas, and transfer the pan to the lower rack of the preheated oven. Be sure the liquid is simmering so that the peas cook properly. If it's not, turn up the oven heat. But don't let the liquid evaporate; add a bit more water if needed. Baste about every 45 minutes with the remaining honey-mustard mixture. If the ham starts to get too dark on top, cover the ham only with foil. Bake for 3 to 3½ hours, until the internal temperature of the ham is about 160°F, or until the peas are almost cooked and the meat shrinks and rides up the bone. The ham should have a dark crust. Remove the ham, and place on a serving tray. Cover with foil and let rest.

SEASON the cabbage with salt and pepper, and add to the pan with the peas. Cover, return to the oven, and cook until the cabbage is tender, about 30 to 40 minutes. If the peas become dry, add a little water.

REMOVE the cabbage gently so as not to break up the pieces and arrange around the ham. Check the peas. If they need to cook more, finish them on top of the stove by putting the roasting pan over two burners. Adjust seasoning.

SLICE the ham, removing the cloves as you do. Serve each diner a piece of the cabbage with the ham, and serve the peas in a bowl.

When I buy the ham for this dish, I prefer the back leg, not the shoulder, or picnic, ham. You want only enough shank removed to allow the ham to fit in the roasting pan. A lot of hams are pre-trimmed of fat. If yours has no excess fat, use a little bacon in place of the trimmings in the first step, as you prepare to cook the vegetables. Ham contains a lot of salt, which will run into the peas during cooking, so don't season the peas until the end, and after you've tasted one.

If you leave the core intact when you cut the cabbage, it will help keep the pieces intact.

CHEF JAMIE'S TIPS

Krewe Meals

Irish Channel Corned Beef and Cabbage

MAKES 6 SERVINGS

*I*magine young Jamie Shannon, just a week on the job as the new chef of Commander's Palace—and St. Patrick's day approaching. Dick Brennan and John Brennan, independently of each other, congratulate Jamie on his new job, say how proud they are of him, and tell him to be sure and get the corned beef right for the upcoming St. Paddy's Day luncheon. It's got to be tender and it's got to be cut right. Believe me, Jamie quickly figured out how important the corned beef is to our family. It's a tradition, and one that we intend to perpetuate—correctly. We've named it after a New Orleans neighborhood.

3 to 3½ pounds corned beef brisket

3 quarts cold water

2½ tablespoons salt

1 bag crab boil, or make your own (page 296; see Chef Jamie's Tips)

¼ cup white vinegar

1 large to medium cabbage, 3½ to 4 pounds, cut into 6 equal parts but with core intact

3 large russet potatoes, peeled and halved

1 pound large carrots, peeled, trimmed, and halved crosswise

3 small onions, halved bottom to top, core intact

1 medium head garlic, cloves peeled

Kosher salt and freshly ground pepper to taste

REMOVE the corned beef from its package, discard the liquid, place the meat in a bowl in the sink, and rinse the meat thoroughly under cold water.

COMBINE the cold water, salt, crab boil, and vinegar in a large pot over high heat. Add the beef and bring to a boil. Boil about 15 minutes, then reduce the heat and simmer for 3 to 3½ hours, or until fork-tender. Remove the meat from the cooking liquid, and set aside.

PLACE a large roasting pan with a lid and a rack over two burners of the stove. Put the cabbage wedges on the rack in the center of the pan, place the potatoes around the cabbage, and rest the carrots between the potatoes and the cabbage. Place the onions on top of the cabbage wedges, and sprinkle the garlic over everything.

REMOVE the bag of crab boil from the cooking liquid and discard it. Pour the liquid over the vegetables, place the meat on top, and turn both burners on high. Bring to a boil. Boil for about 8 minutes, cover, reduce the heat, and simmer until all the vegetables are tender, about 45 minutes.

REMOVE the meat and trim any excess fat. With a sharp carving knife, thinly slice the meat against the grain on the bias. Place the cabbage, potatoes, carrots, onion, and a few cloves of garlic on a serving platter. Place the sliced corned beef on top, and pour a little liquid over everything. Adjust seasoning if needed.

SERVE with prepared horseradish and/or Creole mustard or another coarse mustard.

CHEF JAMIE'S TIPS

Even though some instructions say to cook the meat with the liquid from the package, I like to discard the liquid and rinse the meat. It removes excess blood and old seasoning and results in a fresher flavor and cleaner cooking liquid.

Crab boil gives the dish its New Orleans touch. Most corned beef comes packed in spice or has a small spice container with it. Because packed spice is either removed or washed off when you rinse the meat, the best way to flavor the meat with crab boil is with a premade bag. You can make your own with crab boil (page 296) and cheesecloth to prevent unwanted loose spice all over the final product.

Be sure the corned beef is tender. It is when a fork can be inserted with little resistance.

Adding a little cooking liquid when you serve adds flavor and keeps everything hot and moist. I like Creole mustard or prepared horseradish as an accompaniment, not horseradish cream.

"Could you tell me what the third dish you mentioned was again?" asks the confused and overwhelmed guest. Why do restaurants persist in having servers recite and describe endless numbers of specials? Why would restaurateurs ever make their guests feel embarrassed or intimidated? And why take up so much time that your captain or waiter could better use answering questions or providing other prompt service? Put it on the menu, with a brief but accurate description.

When our family first started serving food in 1946, restaurants simply listed a dish's name with no description. The names in New Orleans were often in French, which made them very intimidating to the uninitiated.

At Commander's, your captain will tell you what the soup of the day is and what kind of fresh fish we have in house. That's it. He or she can then answer your questions about ingredients or dishes. Where do you get your turtles? Is red snapper more tender than flounder?

We believe that in 1946 Brennan's was the first restaurant to put descriptions on the menu. From the start, Owen Brennan and his siblings did not consider intimidation hospitable.

SIDE DISHES AND VEGETABLES

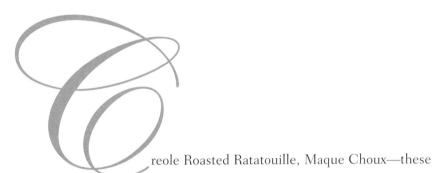

reole Roasted Ratatouille, Maque Choux—these are not the foods your mom forced you to eat by insisting that they were good for you. But the fact is, our guests clamor for these goodies so much that we had to give them their own spot on the menu, on their own, with their own headline.

The way my mother explains it, after World War II, things canned and packaged were all the rage. Fruits and vegetables available all year long were a novelty, apparently an irresistible one. Throughout the country, the loss in flavor and taste went unnoticed by most of a nation happy to be done with war and enamored with life's new conveniences. Canned and frozen everything, dishwashers, televisions, machines that dispensed sandwiches, blueberries all year, and so on and so on. Taste took a back seat to convenience and availability. Supermarkets grew rapidly and farmer's markets died. Famous restaurants printed recipes commonly calling for the syrup in canned fruit cocktail as an ingredient. It was a sad time in our country's gastronomic history.

New Orleans and Louisiana were not immune to this phenomenon. But something kept us from being totally immersed in it. After all, where was the fun in eating crawfish that were already cooked and frozen? No crawfish boiling party? The frozen corn just didn't taste like neighbor Joe's corn you could still get easily on the side of the road. And when I stop on the side of the road to get Joe's corn, I can have a little visit and maybe a taste of boudin. So maybe it was the plain stubbornness of a culture that has always been less impressed with life's novelties.

Nevertheless, Louisiana's vegetables and side dishes have a glorious past and a fertile present.

*M*aque Choux had been lost to the restaurant world until Commander's put it back on the map years ago, but it's as old as New Orleans, going back more than 300 years, when the natives turned the settlers on to corn that had a little hint of a cabbage taste.

¼ pound bacon, cut into thin strips about 1 inch long by ¼ inch wide

6 cloves garlic, peeled and minced

½ small onion, in small dice

1 small bell pepper, in small dice

1 hot pepper, or to taste, seeded and minced

¼ pound (about 10 pieces) small okra, tops removed, thinly sliced

8 ears fresh corn, shucked and kernels removed from cob

Kosher salt and freshly ground black pepper to taste

1 bunch green onions, sliced thin

1 tablespoon butter

RENDER the fat from the bacon in a large skillet over high heat for about 3 minutes, or until crisp. Remove with a slotted spoon and let drain on a paper towel. Add the garlic and onion to the hot bacon fat, and sauté until brown, stirring constantly, for about 2 to 3 minutes. Add the peppers and stir for about 3 minutes. Add the okra and cook for about 2 minutes, stirring constantly. Add the corn and cook for 5 minutes or until tender. (If the pan gets too hot, reduce the heat.) Season with salt and pepper, transfer to a serving dish, stir in the green onions and the butter, and garnish with the crisp bacon.

CHEF JAMIE'S TIPS

Be sure the corn is fresh and not overly starchy. To check, pull down a husk and check the kernels. They should be plump and full of juice, and the silk of the corn should be fresh and not mushy.

Corn starts to break down if it's not refrigerated immediately. The sugars begin turning to starch the moment it's picked. Farm-raised corn that has been iced down is best.

You want to brown but not burn the garlic, onions, and peppers. This is where all the flavor of the dish comes from. Be careful not to overcook the corn and okra. Adjust the temperature when cooking if needed. Also be careful not to break up the okra. Remember that the bacon and bacon fat are salty, so be careful adding salt.

Try to pick small, tender okra. Larger okra can be too woody and need too much cooking time.

Side Dishes and Vegetables

Roasted Vegetable "Lasagna"

MAKES 4 ENTRÉES
OR 8 SIDE-DISH SERVINGS

Everyone, not just vegetarians, likes this dish. It's 100 percent vegetables, no pasta. The vegetables are slow-cooked to bring out the moisture. You get a great grilled taste and a strong, hearty vegetable flavor.

2 medium eggplants, sliced ¼ inch thick, top to bottom (discard end slices, which will have too much skin), 2 to 2¼ pounds total

½ cup extra-virgin olive oil, approximately

3 medium yellow squash, sliced ¼ inch thick, top to bottom

3 medium zucchini, sliced ¼ inch thick, top to bottom

2 medium onions, sliced ¼ inch thick, across, slices kept whole

5 medium tomatoes, sliced ¼ inch thick, across

Kosher salt and freshly ground pepper to taste

10 basil leaves

15 cloves garlic, peeled and minced

¼ cup bread crumbs

2 tablespoons grated Parmesan cheese

PREHEAT the oven to 500°F.

PLACE the eggplant in a large bowl, drizzle about 2 tablespoons of the olive oil on top, and gently toss to give the eggplant a light coating of oil. Arrange the slices as close as possible to each other on a lightly oiled sheet pan without overlapping the slices. Using the same bowl and more oil, repeat with the yellow squash and zucchini. Place the yellow squash and zucchini next to the eggplant, or, if there isn't room, on a second oiled sheet pan.

ADD all but 1 tablespoon of the remaining oil to the bowl. Dip the onion slices in the bowl, keeping the slices whole, if possible, and place them side by side on another sheet pan. Dip the tomato slices in the bowl, and place them on the same pan or, if there isn't room to avoid layering, on a separate pan.

SEASON all the vegetables with salt and pepper, and roast for 13 to 15 minutes, in two batches if you don't have enough room in your oven. The yellow squash and zucchini should be browned on their bottoms, the onions should be starting to brown, and the tomatoes starting to shrink and tenderize.

REMOVE the vegetables and reduce the oven temperature to 350°F.

BRUSH an 8- or 9-inch square pan that's about 2 inches deep with oil. Gently layer about half the eggplant on the bottom of the pan, and layer the yellow squash on top of the eggplant. Press down firmly to pack the vegetables together. Layer the zucchini on top, then the remaining eggplant, and then the onions, pressing down after each. With a spatula, gently cover the onions with the tomatoes. Top with the basil leaves.

COMBINE the garlic, bread crumbs, cheese, any oil remaining in the bowl, and additional salt and pepper, and mix with your hands. Sprinkle the topping evenly over the lasagna. Bake for about 1 hour. Check during that hour, and if the lasagna seems to have a lot of liquid that has come from the vegetables, drain some of it. The lasagna is done when it starts to brown on top and pulls back from the pan a bit. Let it cool about 20 to 30 minutes before slicing or serving. Cut in quarters for entrées, in eighths for side dishes.

Roasting vegetables cooks them, helps add flavor by caramelizing (which is a browning of the starch that turns into sugar), and releases liquid to help the lasagna set up for better cutting and serving.

 CHEF JAMIE'S TIPS

You can assemble this a day in advance and bake it before serving.

Mirliton, Shrimp, and Tasso Casserole

This is Louisiana-style comfort food, and we serve it at casual gatherings as well as at festive holiday meals like Christmas and Thanksgiving. Tasso is a spicy pork that has been cured by smoking. All the ingredients are baked in a custardy mixture, which is about as comforting as food gets. The mirliton, part of the squash family, can be found in Louisiana, California, and Florida, and is known as the chayote elsewhere. It looks like a large pear and its flavor is so mild that it tends to absorb the flavor of whatever it is cooked with.

6 small mirliton or chayote, each about
    9 ounces (they vary in size)

3 tablespoons butter

8 ounces tasso, in medium dice

2 medium onions, in medium dice

Kosher salt and freshly ground pepper to
    taste

1 pound small headless shrimp, peeled
    (if the shrimp start out large, cut
    them in medium dice)

15 cloves garlic, peeled and minced

5 medium eggs

1 cup milk

2 cups fresh bread crumbs

1 bunch green onions (green part only),
    thinly sliced

PLACE the mirliton in a large pot and cover with cold salted water. Bring to a boil, and cook for 1 hour, or until fork-tender. Drain and let cool. (The mirliton should be treated as you would a potato with a very high water content. Do not overcook it, and do not shock the cooked vegetable with cold water to cool or the vegetable will lose its flavor and the casserole turn watery.) Peel the skin from the mirliton with a paring knife, cut in half top to bottom, remove the seed, and mash lightly. Drain off excess liquid.

PLACE 1 tablespoon of the butter in a large pot over medium heat and sauté the tasso for about 4 minutes, or until brown. Add the onions, season with salt and pepper, and sauté for 4 to 5 minutes, or until tender.

STIR in the shrimp and garlic, and sauté for 30 seconds. Add the mashed mirliton, and sauté for 3 minutes, stirring constantly. Remove from the heat and adjust the seasoning. Let cool.

MAKE the custard by whisking the eggs with the milk and additional salt and pepper. Stir the custard into the cooled mirliton.

USE 1 tablespoon of the butter to coat a 3-inch-deep large casserole dish, and pour the mirliton mixture into the dish.

PREHEAT the oven to 350°F.

MELT the remaining butter in a medium saucepan, add the bread crumbs, green onions, and additional salt and pepper, and top the casserole with this mixture.

COVER the casserole with foil and bake for 1 hour in the preheated oven. Remove foil, and bake for 30 to 40 minutes more, or until golden brown.

NOTE: If you cannot find tasso, roll ham in one part cayenne, three parts paprika. This is a good substitute.

Be sure the casserole is not watery. If it is, pierce the topping, lower the oven temperature, and continue cooking until the liquid is absorbed. **CHEF JAMIE'S TIPS**

Honey-Roasted Mashed Opelousas Sweet Potatoes

MAKES ABOUT 8
SIDE-DISH SERVINGS

Roasting sweet potatoes (or yams) intensifies their earthy, sweet flavor. Boiling them, as is so often done, extracts much of their flavor into the water. Opelousas Sweet Potatoes are just too good to be boiled. So we make sweet potato pie, sweet potato hay, and sweet potato succotash, but this one, roasted with honey and butter and whipped, is my favorite. Opelousas is in southwestern Louisiana.

6 sweet potatoes, about 1 pound each
8 tablespoons (1 stick) butter, diced
1 teaspoon ground cinnamon
1/4 teaspoon freshly grated nutmeg

1 cup honey
Kosher salt and freshly ground pepper to taste

PREHEAT the oven to 350°F.

PEEL and quarter the sweet potatoes and place them in a roasting pan. Place the diced butter evenly on top of the potatoes, sprinkle the cinnamon and nutmeg on top, drizzle with the honey, and season them with salt and pepper. Gently pour about 2 cups of water into the pan without washing anything off the potatoes.

COVER and bake for 1½ hours, or until the potatoes are very tender. Remove the cover, stir, and cook for 30 minutes more. The potatoes should have a dark brown color on top and be very tender.

REMOVE the potatoes with a slotted spoon, place them in the large bowl of an electric mixer, and mix until all the lumps are gone. Drizzle in as much liquid from the pan as desired. Turn off the mixer, and scrape the bowl. Continue mixing until the potatoes have the desired consistency. Adjust seasoning, place potatoes in a large casserole dish, and serve.

CHEF JAMIE'S TIPS

I usually incorporate all the pan liquid because it's needed for consistency and it has a lot of flavor.

I like the dark, orange sweet potatoes, not the thin-skinned pale ones. The darker-skin variety is sweeter and has deep orange flesh, while the pale variety is starchy. The medium to large size seem best, with the sweetest ones coming from mid-fall to late winter. Store them in a dry, dark, cool area.

You can add more butter and honey if you wish.

This dish can be made up to 3 days in advance, but keep it covered in the refrigerator.

*Y*ou've heard of twice-baked potatoes? Our Lyonnaise Potatoes are cooked in three steps. First they're baked, then they're fried, then they're sautéed. They're good for brunch, lunch, or dinner and are perfect with our Pan-Seared Sirloin. This classic potato dish should be crispy on top and flavorful, with lots of onion.

6 large russet potatoes

4 cups canola oil, for frying

1 tablespoon butter

1½ large onions, halved top to bottom and thinly sliced

Kosher salt and freshly ground pepper to taste

PREHEAT the oven to 400°F.

SCRUB the potatoes and, with a paring knife, poke a hole all the way through the center of each to speed the cooking process. Place on an oven rack, and bake until done, about 40 to 50 minutes. The skin should be crisp on the outside and the potato tender inside. Let cool completely and refrigerate for about 1½ hours.

HEAT the oil in a large, deep pan to 350°F. Peel the potatoes, slice each into ½-inch-thick rounds, and fry half the potatoes until golden brown and very crisp, about 12 minutes. Place on paper towels to drain and repeat with the remaining potatoes.

MELT the butter in a large, heavy skillet over high heat, add the onions, and season with salt and pepper. Cook for about 11 to 12 minutes, stirring occasionally. When done, the onions should be golden brown. Remove half the onions and set aside. Add half the potatoes to the pan, and toss until well mixed. Season generously with salt and pepper and cook until hot all the way through, about 2½ minutes. Repeat with remaining onions and potatoes.

 CHEF JAMIE'S TIPS

Russet potatoes are also called Idaho potatoes or baking potatoes. Baking the potato first removes a lot of the moisture and helps the potato become very crisp when fried. This can be done in advance or with leftover potatoes.

Be sure to fry the potatoes completely until golden brown and crisp because the next step is simply to heat them up with the onions.

When sautéing onion with potatoes, more butter is not needed. You want them to stay crisp. Season generously.

Side Dishes and Vegetables

Corn Cakes with Sour Cream and Green Onions

MAKES 12 CAKES

*T*hese moist cakes are extremely versatile. You can make them in rings or spread out on a griddle to make them look like thick pancakes. And you can serve them as a savory appetizer or a sweet fritterlike side dish. We often serve them with foie gras or with pork loin and a dollop of sour cream.

³/₄ cup cornmeal, any color

³/₄ cup all-purpose flour

1 tablespoon baking powder

3 medium eggs, separated

¹/₂ cup milk, any kind

3 ears corn, kernels sliced off cobs

4 green onions, thinly sliced

1 tablespoon chopped fresh sage
   (optional)

Kosher salt and freshly ground pepper
   to taste

¹/₂ cup sour cream

8 tablespoons (1 stick) butter, half in
   medium dice, half cut in 2 chunks

SIFT the cornmeal, flour, and baking powder in a large bowl. Make a well in the center of the dry ingredients, and stir the egg yolks and milk into the well until thoroughly incorporated. Add the corn, green onions, sage, salt, and pepper. Mix until the ingredients are well incorporated. In a separate bowl, whip the egg whites to stiff peaks. Fold the beaten whites into the corn mixture, fold in the sour cream, and fold in the diced butter. Adjust salt and pepper.

OVER low to medium heat, in a large, cast-iron skillet, melt 1 of the 2 chunks of remaining butter. Place 6 metal rings, each about 1³/₄ inches in diameter and 1¹/₂ inches deep, in the pan. (Cookie cutters, if they're the right size, would work well.)

AS THE butter melts, gently shake the skillet so the butter coats the sides of the rings. Spoon about 2 to 3 tablespoons of batter into each ring, leaving room for the batter to rise. Cook for about 4 minutes, or until the bottoms have turned golden brown and the tops have begun to thicken and rise.

FLIP the rings by carefully tipping one end of the ring up and sliding a small spatula underneath. Cook on the second side for 2¹/₂ to 3 minutes, or until done. Remove the rings from the pan using the spatula. Let cool about 2 minutes, then remove the cake from each ring, using a sharp paring knife if necessary.

WIPE out the skillet, clean the rings, and repeat with remaining butter and batter.

Flipping the cakes takes a little practice, but you will be happy with the results.

Using the rings makes for a thick, moist cake, but you could also make the cakes as you would pancakes, spooning batter onto the skillet. You'll end up with more cakes. Cook over low heat, so the cake cooks on the inside, not just on the crust.

Creamed Corn with Jalapeño and Thyme

MAKES 8 SIDE-DISH SERVINGS

Corn has been plentiful since the time of the earliest Indian settlers in Louisiana, so it pops up in many incarnations. And nothing could be simpler than this one. In just minutes, you can have a great vegetable side dish. We prefer the sweeter white corn, but any fresh corn on the cob will do. Try this dish with softshell crabs, stuffed deviled crab, veal chops, or our Honey Mustard Pork Tenderloin.

8 ears fresh corn, shucked

1 pint heavy cream

Kosher salt and freshly ground pepper to taste

2 jalapeño peppers, stemmed, seeded, and minced

2 tablespoons fresh thyme

1 tablespoon butter

STAND an ear of corn inside a large bowl, and, using a small knife, remove the kernels, being sure not to cut into the cob. When all the corn has been scraped off, scrape the cob with the back of a knife, break the cob in half, and place in a large pot. Repeat with the remaining corn.

POUR the cream into the pot. It probably won't cover all the cobs. Season with salt and pepper and bring to a boil, taking care not to let the cream boil over. Stir and simmer for about 15 minutes, or until the cream starts to thicken. Using tongs, remove the cobs.

ADD the corn and the jalapeño to the pan and simmer for about 5 minutes, stirring occasionally. The corn should be tender. Add the thyme, stir in the butter, and adjust the seasoning.

CHEF JAMIE'S TIPS

Be sure to remove the silk strands before cutting the corn. A towel helps with this. Scraping the cob with the back of a knife into the bowl, as well as cooking the cob, helps to thicken the mixture, gives it extra corn flavor, and makes the addition of a roux unnecessary.

Lagniappe

TABLE SIGNALS

Most restaurants use signals to improve service. Any restaurant that uses team service should use signals, too. Otherwise, miscommunication can annoy the guest.

For example, isn't it a little irksome when three waiters in a row ask if you would like a drink? Even if taking drink orders is one person's job, someone else should be able to lend a hand. Our solution is a table signal. Our signal is so simple that even our regular customers have never picked up on it unless they happened to ask or we happened to tell. The point is that they're not supposed to notice.

When someone greets your table and takes your drink order, he or she simply places the salt and pepper shakers together, so they're touching. The touching salt and pepper shakers are a signal to anyone else who approaches the table that the drink order has already been taken. So don't ask again.

It's simple, but it works. See what table signals you notice in restaurants from now on.

Roasted Garlic and Buttermilk Mashed Potatoes

MAKES 8 SERVINGS

The Brennan family is Irish, Chef Jamie Shannon is Irish, and we're serious about potatoes. In fact, John Brennan, Lally's late father, had a machine to pre-cut potatoes for restaurants and ran a company that did that. And as you can see from the recipes in this book, we also like garlic. So we're proud of our version of garlic mashed potatoes. We fry the garlic, add it to the butter, and combine it with buttermilk for a rich, Southern side dish not to be missed.

2½ pounds boiling potatoes, white or red

1½ tablespoons kosher salt

½ pound (2 sticks) butter, 1 stick whole, 1 stick in ¼-inch slices

1 large head garlic, cloves peeled, half sliced very thin, half left whole

1½ cups buttermilk

1 cup plus 1 tablespoon sour cream

Kosher salt and freshly ground pepper to taste

SCRUB the potatoes, place them in a large pot, cover with cold water by 1 inch, and add the salt. Bring to a boil and simmer until a knife pierces the potatoes with no resistance, about 30 to 40 minutes. Drain them in a colander.

MELT the whole stick of butter in a small skillet over medium heat. When the butter is hot and starting to brown, add the sliced garlic and stir with a slotted spoon, separating any pieces that stick. Stir to fry evenly, until brown and crisp, about 2 minutes. Remove with the spoon, drain on a paper towel, and season with salt and pepper. Add the whole garlic cloves to the pan and cook over medium heat for about 1½ minutes, or until tender.

IN A small saucepan over medium heat, bring the buttermilk to a simmer but do not allow it to boil.

WHEN the potatoes are cool enough to handle, peel them. Pass half the potatoes through a food mill or ricer set over a pot. Then remove the whole garlic from the pan and pass the cloves through the mill. Pass the remaining potatoes through the mill. Stir in the melted butter and turn on low heat. Stir in the buttermilk. Turn off the heat. Stir in the sliced butter and 1 cup of sour cream and season with salt and pepper. Sprinkle the garlic chips on top, and serve. Garnish the top with the remaining tablespoon of the sour cream.

The round white or red potatoes are called boiling potatoes, and they contain less starch. My favorites are Yukon Gold and fingerling potatoes. Round potatoes are *not* new potatoes; new potatoes are just young potatoes.

Don't peel the potatoes until after they're cooked. During cooking, the peel protects the potato from absorbing water. And don't overcook the potatoes, or they will absorb water. Don't run them under cold water after cooking; instead, let them cool by themselves. Using a food mill or ricer helps avoid overmixing the potatoes and pulling out too much starch. Be sure to serve the potatoes while they are hot. Pay attention to their temperature because you'll be adding cold ingredients.

Be sure to have plenty of salt in the water when you're cooking the potatoes. Adding salt at the end is not the same.

The whole garlic cooks quickly because the cloves are peeled and they go directly into hot fat.

Boiled Rice

ice is the major staple of Louisiana cooking, and it's *always* called boiled rice, not steamed rice, probably because you keep the water boiling. With so many meandering rivers, lakes, streams, and bayous slicing through the state, Louisiana has lots of the boggy flatlands where rice thrives almost effortlessly. It's so abundant that we're always using it to stretch a meal for unexpected guests. We serve boiled rice in cakes, as hot calas (rice cakes served with cane syrup), in rice dressing, in stuffing, in jambalaya, with red beans, and on and on. We serve long-grain and short-grain. Our rice is unusual in that it starts on the stovetop and finishes in the oven. This is a true Creole technique. This is the perfect amount for our gumbos, though you'll need more for our beans and rice.

1 cup long-grain rice, such as basmati	Kosher salt and freshly ground pepper to
1 quart water	taste
1 teaspoon salt	1 tablespoon butter, cut into pieces
2 bay leaves, fresh if possible	

PREHEAT the oven to 325°F. Wash the rice three times with cold water, each time stirring the rice with your hands, then dumping out the water. Drain rice thoroughly.

BRING the water and salt to a rolling boil in a large ovenproof pot that has a lid, add the rice and bay leaves, and stir occasionally and gently with a wooden spoon until the water returns to a boil. Stirring will release the starch, so avoid overstirring, and, when boiling, do not stir at all. The boiling prevents the rice from sticking.

COVER the pot but with the lid slightly ajar to let steam out. Continue boiling for about 12 minutes or until the grains soften and water appears to dissipate. The grains will swell and become tender to the touch.

DRAIN the rice by creating a small opening between the cover and the pot. Season with additional salt and pepper, and dot it with the butter.

REMOVE lid and place in the preheated oven for 5 to 6 minutes, taking care not to brown it. Do not stir. Remove the rice from the pot, and place it in a serving bowl to prevent carryover cooking.

I'm always amazed at how many people don't know how to cook rice properly. Follow these directions—particularly the triple rinsing—and you'll end up with perfect rice every time. I like to use basmati rice. And never use converted rice, which is pre-cooked.

You're probably accustomed to a much smaller ratio of water to rice. The process of dumping the excess water, then finishing the cooking in the oven is what we call "sweating the rice."

Lagniappe

LONG-GRAIN RICE

Popcorn rice, so named because it smells like popcorn as it cooks, is the long-grain rice we use. It was developed by the Louisiana State University agriculture department. Long-grain rice produces grains that are still distinct after cooking, so they separate and don't bind to each other. The grains are less moist and lighter. Basmati rice, another long-grain rice, one with a lively fragrance, is probably more widely available and would work well with any of our recipes.

*W*e make this with our indigenous vegetables, depending on whatever is fresh at the time—Plaquemines Parish squash, eggplant, Creole or vine-ripened tomatoes, Vidalia onions, etc. Make this in the summer or early fall, when these vegetables are in season in your area, but use whatever is fresh and good, along with a good olive oil. Make it hot for dinner, then eat the leftovers cold for lunch the next day. It's great either way.

2 medium eggplants, skin on, in small dice

1 medium zucchini, in small dice

2 small yellow squash, in small dice

2 bell peppers, any color, in small dice

2 jalapeño peppers, seeded, stemmed, and cut in small dice

15 cloves garlic, peeled and minced

2 medium to large tomatoes, in small dice

2 medium onions, in small dice

1/4 cup extra-virgin olive oil

1 tablespoon chopped fresh thyme

2 tablespoons chopped basil

Kosher salt and freshly ground pepper to taste

PREHEAT the oven to 400°F.

PLACE the diced eggplant to soak in about a quart of salted cold water. After the other vegetables are cut, drain the eggplant.

TOSS the eggplant, squash, bell peppers, jalapeños, garlic, tomatoes, and onions in the olive oil. Add the thyme, basil, salt, and pepper, place in a large roasting pan, and roast in the preheated oven for 1 hour. Gently mix the vegetables from top to the bottom, but be careful not to break them up. Roast for 30 minutes more. The vegetables should be brown and colorful.

Dirty Rice

This rice is no mere accompaniment. It's a lusty, earthy classic that satisfies the Creole sensibilities in us all. Chef Jamie says there are two keys to great rice: First, rinse the rice three times, just as you would spinach. Second, stir the rice as little as possible—and not at all while it's actually cooking.

1 tablespoon vegetable oil

½ pound chicken gizzards and hearts, cut in small dice

1 tablespoon Creole Meat Seasoning (page 293), or to taste

2 teaspoons dried thyme

2 teaspoons dried sage

2 teaspoons dried marjoram

2 medium onions, in medium dice

2 medium bell peppers, in medium dice

15 cloves garlic, peeled and minced

2 cups long-grain rice, washed and rinsed 3 times, drained

4 cups cold water

1 pound liver, preferably chicken but any kind will do, ground or minced

Kosher salt and freshly ground pepper to taste

1 bunch green onions, thinly sliced

½ cup finely chopped fresh parsley

PREHEAT a large, heavy pot. Heat the oil until it's hot, add the gizzards and hearts, Creole seasoning, thyme, sage, and marjoram, and sauté over medium-high heat for 5 minutes or until golden brown. Add the onions, peppers, and garlic, and sauté for 8 minutes more, or until browned and tender. Gently stir in the rice. Add the water and bring to a boil, stirring only briefly and gently to make sure the rice is not sticking to the bottom of the pot. Cover and simmer for 13 to 15 minutes, or until the rice absorbs most of the liquid and is tender. If the rice is not tender at this point, add a bit more liquid and continue cooking.

REMOVE from the heat. Fold the liver into the rice mixture with a fork, season with salt and pepper, cover, and set aside for 10 to 12 minutes. The heat from the rice will cook the liver. With the fork, gently stir in the green onions and parsley. Transfer to a serving bowl.

_N_ouvelle cuisine taught us to cook vegetables al dente. Well, phooey, says Chef Jamie. Upset at the trend to barely cooked, crispy, blanched vegetables, Jamie was vindicated one day while talking to his idol, Julia Child. Jamie said he just didn't understand this phenomenon, and Julia agreed: "Al dente green beans? Blah. What's wrong with people cooking their vegetables?" The two agreed that al dente asparagus is good on a salad, but not with an entrée. These are tender and delicious.

4 pounds large asparagus spears, stems removed where the tender stalk begins

1 medium onion, halved top to bottom and thinly sliced

2 red bell peppers, thinly sliced

8 tablespoons (1 stick) butter, thinly sliced

2 cups water

Kosher salt and freshly ground pepper to taste

PREHEAT the oven to 400°F.

LAYER the asparagus across the bottom of a roasting pan, and distribute the onion and pepper slices and the butter pieces evenly over the asparagus. Add the water, and season with salt and pepper.

COVER with foil and bake 30 to 40 minutes, or until the asparagus is cooked. Remove the foil, and bake for 20 minutes more, until the asparagus is fork-tender and at least half the liquid has evaporated.

SERVE with some peppers and onions on top of each serving and some liquid spooned over.

This is my favorite way to eat asparagus. The liquid is as good as the vegetable itself. You can remove the tough stem ends of the asparagus by snapping them off or by simply cutting them off.

CHEF JAMIE'S TIPS

Side Dishes and Vegetables

257

Roasted Cauliflower

Chef Jamie remembers the first time he ever saw a 6-pound cauliflower. It had been sent to Ella and Dottie Brennan as a gift from up the road—from a farm run by the prisoners at Angola Penitentiary (the sender of the gift shall remain anonymous). Don't boil the cauliflower and let the flavor dissipate into the liquid. Overcooking will also lessen the intense flavor. Treat it gingerly. It's great with veal chops, rack of lamb, even redfish.

2 medium heads cauliflower, cored and cut into large florets

1 cup water

8 tablespoons (1 stick) butter, 4 tablespoons diced, 4 tablespoons melted

Kosher salt and freshly ground pepper to taste

1 cup fine dry bread crumbs

1 cup grated Romano cheese

1 cup chopped fresh parsley

PREHEAT the oven to 375°F.

ARRANGE the cauliflower neatly in a roasting pan, add the water, place the diced butter evenly over the florets, and season lightly with the salt and pepper. Bake uncovered for 30 minutes. Most of the liquid will evaporate and the cauliflower should be about half-cooked.

THOROUGHLY combine the melted butter, bread crumbs, cheese, and parsley, and sprinkle the mixture evenly over the florets. Return the pan to the oven, and cook for another 25 to 30 minutes, or until the cauliflower is tender but not overcooked. The topping should be golden brown, not burned.

Honey-Glazed Tarragon Carrots

MAKES 8 SIDE-DISH SERVINGS

*T*his dish highlights the contrasting styles between North and South. In New Orleans, we often like our veggies cooked down with other ingredients. In the North, we often encounter blanched, crisp vegetables with a touch of butter, salt, and pepper. Carrots can add that perfect touch of color to a plate, and they're available year round. The tarragon and the honey add a new dimension to the carrots that lends personality to the plate.

3 pounds medium carrots, peeled and sliced on the bias 1/4 inch thick

8 tablespoons (1 stick) butter, diced

3/4 cup honey

1/2 cup water

Kosher salt and freshly ground pepper to taste

Juice of 1 lemon

2 tablespoons chopped fresh tarragon

PREHEAT the oven to 350°F.

PLACE the carrots in a large casserole that has a lid. Add half the butter, half the honey, and the water, salt, and pepper. Stir and bake, covered, for 20 minutes, or until the carrots begin to tenderize and turn bright orange. Remove the cover and stir. Bake 20 to 40 minutes more, until the carrots are done and most of the water has evaporated. Remove the casserole from the oven and place it on top of the stove.

THE CARROTS should be tender and be sitting in a creamy, syrupy glaze. Adjust the consistency of the liquid, if necessary, by removing the carrots and cooking a bit more to thicken or by adding a little water to thin. Return the carrots to the pan, add the remaining butter and honey over medium heat, then add the lemon juice and tarragon. Stir, adjust seasoning, and serve hot.

CHEF JAMIE'S TIPS

I like to cook the vegetables from a raw state in the oven because you don't lose a lot of flavor blanching them.

Substitute dill for the tarragon, if you'd like, or orange juice for the lemon juice.

Side Dishes and Vegetables

Pear Parsnip Purée

*I*f you don't have fresh, ripe pears, don't bother making this dish. This great combo goes well with any meat or roasted fish. We serve it during the winter holidays, and it's fun to watch intrigued customers try to figure out what it is when they've forgotten the menu description. Then they ask for the recipe.

3 pounds parsnips, peeled and roughly chopped into 1-inch lengths	6 medium ripe pears, peeled, cored, and quartered
4 cups milk	8 tablespoons (1 stick) butter, cut in 1/2-inch dice
Kosher salt and freshly ground white pepper to taste	1 tablespoon honey or sugar, or to taste
	1/2 cup water

PREHEAT the oven to 350°F.

PLACE the parsnips in a medium pot, add the milk, salt, and pepper, bring to a boil, then simmer for 20 minutes, or until the parsnips are tender. Remove the parsnips from the milk and set aside.

TRANSFER the pears to a small roasting pan. Add half the diced butter, sprinkle with salt and pepper, and drizzle the honey on top. Add the water to the pears, and bake for 20 to 25 minutes, or until the pears are fully cooked and very tender and most of the liquid has evaporated.

ADD the pears and any remaining liquid to the parsnips, and purée the mixture with a hand blender, a food processor, or a ricer. If the mixture seems too thick, add a little of the hot milk mixture. Add the remaining butter, and adjust seasoning.

CHEF JAMIE'S TIPS

Parsnips can be found most of the year, but are best after the first frost has turned their starch into sugar. Pears are usually at their best in the late fall. If the pears are not ripe, make something else. Be sure the parsnips are fully cooked. They tend to be woody when they're not.

I like to add some of the liquid that remains after it comes out of the oven and let it melt over my purée.

This is a great dish with meat and poultry, but I've also enjoyed it with fish. It makes a special holiday dish.

DESSERTS

he eyes of people who have just eaten one of these desserts

give off a certain look. When we ask how they enjoyed the Bread Pudding

Soufflé with Whiskey Sauce, for example, they often push back in their

chairs, take a deep breath, or roll their eyes a bit as if to say, "This is the liv-

ing end."

Then they may start to describe the allure of the dessert. We love

to hear it, and we already know. We've seen the look before, and we've had

it on our own faces, too. You see, we believe that if you don't revel in the

unabashed decadence of desserts at a fine restaurant (whether it's Commander's Palace or Le Cirque or Aureole or Union Square Cafe), well, when *do* you let your guard down? Go for it! That's what we do.

Now, when it comes to deciding between Dottie Brennan's favorite, Lemon Flan; the popular in-house favorite, Creole Cream Cheese Cheesecake; the quintessential Bread Pudding Soufflé; and the rich Chocolate Molten Soufflé—well, *there's* a problem.

You may want to make the Ponchatoula Strawberry Shortcake or Ruston Peach Pie for a small dinner party at home, but when the event is bigger, we like to set out trays of desserts and glasses of Champagne in a separate room so that people can serve themselves. To make it festive, we use flowers and candles between rows of pralines or slices of pecan pie or a pretty citrus pound cake.

As for the calories, I long ago learned to take the advice of my Aunt Dottie Brennan, whose model-thin figure has long been the envy of the rest of us. She simply says not to waste calories on junk, like bad potato chips and lackluster desserts. Make your calories worthwhile.

There will be no calorie-regretting or remorse with this dessert lineup. They are shockingly good.

Lagniappe

BEST VALUE IN NEW ORLEANS

I was thrilled when the renowned economist Milton Friedman, his wife, and two charming Tulane professors dined at Commander's. When he asked about business, I said things were good and we were very lucky. One of the professors said, "At Commander's prices, I guess things are good." Before I could even say that Food & Wine *magazine's September 1998 issue had just named Commander's Palace the best value in New Orleans, Friedman looked around at the full dining room and said, "I'd say they've got the prices figured just right." Now I was really having fun.*

People often associate all fine dining with high prices. Higher than fast food? Sure. But for fine food, warm and pampering service, and gracious ambiance? No.

We know we could charge more. After all, many others in New Orleans do. But we won't do it just because we can. We want to run the restaurant efficiently, provide you with the best dining experience you can remember, make a fair profit, and leave you knowing that Commander's Palace is a great value.

Bread Pudding Soufflé with Whiskey Sauce

hen I eat Bread Pudding Soufflé, I always think of the Commander's saying, "If it ain't broke, fix it anyway." Bread pudding was already near perfection, but we combined Creole bread pudding with the light texture of a meringue and ended up with the restaurant's signature dessert, the single most sought-after dish in our family's restaurant history. The whiskey sauce itself is divine but particularly so when generously poured over the piping hot soufflé. Take it from me, this is no light dessert. Make the bread pudding and the sauce in advance, the meringue just before assembling and baking.

Bread pudding:

³/₄ cup sugar

1 teaspoon ground cinnamon

Pinch of freshly grated nutmeg

3 medium eggs

1 cup heavy cream

1 teaspoon pure vanilla extract (use a high-quality extract, not an imitation)

5 cups day-old French bread, cut into 1-inch cubes (see Note)

¹/₃ cup raisins

Whiskey sauce:

1¹/₂ cups heavy cream

2 teaspoons cornstarch

2 tablespoons cold water

¹/₃ cup sugar

¹/₃ cup bourbon

Meringue:

9 medium egg whites, at room temperature

¹/₄ teaspoon cream of tartar

³/₄ cup sugar

PREHEAT the oven to 350°F. Grease an 8-inch square baking pan.

TO MAKE the bread pudding, combine the sugar, cinnamon, and nutmeg in a large bowl. Beat in the eggs until smooth, then work in the heavy cream. Add the vanilla, then the bread cubes. Allow the bread to soak up the custard. Scatter the raisins in the greased pan, and top with the egg mixture, which will prevent the raisins from burning. Bake for approximately 25 to 30 minutes or until the pudding has a golden brown color and is firm to the touch. If a toothpick inserted in the pudding comes out clean, it is done. It should be moist, not runny or dry. Let cool to room temperature.

TO MAKE the sauce, bring the cream to a boil, combine the cornstarch and water, and add the mixture to the boiling cream, stirring constantly. Return to a boil, then reduce the heat and cook, stirring, for about 30 seconds, being careful not to burn the mixture. Add the sugar and bourbon, and stir. Let cool to room temperature.

PREHEAT the oven to 350°F, and butter six 6-ounce ceramic ramekins.

TO MAKE the meringue, be certain that you use a bowl and whisk that are clean and that the egg whites are completely free of yolk. This dish needs a good, stiff meringue, and the egg whites will whip better if the chill is off them. In a large bowl or mixer, whip the egg whites and cream of tartar until foamy. Gradually add the sugar, and continue whipping until shiny and thick. Test with a clean spoon. If the whites stand up stiff, like shaving cream, when you pull out the spoon, the meringue is ready. Do not overwhip, or the whites will break down and the soufflé will not work.

IN A large bowl, break half the bread pudding into pieces using your hands or a spoon. Gently fold in a quarter of the meringue, being careful not to lose the air in the whites. Place a portion of this mixture in each of the ramekins.

PLACE the remaining bread pudding in the bowl, break into pieces, and carefully fold in the rest of the meringue. Top off the soufflés with this lighter mixture, to about 1½ inches over the top edge of the ramekin. With a spoon, smooth and shape the tops into a dome over the ramekin rim.

BAKE immediately for approximately 20 minutes or until golden brown. Serve immediately. Using a spoon at the table, poke a hole in the top of each soufflé and spoon the room-temperature whiskey sauce into the soufflé.

NOTE: New Orleans French bread is very light and tender. Outside New Orleans, use only a light bread. If the bread is too dense, the recipe won't work. We suggest Italian bread as the most comparable.

New Orleanians like their spiked foods spiked, which is why the whiskey sauce for this recipe uses what might seem like a generous amount of bourbon. Cut the amount of bourbon if you'd prefer. A standard crème anglaise would make a good alcohol-free alternative sauce.

 CHEF JAMIE'S TIPS

Creole Bread Pudding

MAKES 8 SERVINGS

*M*uch as we all love Commander's Bread Pudding Soufflé, sometimes plain Creole Bread Pudding is the most soul-satisfying taste of all. But do it right. One day, while my mother and I were nibbling on some bread pudding, I watched her eyebrow go up as she discovered a morsel of dry bread. It hadn't soaked thoroughly, a cardinal sin. When pastry chef Tom Robey walked by, Mom pointed to the dry morsel. She didn't have to say a word. Tom shook his head and went off to explain to a protégé how we don't rush things at Commander's. Originally created as a way to utilize day-old bread, this dessert, along with pecan pie and crème caramel, is a must for any New Orleans restaurant.

1 tablespoon butter

12 medium eggs, beaten

3 cups heavy cream

2 tablespoons pure vanilla extract (use a high-quality extract, not an imitation)

2 cups sugar

1 teaspoon ground cinnamon

$1/2$ teaspoon freshly grated nutmeg

4 ounces day-old French bread, sliced 1 inch thick (see Note)

1 cup raisins

PREHEAT the oven to 250°F.

BUTTER a large ($11 \times 8^{1}/_2 \times 3$ inches) casserole dish and set aside. (Once in the oven, the casserole will sit inside a larger pan. A roasting pan would be good.) Mix the eggs, cream, and vanilla in a large bowl, and combine the sugar, cinnamon, and nutmeg in a separate bowl. This helps to evenly distribute the spices. Add the sugar mixture to the egg mixture, and combine thoroughly.

PLACE the raisins in the bottom of the buttered casserole, and add the bread slices in a single layer. Gently pour the custard over the bread, making certain that all the bread thoroughly soaks up the custard. Cover the casserole with foil, place in a larger dish (the roasting pan, if that's what you decided to use) partly filled with hot water, and bake for $2^{1}/_2$ hours. Remove the foil, and increase the oven temperature to 300°F. Bake for 1 hour more, or until the pudding is golden brown and slightly firm. Use a spoon to make sure the custard is fully cooked; it should be moist but no longer runny. If you're unsure whether it's done, remove it from the oven and let it cool while it remains sitting in the water bath; the carryover effect will keep it cooking but it will not overcook. Serve slightly warm with the same whiskey sauce as for Bread Pudding Soufflé with Whiskey Sauce (page 264).

NOTE: New Orleans French bread is very light and tender. Outside New Orleans, use only a light bread. If the bread is too dense, the recipe won't work.

Some people prefer whole slices of bread, while others like the bread crumbled. Do it your way.

 CHEF JAMIE'S TIPS

Creole Cream Cheese Cheesecake

MAKES 8 SERVINGS

Of all the desserts at Commander's, this is my favorite, even though I've never been a major cheesecake fan. Maybe it's because this one is much lighter yet still tastes rich, sweet, and soul-satisfying. The critical ingredient here is Creole Cream Cheese. We can find no perfect substitute, and we can't find any place that still sells it. So we make our own. We've provided a recipe that tells you how to make it. In a pinch, you can use sour cream, but the results will be different.

Crust:

2 cups graham cracker crumbs

1/2 cup sugar

8 tablespoons (1 stick) butter, melted

Filling:

2 1/2 pounds softened cream cheese (store-bought is fine)

1 1/4 cups sugar

1 1/4 cups Creole Cream Cheese (page 309)

3 medium eggs

Topping:

3/4 cup sour cream

2 tablespoons sugar

For serving:

Caramel Sauce (page 281) (optional)

MAKE the crust by combining the graham cracker crumbs, sugar, and melted butter in a mixing bowl. Mix thoroughly by hand, and press the crumbs evenly over the bottom and up the sides of a 9 × 3-inch springform pan. Refrigerate.

PREHEAT the oven to 250°F.

TO MAKE the filling, use the large bowl of a mixer with the paddle attachment to combine the softened cream cheese and sugar. Mix until smooth, occasionally scraping the bowl with a spatula. Add the Creole cream cheese and mix until smooth. Add the eggs one at a time, scraping the bowl with a spatula and mixing until smooth after each addition. Pour the batter into the prepared crust and bake for 2 hours, until the center of the cake is firm to the touch. Let the cake cool while you make the topping.

COMBINE the sour cream and sugar and, when the cake is almost at room temperature, spread the mixture over the top with a spatula. Refrigerate until completely chilled, preferably overnight.

TO SERVE, release the sides of the springform pan, and cut the cake with a long knife dipped in very hot water and wiped with a clean towel after each slice. Smooth the sides of each piece with the knife. Place on a serving plate. If you wish, drizzle caramel sauce over the top and down the sides of the cake.

 CHEF JAMIE'S TIPS

When you're coating the pan with the crumb mixture, be sure the corners are not too thick with crumbs. When you mix the batter, don't overmix or you'll incorporate too much air and the cheesecake won't set up properly.

The trick to this cake is long, slow baking. You don't want the top to crack or the cake to rise. And while the cake is baking, it should not have any color on top. If you're not sure it's done, turn off the oven, let the cake sit for 30 minutes, and remove it from the oven.

Pecan Pralines

*W*alk through the French Quarter and the French Market, and every so often you'll pass a doorway from which wafts the aroma of burnt sugar or molasses—not a bitter smell, but a sweet, intoxicating one. It can mean only one thing: pralines (pronounced PRAW-leens, not PRAY-leens). When it comes to pralines, we don't like chocolate pralines or chewy pralines—just classic cream-and-sugar pecan pralines, made with only one Commander's addition, orange zest, and served without further adornment.

Zest of ½ orange (see Chef Jamie's Tips)	2 cups sugar
2 cups heavy cream	2 cups chopped pecans

TIMING is critical for this recipe, so line two or three cookie sheets with wax paper or parchment and place them as close to the hot pot as possible.

WITH A zester or a sharp paring knife, remove the zest, then chop it fine.

PLACE the zest, cream, and sugar in a large, heavy pot over medium-high heat. (Be sure to use a large pot, and be sure it's heavy. This mix can easily overboil and create a mess. A 4-quart pot works well.) Stir constantly and watch carefully as you bring the mixture to a boil. Reduce the heat to medium-low, and keep the mixture at a vigorous simmer for 15 to 17 minutes. As the mixture simmers, stir occasionally to break down the froth that comes to the top.

AFTER about 15 minutes, the mixture will stabilize, stop trying to climb up the sides of the pot, and start to reduce and caramelize. Stir occasionally, making sure that the mixture isn't burning on the bottom, until the mixture starts to pull together, releases from the side, and turns brown—about 5 to 7 minutes more. If the mixture seems to pull together without turning brown, increase the heat, but be aware that it could take only seconds to start browning.

ADD the pecans. When the mixture becomes one large clump, immediately remove the pot from the heat. Working quickly with two spoons (using one to scoop the mixture and one to scrape), place spoonfuls of the mixture onto the cookie sheets. The size will depend on the number of pralines you want; this formula will give you about 3 dozen bite-size portions.

LET COOL to room temperature, about 45 minutes.

NOTE: The mixture and saucepan are extremely hot and can easily burn your work surface.

Timing is so important to this recipe that in addition to having the cookie sheets ready, consider having a helper when it comes time to spoon the hot mixture onto the sheets. This recipe might require practice.

Citrus zest can add a great touch to your Creole cooking. The zest is the colored, outer part of the citrus. When you remove it, be sure to avoid the white pith, which is very bitter, underneath.

 CHEF JAMIE'S TIPS

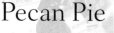

Pecan Pie

ecan pie is the reason we exercise. This is seriously sweet and seriously New Orleans. In fact, pecan pie, crème caramel, and bread pudding are the three all-time classic New Orleans desserts. Variations on pecan pie include chocolate pecan pie and bourbon pecan pie, but I love this traditional recipe.

Pie Dough (page 295), at room
    temperature
Flour, for rolling out dough
6 medium eggs
1¹/₃ cups sugar

1¹/₃ cups light corn syrup
1 tablespoon butter, melted
1 teaspoon vanilla extract
¹/₄ teaspoon salt
2¹/₂ cups pecan halves

SPRINKLE the work surface with flour. Flatten the pie dough slightly with your hands into a round shape, sprinkle the dough and a rolling pin with flour, and roll out the dough evenly, working from the center out. Pinch the dough to eliminate cracks. If the underside of the dough or the rolling pin sticks, sprinkle with additional flour. Roll to about ¹/₈-inch thickness.

PLACE a 9-inch pie pan upside down in the center of the dough. Add one inch for an overhang and cut out a circle of dough around the pie pan. Remove the pan, and brush off any excess flour. Push the dough into the bottom and against the sides of the pan, being careful not to tear the dough. Fold the edge of the dough under, and crimp the edges. Chill the crust while you make the filling.

WHISK the eggs in a large bowl. Add the sugar, corn syrup, melted butter, vanilla, and salt, and mix until smooth. Preheat the oven to 250°F. Scatter the pecans over the chilled crust, and pour the filling over the pecans. Use your fingers to blend gently until the pecans are evenly distributed. Be careful not to tear the dough. Bake for 2 hours and 45 minutes, until the center is set and the crust is golden brown.

CHEF JAMIE'S TIPS The pie will rise lightly in the center when it's finished. Don't allow it to rise too much because it can easily overcook, causing a dark filling and a dry, cracking pie. Perfect pecan pie should have a golden filling. The secret is long and slow cooking. If you're not positive that the pie is done, turn off the oven and let the pie rest in the oven for 15 minutes. Always be sure your pie pan is clean and that the dough has no holes. Otherwise, the filling will leak and the pie will stick. We *never* refrigerate pecan pie at the restaurant. You shouldn't either.

*Y*ou won't see these treats nearly as often today as you'll see pralines, but they're every bit as decadent—somewhat like funnel cakes but drier, crispier, and best served with cane syrup and a sprinkle of toasted chopped pecans. The name? Well, as they fry, you use a fork to twirl the centers, giving them the look of a pig's ear—or so thought some long-ago Acadian *bon vivant*.

2 cups all-purpose flour plus additional for dusting	3 medium eggs
2 teaspoons baking powder	3 cups solid vegetable shortening or canola oil
½ teaspoon kosher salt	Powdered sugar, for dusting
8 tablespoons (1 stick) butter, at room temperature	½ cup toasted chopped pecans (optional)
	Cane syrup, molasses, or honey

SIFT the 2 cups of flour, baking powder, and salt together in a small bowl. Cream the butter in a large bowl by hand or using an electric mixer on medium speed. Mix until light and fluffy, about 2 to 3 minutes. Add the eggs one at a time, mixing well after each addition. Add the dry ingredients a half-cup at a time, and mix until completely blended.

USE your hands to shape the dough into a ball. Lightly dust a work surface with flour, and with the palms of your hands roll the dough into a 16-inch-long tube. Slice the dough into sixteen 1-inch pieces, and roll each piece between your hands into a ball. Dust your work surface and rolling pin with flour, and roll each ball into an 8-inch circle ⅛ inch thick. Dust the surface with flour as you go, to prevent sticking.

HEAT the vegetable shortening in a 10-inch cast-iron skillet to 350°F on a deep-fry thermometer. Place a round of dough in the hot oil, and immediately poke the center of the dough with a long-handled fork. With the fork at a 45-degree angle to the pan, twist the fork so that the dough folds in on itself. Repeat with 2 more rounds of dough. Fry until golden brown, about 2 minutes, then flip the dough and fry the opposite side until it, too, is golden brown, another 2 minutes.

LET drain on a rack set over a cookie sheet or on paper towels. Fry each piece in the same manner, and generously dust the fried pieces with powdered sugar while they are hot. Sprinkle with the toasted chopped pecans, if desired, and pour on some cane syrup, molasses, or honey. These are best eaten while they are still warm.

Calas

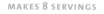

Calas may be old and almost forgotten, but they're a Creole favorite, traditionally served for breakfast with fresh fruit or fruit preserves and steaming dark chicory coffee. They're made with a pastry of rice, flour, and sugar, then are deep-fried and sprinkled with cane syrup and powdered sugar.

1 recipe Boiled Rice (page 252)

2 cups all-purpose flour

2 teaspoons baking powder

1½ teaspoons ground cinnamon

1 teaspoon freshly grated nutmeg

½ teaspoon kosher salt

4 medium eggs

3 tablespoons granulated sugar

3 cups solid vegetable shortening or canola oil, for frying

Powdered sugar, for dusting

SPREAD the cooked rice on a cookie sheet to cool completely. Sift together the flour, baking powder, cinnamon, nutmeg, and salt in a bowl, and set aside.

COMBINE the eggs and granulated sugar in a large bowl. Whip together using an electric mixer on medium speed until the mixture is light and fluffy, about 2 to 4 minutes. Fold in the cooked rice using a wooden spoon. Add the dry ingredients a half cup at a time, mixing well after each addition.

HEAT the vegetable shortening in a 10-inch cast-iron skillet to 350°F on a deep-fry thermometer.

MOISTEN your hands and roll the rice mixture between your hands, forming twenty-four 2-inch balls. Fry half the balls in the hot oil until they are golden brown on one side, about 3 to 4 minutes. Turn the balls over and cook another 3 to 4 minutes. Drain the balls on a rack set over a cookie sheet lined with paper towels, and dust with powdered sugar. Fry the second batch in the same way, then dust the second batch with powdered sugar, and serve.

SPRINKLE with cane syrup, if you wish, or they can be served with preserves (fig preserves are especially good).

Lagniappe

DINNER WITH TRUMAN CAPOTE

Between my mother and my Aunt Adelaide, the house I grew up in was the scene of more spontaneous gatherings and parties than I can recount. Most often, Mom or Aunt Adelaide would be entertaining old friends or brand-new ones they met in the restaurant (they never knew a stranger) and who they would invite home to continue whatever fun they had struck up at the restaurant. People I encountered at home with no warning were Raymond Burr, Danny Kaye, Carol Burnett, Phil Harris and wife, Alice Faye, Rock Hudson, Phyllis Diller, David Brinkley, and on and on.

But one year as Aunt Adelaide's birthday approached, my mother could not come up with gift ideas, so she asked Adelaide what she'd like. After some thought, Aunt Adelaide, having met and been intrigued by Truman Capote, told my mother she'd like to have dinner with Truman Capote. So, on her birthday, I answered the door and there was this short, peculiar-looking man in a blue velvet jodhpur outfit with a red bow on his head. My mother gave my aunt Truman Capote for her birthday.

Ponchatoula Strawberry Shortcake

MAKES 6 LARGE SERVINGS
OR 8 MODERATE SERVINGS

*I*magine a leisurely Sunday morning: You start with strong, black coffee, ease into a breakfast of homemade buttermilk biscuits, fresh Ponchatoula strawberries and sugar, and whipped sweet cream on top. If you happen to have a French Quarter apartment window with a view of banana trees blowing against the neighbor's peeling plaster and wrought iron, well, that's what living in New Orleans is all about. And if not, this dish will help you imagine it.

Biscuits:

4 cups all-purpose flour

$\frac{1}{2}$ teaspoon kosher salt

$1\frac{1}{2}$ tablespoons baking powder

$\frac{1}{4}$ cup granulated sugar

$\frac{1}{2}$ pound (2 sticks) butter, cold and cut into 1-inch cubes

$1\frac{1}{2}$ to 2 cups buttermilk

1 teaspoon baking soda

Strawberry mix:

4 pints reddest strawberries (smaller berries are generally the sweetest)

3 cups granulated sugar (adjust for the sweetness of the berries and your taste)

Topping:

$1\frac{1}{2}$ cups heavy cream, very cold

$\frac{1}{4}$ cup granulated sugar

For serving:

Powdered sugar, for dusting

PREHEAT the oven to 400°F.

TO MAKE the biscuits, sift the flour, salt, baking powder, and sugar in a large bowl. Gently work in the butter with 2 knives or your hands, breaking it into pea-size pieces but taking care not to overwork the dough. Form a well in the center of the mixture, add $1\frac{1}{2}$ cups of the buttermilk mixed with the baking soda, and lightly fold the mixture so that it's just sticky and the dry ingredients just moistened. If needed, add the additional buttermilk. The idea is to create layers so the butter will steam and serve as a leavening agent to help the biscuits rise. The less you handle the dough, the flakier the biscuits will be.

ON A WORK SURFACE lightly dusted with flour, flatten the dough to $1\frac{1}{2}$-inch thickness. Using a flour-dusted cutter $2\frac{1}{2}$ inches in diameter, cut the dough into 6 or 8 biscuits. Set the biscuits touching each other in an ungreased pie tin so that they stay moist while they bake. Bake biscuits for 20 to 25 minutes. Do not overbake; remember that the final 10 percent of the cooking will happen after they are removed from the oven.

WASH and hull the strawberries, and cut them in half; if they are large, cut them in quarters. One hour before serving, combine the berries and the sugar. The berries will secrete a juice mixture that should not be gritty from the sugar. The sugar mixture should be of a syruplike consistency.

TO PREPARE the topping, put the chilled heavy cream in a chilled bowl and whip with a whisk or an electric mixer. When the cream starts to thicken, add the sugar and whip to the desired consistency. Do not overwhip.

THE BISCUITS should be served warm (prepare and chill the dough the day before, if you wish, and bake before serving) but not so warm that they cause the whipped cream to melt.

TO ASSEMBLE, split the biscuits horizontally, and dust the top halves with powdered sugar. Place the bottom half of each biscuit on a dessert plate and top each with a portion of the strawberry mixture and some of the syrup. Top with a dollop of the whipped cream, and top each with a sugared biscuit top.

Ruston Peach Pie

MAKES ONE 9-INCH PIE

*D*ivine intervention never hurt a recipe, especially this one. It all started when our buyer met a preacher on a retreat and learned that he was a farmer, too. His peaches are fantastic, but he can't be bothered to drive to New Orleans. So we drive 200 miles to Ruston, La., every week during peach season. Ruston peaches are smaller than Georgia peaches, but they're very sweet.

1½ recipes Pie Dough (page 295)

⅓ cup all-purpose flour, plus extra for dusting

7 medium-ripe peaches (about 1¾ pounds), peeled and sliced ¼ inch thick

2 tablespoons fresh lemon juice

1 cup plus 2 tablespoons sugar

2 tablespoons butter, cubed

1 medium egg

2 tablespoons water

DIVIDE the prepared pie dough into 2 balls, wrap them in plastic, and refrigerate until chilled completely, about 3 hours.

REMOVE one ball of dough from the refrigerator. Let it sit for 15 minutes, then unwrap, dust with flour, and flatten it into a disk. Lightly dust the work surface, a rolling pin, and both sides of the dough with flour. Roll the dough into a large circle about ⅛ inch thick, rolling from the center out. Continue to lightly flour all surfaces as needed, especially underneath the dough.

PLACE a 9-inch pie pan upside down over the pie dough. Cut out a circle of dough, allowing an extra 2 inches around the pan for an overhang. Press the dough into the bottom and up the sides of the pan. Roll out the second ball of dough in the same manner, this time extending the circle only 1 inch beyond the edge of the pan. Place the pan with one crust, along with the second crust, on a cookie sheet and refrigerate.

PREHEAT the oven to 350°F.

TOSS the sliced peaches and the lemon juice in a large bowl, add the 1 cup of sugar and ⅓ cup of flour, and mix. Taste the peaches, and adjust the sugar if needed. Add the butter, and pour the mixture into the prepared crust.

WHISK the egg with the water and, using a pastry brush, brush the entire rim of the pie crust with the egg wash. Place the second pie crust over the top of the peaches. Fold the overlapping dough from the top crust over and underneath the bottom crust. Seal and crimp the edges with the tines of a fork or flute it by pushing the dough between your thumb and index finger. Cut vents in the top crust with a paring knife to allow steam to escape while baking.

BRUSH the entire top with the egg wash, then sprinkle the 2 tablespoons of sugar on top. Bake for 50 to 60 minutes, or until the crust is golden brown and the filling is bubbling. Let cool to room temperature, about 3 hours, before serving.

Depending on the ripeness of the peaches, you may want to add a tablespoon of flour. The riper the peaches, the more liquid they'll contain and the more flour you'll need.

And here's a great trick that makes peeling peaches easy. Submerge them in boiling water for a minute or two, then plunge them into a bowl of ice water. The peel should slide right off.

Egg wash serves two purposes in this recipe. First, it is a great "glue," sealing together layers of dough. Second, when it's brushed over the top of a baked good, it gives a nice, shiny, golden brown crust.

Blackberry Cobbler

MAKES 8 SERVINGS

*I*n our fruit cycle, blackberries come right after strawberries. Strawberry season is short, just a couple of months, but the season for wild blackberries is even shorter—from early May through the first week of June. Everybody has a favorite spot for picking them. My best luck has always been on the route to water skiing, along the nearby Jordan River in the thick shrubs. The bushes prick you, but the effort is worth it.

2 recipes Pie Dough (page 295)

4 pints blackberries (see Note)

1¼ cups sugar, plus additional for
     sprinkling

⅓ cup all-purpose flour

6 tablespoons butter, cut in ½-inch pieces

1 medium egg

2 tablespoons water

CHILL the finished pie dough for 3 hours. Preheat the oven to 350°F.

BUTTER and flour eight 8-ounce ramekins. Roll out the dough to ⅛-inch thickness, and cut out 8 circles large enough to fit the bottom and sides of the ramekins. Place a pastry circle in each ramekin and, using your fingers, press the dough snugly against the sides and bottom. Reroll the scraps to ⅛-inch thickness, and, using a knife or a pastry wheel, cut 32 lattice strips of dough, each 1 inch wide and 4 inches long.

TOSS together the blackberries, the 1¼ cups of sugar, the flour, and butter, and divide the mixture among the ramekins. Lay 2 lattice strips parallel to each other on top of the berries, and lay 2 more perpendicular to the first pair, creating a basketweave effect. Trim any excess dough around the edges.

WHISK the egg with the water to make an egg wash. With a pastry brush, brush the tops of the cobbler with the egg wash. Sprinkle the tops with additional sugar, place the ramekins on a cookie sheet, and bake for about 50 to 55 minutes, until the crust is golden brown and the filling is bubbling. Creole Cream Cheese Ice Cream (page 215) makes a great accompaniment.

NOTE: Instead of blackberries, good substitutes are blueberries, peaches, strawberries, and rhubarb.

*D*ripping over the sides of my Creole Cream Cheese Cheesecake, this thick Caramel Sauce is like a liquefied praline. Creole cooking uses a lot of sugar in various forms, like the caramelized sugar used here. The widely obsessed-upon praline is indeed a variation of caramel. Dribble this sauce over homemade vanilla or Creole Cream Cheese Ice Cream (page 215). Use a candy thermometer for best results.

1 cup sugar

2 tablespoons light corn syrup

3 tablespoons water

²/₃ cup heavy cream

IN A heavy pot, combine the sugar, corn syrup, and water. Cook over high heat, stirring constantly until the sugar is dissolved. Bring to a boil and cook over medium to high heat without stirring for about 5 minutes or until the mixture turns amber. This mixture can burn easily, so be careful. If you use a candy thermometer, cook until the thermometer reads 320°F to 340°F (no higher, or the sugar will burn).

REMOVE the pot from the heat and slowly stir in the cream. The mixture will boil and emit very hot steam, so again, be careful. Return to the heat, and bring to a boil again, then set aside to cool.

Corn syrup is added to the sugar syrup to prevent a process called crystallization. Instead of being smooth and creamy, crystallized caramel sauce is grainy with small bits of undissolved sugar.

 CHEF JAMIE'S TIPS

The sugar syrup pulls into a ball and hardens when a drop of it is put into a cup of ice water. The stages of sugar cooking are: soft ball 240°F, hard ball 260°F, soft crack 280°F, hard crack 310°F, and caramel 320°F to 345°F. Sugar syrup burns and is unusable at 350°F. The darker or the higher the temperature of your caramel, the nuttier and less sweet it will taste.

Citrus Pound Cake

Citrus Pound Cake is a more subtle dessert pleasure than Chocolate Molten Soufflé or bourbon pecan pie. It's like the difference between a rowdy afternoon at the Jazz and Heritage Festival and a quiet afternoon reading on a secluded beach house porch with a salty breeze rippling the pages of your novel. Either one is a glorious way to spend an afternoon and any of those desserts would be a glorious way to end a meal.

½ pound (2 sticks) plus 1 tablespoon butter, softened	1 tablespoon *each* lemon zest and lime zest (see Note)
2¼ cups all-purpose flour	Pinch of kosher salt
2 cups sugar	¼ teaspoon baking powder
5 medium eggs	¼ cup lemon and lime juices, combined in any proportion (see Note)

PREHEAT the oven to 325°F. Grease a 9 × 5-inch loaf pan with the 1 tablespoon of butter. Dust the sides and bottom of the greased pan using 2 tablespoons of the flour.

IN AN electric mixer, cream the remaining butter with 1½ cups of the sugar at medium speed for about 30 seconds. Scrape the bowl and add the eggs, lemon zest, and lime zest, and mix on high speed for about 1 minute, or until the mixture is the consistency of whipped butter.

WHISK together the remaining flour, salt, and baking powder, and, with the mixer on low speed, add to the butter mixture and mix for about 15 seconds. Scrape the bowl, turn the mixer to medium speed, and mix for 30 seconds, or until all the ingredients are well incorporated.

SCRAPE the batter into the prepared loaf pan, shaking gently to distribute evenly. Bake for 70 to 80 minutes, or until the cake is firm and a toothpick inserted in the center comes out clean.

MIX the remaining ½ cup of sugar with the lemon and lime juices, dissolving as much as possible. After the cake is removed from the oven, poke a few holes in the top and pour the syrup over the cake. Allow all the syrup to soak in.

LET the cake cool completely, and serve. It goes especially well with sorbet, ice cream, or fresh fruit and Creole Cream Cheese (page 309), Crème Fraîche (page 308), or whipped cream.

NOTE: When the fruit is in season, limes and lemons can be much larger and juicier, so be prepared to vary how many pieces of fruit you'll need. The zest is the colored outer part of the fruit. You can remove it with a special zester or a common potato peeler. But do not use the white pith, which is bitter.

Lemon Flan

*D*ottie Brennan complained loudly for years that we needed a great lemon dessert, something light and lemony. We tried and we tried, but nothing hit the mark—until we presented her with this Lemon Flan topped with a light, cinnamon-flavored phyllo sugar crisp. The contrasting textures of the crisp phyllo and the smooth lemon flan have an appeal similar to that of crème brûlée. This Lemon Flan holds its own and then some in our powerhouse dessert lineup, but more important, Aunt Dottie loves it!

Preparing the ramekins:

1 tablespoon butter, melted

3 tablespoons sugar

Flan:

1½ pounds cream cheese

1½ cups sugar

1½ cups fresh lemon juice (about 13 small lemons)

6 medium eggs

⅓ cup light rum

Lemon curd sauce:

4 medium egg yolks

¾ cup fresh lemon juice (about 7 small lemons)

¾ cup sugar

¼ cup light rum

Phyllo topping:

¼ teaspoon ground cinnamon

¼ cup sugar

4 sheets phyllo dough

4 tablespoons butter, melted

PREHEAT the oven to 250°F. Brush 8 ramekins, each with a capacity of 10 ounces, with melted butter, then dust each with sugar.

TO MAKE the flan, cream the cream cheese and the sugar in the large bowl of an electric mixer at medium speed until well blended. Scrape the bowl with a spatula, add the lemon juice, mix well, and scrape the bowl again. Add the eggs and the rum, continue mixing until the ingredients are well incorporated and free of lumps, and pour the mixture into the prepared ramekins. Place the ramekins in a roasting pan with 1 inch of hot water in the pan. Bake for 80 to 90 minutes, until the custard is set and firm to the touch but doesn't stick to your finger. Let cool in the water bath for about 1½ hours.

NEXT, prepare the lemon curd sauce. Place the egg yolks in a medium bowl. In a small saucepan, bring the lemon juice, sugar, and rum to a boil, and slowly pour the hot mixture into the bowl while whisking the egg yolks. Return the entire mixture to the saucepan, and cook over low heat for 2 to 3 minutes, until the sauce thickens slightly and reaches a temperature of 160°F. Do not let the sauce boil or it will curdle. Strain the sauce and set aside to cool.

PREHEAT the oven to 350°F and make the phyllo topping. Combine the cinnamon and sugar in a small bowl. Remove the phyllo dough from the package, and unroll it on a work surface. Separate one sheet of dough and place it on a cutting board. (Keep the remaining phyllo covered with a clean, damp towel while you work to prevent it from drying out.) Brush the phyllo sheet with about 1 tablespoon of the melted butter and sprinkle with a quarter of the cinnamon sugar. Place a second sheet of phyllo dough on top, brush with another tablespoon of melted butter and sprinkle with a third of the remaining cinnamon sugar. Repeat with a third and fourth sheet of phyllo, brushing each sheet with the remaining melted butter and sprinkling with equal amounts of the remaining cinnamon sugar.

USING the bottom of a ramekin as a guide, cut eight circles of phyllo dough with a paring knife. Place the circles on a greased sheet pan and bake in the preheated oven for 7 to 8 minutes, or until golden brown.

TO SERVE, run a paring knife around the inner edge of each ramekin to loosen the custard. If necessary, tap the side of the ramekin with the palms of your hands. Invert each custard onto a dessert plate, drizzle a portion of the sauce around the custard, and place a baked phyllo circle on top of each custard.

 CHEF JAMIE'S TIPS

These custards are very delicate, so be careful when you remove them from their ramekins. Be sure they are thoroughly cooled. The sauce, flan, and crisps can be made in advance, though be sure to keep the crisps in a cool, dry place.

Caramel Cup Custard

his dessert is also known as Crème Caramel, but whatever it's called, there must not be any bubbles in it and it's best never to refrigerate it or the consistency will change too much. *My* mom, Ella Brennan, says that *her* mom, Nellie Valentine Brennan, would leave it out all day at room temperature. We make ours just before service. Nellie would like it that way.

Caramel:

¼ cup water

1 tablespoon light corn syrup

1 cup sugar, free of lumps and impurities

Custard:

1½ cups milk

1½ cups heavy cream

1 vanilla bean, split lengthwise, seeds
    removed by scraping with the back of
    a paring knife, and scrapings saved, or
    1 tablespoon high-quality vanilla
    extract

5 medium eggs

1 cup sugar

¼ teaspoon kosher salt

HAVE ready near the stove eight 6-ounce ramekins and a towel soaking in a bowl of ice water.

FIRST, make the caramel: Put the water in a small saucepan, stir in the corn syrup, and bring to a boil over high heat. Add the sugar, stir, and bring back to a boil. Reduce the heat to medium-high, and cook, giving the pan an occasional gentle swirl and wiping up any hard crystals, which could cause lumps, from the edges. Cook for about 7½ to 8 minutes, or until the caramel starts to darken slightly, turning the color of honey.

NOW WORK quickly. Lightly wring out the soaking towel, fold it three times, and place it on the work surface. Remove the saucepan of caramel from the stove and place it on the towel. Quickly spoon 1½ tablespoons of caramel into each ramekin. Let cool for about 20 minutes.

TO MAKE the custard: Preheat the oven to 250°F and bring about 2 quarts of water to a boil for use as a water bath. Combine the milk, cream, vanilla bean, and reserved bean scrapings, or extract, in a saucepan, and cook over medium heat for 3 to 5 minutes, stirring occasionally, until the mixture almost simmers—it should register about 175°F. Remove from the heat. Do not let the mixture boil.

IN A large bowl, whisk together the eggs, sugar, and salt, and add the warm milk mixture in a slow stream. Swirl the pot to release any remaining vanilla seeds and keep them from sticking to the bottom of the pan. Continue pouring until the two mixtures are combined, and strain through a fine sieve. Swirl the last couple of ounces in the bowl to release any remaining vanilla, and strain.

DIVIDE the custard evenly among the ramekins.

PLACE a roasting pan on a rack in the oven, position the ramekins in the pan so that they are not touching, gently add the boiling water to the pan, and bake for about 2 hours, or until done. The custard should be firm. Test by tapping a spoon on the edge of the ramekin. If nothing happens, it's done; if it's not quite done, you'll see rippling toward the center.

REMOVE the roasting pan from the oven and let the custards, still in the water bath, cool to room temperature for about 1 hour. Remove the ramekins from the water bath and continue cooling on a wire rack for about 30 minutes more. Do not refrigerate.

TO UNMOLD, run a paring knife around the perimeter of each ramekin. Place a dessert plate on top of each ramekin, and invert. Set each plate on a work surface and gently shake the ramekin to release. Serve immediately at room temperature.

 CHEF JAMIE'S TIPS

Caramel can go from perfect to burnt in seconds. Don't be discouraged if your first couple of attempts don't work. It takes practice. You need to work fast and be safe. The purpose of the soaked towel is to stop the cooking and prevent burning the caramel. The caramel can be made up to a day in advance.

Many cooks prefer their caramel a little lighter than I do. That's because I like the way the slight bitterness of the darker caramel contrasts with the sweetness and creaminess of the custard.

I also like using fresh vanilla in my custard. Some cooks don't like the specks, but they don't bother me. I think the flavor is so much better than what many extracts will yield.

At Commander's, we cook most of our custards in a 225°F convection oven, which is equivalent to about 250°F in a conventional oven. This slow cooking virtually guarantees a perfect texture—without any of the bubbles that indicate overcooking and with no skin on the bottom.

The custard should be smooth, rich but not eggy, and barely able to sit up on its own.

Chocolate Molten Soufflé

MAKES 8 SERVINGS

*R*emember baking chocolate cake as a kid and licking the batter off the spoon and bowl? Believe it or not, that was the inspiration for this soufflé. You put your spoon into this all-chocolate soufflé and find warm, gooey, chocolate lava in the center. It's not even on the Commander's menu, yet it's still one of our top sellers. You've got to ask for it. We're afraid that if we put it on the menu, we wouldn't sell much of anything else. We keep it a secret for our regulars and for those in the know—which now includes you.

12 tablespoons (1½ sticks) butter, softened	8 medium eggs
1 pound semisweet chocolate, in small pieces (see Chef Jamie's Tips)	1½ cups sugar
	1½ cups all-purpose flour

White chocolate sauce:

1 cup heavy cream	8 ounces white chocolate, in small pieces

For serving:

Powdered sugar, for dusting

PREHEAT the oven to 350°F.

USE 2 tablespoons of the butter to grease 8 ramekins or ovenproof coffee cups, each with a 6-ounce capacity. Check to see that all surfaces are completely covered with butter, especially the corners.

PLACE the remaining 10 tablespoons of butter with the chocolate pieces in the top part of a double boiler or in a medium bowl set over a saucepan of barely simmering water, and melt completely, stirring occasionally with a rubber spatula.

BREAK the eggs into the workbowl of a food processor, add the sugar and the melted chocolate, and process until the mixture is smooth, about 15 seconds. Add the flour, and process for another 10 seconds. Scrape down the inside of the workbowl with the spatula and process until smooth, about 10 seconds more.

POUR an equal amount of the batter into each ramekin. Place the ramekins on a baking sheet, and bake in the preheated oven for about 20 minutes, until the mixture begins to rise and the center is still slightly soft to the touch. Remove the soufflés from the oven, but don't let them cool for more than a couple of minutes before you carefully invert them onto serving plates.

WHILE the soufflés are baking, make the white chocolate sauce. Bring the heavy cream to a boil in a medium saucepan. Turn off the heat, add the white chocolate pieces, and stir with a rubber spatula or wooden spoon until the chocolate has melted completely.

TO SERVE, sprinkle each soufflé generously with powdered sugar, and spoon the white chocolate sauce around the perimeter. Serve warm.

Use the best-quality semisweet chocolate you can find.

CHEF JAMIE'S TIPS

   You can make the batter ahead of time and refrigerate it in the ramekins. If it's coming out of the refrigerator, bake as described in the recipe but for 25 minutes instead of 20. You could also make the sauce ahead of time. Refrigerate it and reheat over a pot of barely simmering water until it's warm and completely melted.

COMMANDER'S

KITCHEN PANTRY

*I*f you keep your pantry and fridge stocked with a dozen or so basic ingredients, you've already won half the battle. It's like starting the ball game at half time with you in the lead. (Wonder if that would help the Saints?) Whether you're pulling together an elaborate Chef's Table–type dinner or spontaneously creating a snack to satisfy your Creole sensibilities, having a great stock, a Creole seasoning mix, some filé, or some Creole Cream Cheese on hand is the secret to Creole cooking nirvana.

Following the recipes in this chapter you'll find a helpful list of ingredients and cooking terms that occur throughout the book.

Creole Mayonnaise

MAKES ABOUT 3 CUPS

This mayonnaise is so good that my family bottled and marketed it in the mid-'80s. Maybe you bought some. Try it once and you'll never go back to jarred supermarket mayonnaise.

1 medium egg

2 tablespoons lemon juice

½ medium white onion, diced

2¼ cups canola, vegetable, or corn oil

1½ teaspoons hot sauce

1 tablespoon freshly ground black pepper

Kosher salt to taste

PLACE the egg, lemon juice, and onion into the workbowl of a food processor and purée. With the motor running, slowly add half the oil. Then add the hot sauce, pepper, and salt. Stop the motor, scrape the sides of the bowl with a rubber spatula, and, with the motor running again, slowly add the remaining oil. Taste and adjust salt. Store, covered, in the refrigerator for a week.

NOTE: This recipe can easily be doubled.

CHEF JAMIE'S TIPS This mayonnaise might be a little thin for your taste. That's because of all the seasoning. If you'd like it thicker, you can use a bit more oil or egg, but be sure to add more salt and pepper.

I have childhood memories of cooks reaching into the pocket of their chef's coats for a touch of seasoning. Each chef had his own special seasoning blend that he would secretly mix and use. Sometime in the 1970s, Commander's kitchen started making batches of its own blends and insisting that our cooks use them, a practice that has spread throughout New Orleans restaurant kitchens and beyond. Here's our blend for seasoning steak and game.

1 cup table salt

3/4 cup onion powder

3/4 cup garlic powder

3/4 cup freshly ground black pepper

1 tablespoon cayenne pepper, or to taste

3/4 cup paprika

COMBINE all ingredients and mix thoroughly in a food processor or in a large mixing bowl. Store in a glass jar or plastic container. It will keep indefinitely.

 CHEF JAMIE'S TIPS

Be careful of what we call cayenne cloud when mixing. Cayenne cloud can cause burning if you put your face too close to the mixing bowl before everything has settled back down. Also, note that the intensity of spices varies with age, location, and season, so always taste and adjust recipes.

Creole Seafood Seasoning

MAKES ABOUT 2 CUPS

*I*f there is any "magic" to our cooking, it's in seasoning mixes such as this. With this mixture, we try to unmask the depth of flavor in our native seafood, not overpower it. We want every bite to display a full flavor profile, so we liberally sprinkle seasoning on the entire piece of fish. That means both sides. Make a decent-sized batch of this mixture so it will always be handy, then rub it or sprinkle it on the food. Remember, mixtures such as this one cost very little to make yourself but quite a lot if you buy them at retail.

⅓ cup table salt	2 tablespoons dried oregano
¼ cup granulated or powdered garlic	⅓ cup paprika
¼ cup freshly ground black pepper	3 tablespoons granulated or powdered
2 tablespoons cayenne pepper, or to taste	onion
2 tablespoons dried thyme	
2 tablespoons dried basil	

THOROUGHLY combine all ingredients in a blender, food processor, or mixing bowl, and pour the mixture into a large glass or plastic jar. Seal it so that it's airtight. It will keep indefinitely.

CHEF JAMIE'S TIPS   Cayenne pepper is the main source of heat in this mixture. If you wish, reduce the quantity by as much as half.

*M*aster this recipe and it will be one of the most versatile recipes in your kitchen, good for pecan pie, crawfish pie, chicken potpie, and on and on.

1½ cups all-purpose flour
Pinch of salt

8 tablespoons (1 stick) butter, at room
    temperature
5 to 6 tablespoons ice water

COMBINE the flour and salt in a medium bowl. Using your hands, gently work the butter into the flour until the butter pieces are each about the size of a dime. Make a well in center of the mixture, and pour 5 tablespoons of the ice water into the well. Fold gently to incorporate, using the additional tablespoon of water if the dough is too dry and crumbly. Fold until the dough comes together. Do not overwork the dough. Wrap the dough in plastic wrap and refrigerate for at least one hour.

REMOVE dough from the refrigerator and roll out according to the directions in recipes using pie dough.

Machines such as food processors seem to overwork this dough, so make it by hand. Use a good-quality, fresh butter.

 CHEF JAMIE'S TIPS

Crab Boil

*M*ost New Orleanians use Zatarain's Crab Boil when cooking crabs, crawfish, and shrimp, but you can't get it everywhere, especially on the West Coast. You can, however, buy all the ingredients you need at any grocery to make your own. That way, you can adjust the boil to your taste, perhaps with more bay leaf or fewer pepper flakes. Enclose the ingredients in a cheesecloth pouch tied with kitchen twine or a rubber band so the spices don't get loose in the water. Jamie says you can use a clean, thin sock. I say you should go with the cheesecloth.

½ cup mustard seeds	2 tablespoons whole allspice
¼ cup dried red pepper flakes	12 whole cloves
¼ cup whole peppercorns	6 tablespoons coriander seeds
20 bay leaves, crumbled	1 tablespoon dill seed

COMBINE all ingredients.

CUT 2 pieces of cheesecloth, each about 2 feet by 1 foot. Fold over each of the two pieces of cloth so that each is double thickness. Place half the ingredients in the center of each piece of cloth. Wrap and tie both bags with kitchen twine. Use as directed in recipes calling for crab boil, or place in boiling water to give a New Orleans flavor to many recipes.

A SMALL BOIL, for which this recipe yields the right amount, is the kind you'd prepare indoors. But you'd need more for the larger, outdoor boil you might prepare for a huge gathering.

CHEF JAMIE'S TIPS Be sure that the mustard seeds can't come through the cheesecloth. Tie the cloth very well, but leave a little room for the spices to expand.

*R*avigote is a classic cold French sauce served with chilled shell-fish that has long been a favorite in New Orleans and at Commander's. The oldest Commander's menus featured Crabmeat Ravigote. Suffice it to say anything that has survived that long on our constantly evolving menu is a classic and a local favorite.

1 cup Creole Mayonnaise (page 292)

¹/₂ cup Creole mustard or coarse-ground
    German mustard

1 tablespoon capers, drained and coarsely
    chopped

1 medium egg, hard-cooked and diced
    small

1¹/₂ teaspoons prepared horseradish

Kosher salt and freshly ground pepper
    to taste

2 green onions, thinly sliced

IN A large bowl, combine the mayonnaise, mustard, capers, egg, and horse-radish. Season with salt and pepper. Fold in the green onions. Cover and re-frigerate. It will keep for a few weeks. Use in recipes as specified.

Creole Tartar Sauce

MAKES APPROXIMATELY 2 CUPS

Our tartar sauce definitely has a little kick, what with the addition of our Creole Seafood Seasoning, onion, hot sauce, and more. We use it on our fried catfish, on fried seafood, with vegetables, and most importantly, on a Po' Boy. Want to make a to-die-for Oyster Po' Boy? Easy: Spread this Creole Tartar Sauce on hot French bread, and add Creole or vine-ripened tomato slices, Vidalia onion slices, and quick-fried oysters.

1 cup chopped kosher dill pickles, or pickle
    or relish of your choice
1 bunch green onions, thinly sliced
1½ tablespoons Creole mustard or other
    coarse mustard
2 teaspoons prepared white horseradish

1½ teaspoons hot sauce, or to taste
2 teaspoons Creole Seafood Seasoning
    (page 294) or any Creole seasoning
    mix, or to taste
1 cup mayonnaise

PLACE the chopped pickles, green onions, mustard, horseradish, hot sauce, Creole seasoning, and mayonnaise in a bowl and mix well. Adjust the seasoning if needed. Store, refrigerated, in an airtight container for up to 2 weeks. Serve on fried fish or seafood or with raw vegetables.

CHEF JAMIE'S TIPS If you want to tone down the spiciness, add more mayonnaise.

Crystal Hot Sauce Beurre Blanc

MAKES ³/₄ CUP

*H*undreds of hot sauces are available in Louisiana, but we have long preferred Crystal Hot Sauce and Tabasco. I sprinkle some Crystal on my Oyster Po' Boys. I know a guy who even likes Crystal Hot Sauce on his eggs. Of course, he owns the company. He's Alvin Baumer, and I profess to being a lifelong Crystal user even before he married my cousin, Brennan. Their son—his name is really Pepper—loves Crystal on everything, too. Sometimes a traditional beurre blanc needs a little kick, and here's how we give it that kick.

¹/₃ cup Crystal Hot Sauce (another hot
    sauce can be substituted)
2 tablespoons minced shallots
6 medium cloves garlic, peeled and minced

¹/₄ cup heavy cream
6 tablespoons unsalted butter, softened
Kosher salt to taste

PLACE the hot sauce, shallots, garlic, and cream in a small saucepan. Over medium heat, simmer until reduced by half, stirring frequently. Slowly whip the softened butter, a bit at a time, into the pot, being careful not to let the sauce break. (The cream acts as a stabilizer.) Strain and keep the sauce warm. Add salt.

CHEF JAMIE'S TIPS

Because of the high acidity of this sauce, you may need to take it off the heat as you add the butter to keep it from breaking, which would require you to start over. If it seems to get too thick, return it to the heat.

Dark Roux

MAKES 2¼ CUPS

*D*on't burn it. Dark Roux is behind one of the wonderful aromas that come from Commander's every day—a deep, nutty smell that permeates the neighborhood and gets the locals asking, "Something smells good, what are y'all cooking?" Roux is just a mixture of flour and fat, usually oil or butter. You simmer and stir them until you get the color you want. Dark Roux turns the perfect color in an almost unnoticeable instant. Cook it just a moment too long and it'll break and taste bitter. It's like riding a bike—there may be trial and error, and you need to watch where you're going, but once you get it, you've got it for life.

1 cup corn, vegetable, or safflower oil	2 stalks celery, in small dice
1 cup all-purpose flour	1 medium bell pepper, in small dice
1 medium onion, in small dice	10 cloves garlic, peeled and minced

BE SURE to use a clean, dry pot that's large enough so that the oil comes no more than a quarter of the way up the sides. Heat the oil in the pot over high heat for about 5 to 6 minutes, or until the oil just starts to smoke. Gently add a third of the flour, stirring constantly with a wooden spoon. Cook for 30 seconds, stirring constantly. Add another third of the flour and stir constantly for 30 seconds more, or until well incorporated. The roux should be a dark shade of brown. Add the remaining flour and stir, cooking for 30 to 45 seconds or until the roux is the color of milk chocolate.

PLACE the pot on a cool burner, add the onion immediately, stir to incorporate thoroughly, add the celery, and stir again. Add the bell pepper and garlic. Scrape the bottom of the pot.

LET COOL for about 1 hour. Remove any excess fat that may rise to the surface. The roux will keep in an airtight container in the refrigerator for about two weeks. Use it as called for in recipes throughout this book and in such dishes as gumbos or turkey gravy.

CHEF JAMIE'S TIPS Be sure the flour is free of lumps and impurities. Any impurities in the flour will burn and leave specks in the roux.

Use an oil with a high smoking point, such as corn, safflower, soybean, or peanut oil. (We don't use peanut oil at Commander's because some people are highly allergic to it.)

The oil and pot must be free of any other moisture, which can make the oil boil over and splatter. Hot oil is dangerous, so don't leave oil unattended while it's heating, and add flour just as it starts to smoke.

The reason you add the flour a third at a time is that flour contains moisture, especially in humid places, such as New Orleans. Moisture will make oil steam, foam, and climb up the pot, and that can be dangerous. And even so, adding that much flour at once would cool the oil too much.

When stirring the roux, be sure to scrape the bottom and sides of the pot, which is where most of the color comes from and where there's the biggest chance of burning.

The roux should smell nutty, not burnt, and it should have a dark brown color without specks. If the roux is burnt, or if it smells burnt, discard it after it cools.

Add the vegetables immediately after the desired color has been reached and the roux has been removed from the heat. Do not add all the vegetables at once. Liquid from the vegetables will make the roux foam up. Stir and be sure to scrape the bottom of the pot. Adding the vegetables cooks and caramelizes them, stops the roux from cooking, adds flavor, and makes the roux darker.

A dark roux is used for flavor as well as for thickening. Like all roux, you want to simmer it when it's added to liquid.

Some recipes use a lighter colored roux. When recipes in this book use such a roux, the directions are incorporated in the recipes. One big difference is that you don't cook it as long, but the lighter roux might use butter whereas a dark roux uses only oil as the fat.

Garden Hot Sauce

*A*lthough New Orleans offers some of the world's greatest commercially available hot sauces, it's easy to make your own. You can buy hot peppers or grow them in your garden, as Chef Jamie does. He and the other cooks had so many peppers that they got a wine barrel and began marinating their peppers as an ingredient for Commander's Bloody Mary. (You can see the barrel as you pass through the kitchen.) And with your own customized label, you've made this sauce into a great gift.

1½ pounds ripe hot peppers (cayenne, jalapeño, habañero, etc., or a combination)	1 cup kosher salt 3 cups white vinegar

RINSE the peppers with cold water and dry them with a paper towel. Remove the stems and chop them coarsely. Place the chopped peppers in a stainless bowl, sprinkle the salt on top, stir, cover with plastic wrap, and place in a cool, dry area for 2 days, stirring every 12 hours. All that salt is there mostly to promote ripening of the peppers.

ADD the vinegar, and purée with a hand blender or in a food processor. Place in a sterilized glass jar with a fresh lid, and refrigerate.

AS TIME goes by, whenever you have an excess of ripe peppers, again wash, remove stems, chop and add to the jar. (The salting step isn't necessary for these additions.) When the jar is filled, remove the sauce, purée if you wish, place it in a clean jar, and age it until it reaches the desired flavor—at least 2 months, or longer.

USE as the hot sauce in many recipes.

NOTE: Use rubber gloves when handling hot peppers, or wash your hands thoroughly before touching your eyes or any skin.

CHEF JAMIE'S TIPS

I don't look for heat alone in my pepper sauce. Making heat is easy. Rather, I search for a true pepper flavor. Ripe peppers result in the best of flavors and colors. The variety of pepper will largely determine the heat level. Combinations are great. And add sweet peppers if you don't like the heat. Or use whatever varieties are best at the time you make this sauce.

I don't like to strain my hot sauce. I like the chunks and rustic look with the seeds. I put it in some clean, funky-looking bottles with corks or lids.

Always shake before using. A well-aged sauce won't need to be shaken as much. And these sauces can be well aged, up to six months when refrigerated.

*ey, Cooker Man, I've got some figs for you." That's what the kids in Chef Jamie's neighborhood yell out to him when they've collected some figs. One day, Jamie gave a kid a few bucks for some figs, so the little capitalists caught on that the big guy with the white coat on the Harley-Davidson would pay you a couple bucks for figs you could find on the ground. So began our own little fig industry. This hot, sweet sauce is just one way we use all those figs.

1 tablespoon butter

1 medium onion, coarsely chopped

1 dried habañero pepper, finely chopped (this pepper is extremely hot, so use less if you wish)

1 cup cane vinegar or cider vinegar

½ cup light or dark molasses (substitute honey or brown sugar if you wish)

4 cups tightly packed fresh figs, stemmed

2 bottles (12 ounces each) dark beer

Kosher salt and freshly ground pepper to taste

MELT the butter over high heat in a large saucepan, add the onion and habañero pepper, and cook for about 6 minutes or until onion is caramelized. Add the vinegar and molasses, and bring to a boil, stirring occasionally. Add the figs while stirring. Return to a boil, then reduce to a simmer and cook for 10 minutes. Add the beer, and bring to a boil. Season with salt and pepper, and simmer for 15 minutes.

PURÉE the mixture using a hand-held blender, standing blender, or food processor. Adjust the consistency by adding a little water or boiling to reduce the mixture. Adjust the flavor to your liking by adding salt, pepper, habañero peppers, vinegar, or molasses. Store, refrigerated, for several weeks. Use as directed elsewhere in this book or to accompany flank steak, pork, chicken, or even hamburgers.

Be careful about adding more habañero, especially in the beginning. As the sauce cooks and after it has been puréed, it will get hotter, especially if you let it sit for a while. Other peppers may be substituted. And other fruits, such as plums, peaches, even apples or oranges, can be substituted.

CHEF JAMIE'S TIPS

Homemade Barbecue Sauce

*L*ook at these ingredients. How could it not be good? This sauce will perk up even a backyard burger on the grill. I like to baste some spicy andouille sausage with this and make a Smoked Barbecue Sausage Po' Boy. Whew!

1 tablespoon butter	8 ounces fresh gingerroot, peeled and coarsely chopped
2 medium onions, coarsely chopped	1 cup dark molasses or honey
2 medium bell peppers, coarsely chopped	7 ounces tomato paste (about 1 can)
1 small head garlic, cloves peeled and coarsely chopped	½ cup hot sauce, or to taste
Kosher salt and freshly ground pepper to taste	1 cup packed brown sugar, light or dark
12 ounces vinegar (cane, cider, or white)	12 ounces beer (any kind; use your favorite)
	Cayenne pepper to taste (optional)

PLACE the butter in a saucepot over high heat, and bring to the smoking point, about 1 to 1½ minutes. Add the onions, peppers, and garlic, and season with salt and pepper. Cook, still over high heat, until the vegetables are very brown, about 15 to 20 minutes, stirring constantly so as not to burn the bottom of the pot.

ADD the vinegar and the ginger, stir, and bring to a boil. Add the molasses, tomato paste, hot sauce, and brown sugar, stir, and bring to a boil. Add the beer, bring to a boil again, then simmer for 1 hour, stirring occasionally.

PURÉE with a hand blender or in a food processor. Taste and adjust seasoning. If it's not hot enough for your taste, add cayenne. If the sauce is too thick, add a bit more beer or water, cover, and simmer for about 15 minutes, stirring occasionally to prevent the bottom from burning.

USE in recipes calling for barbecue sauce. This will go beautifully on your next batch of ribs or on chicken, pork chops, flank steak, or pork tenderloin.

CHEF JAMIE'S TIPS

I'm assuming that whatever meat you use this sauce on is itself well seasoned, so the sauce isn't heavily seasoned. It will keep in the refrigerator for about 3 months. It's best after a couple of weeks, and it goes great on all meats and game.

Why not make our own?" That innocent question often marks the beginning of a new adventure for Commander's. Worcestershire was one of those staples that we always took for granted. Now a wooden keg with a spigot sits proudly in the kitchen and is tapped all day long. This sauce is integral to countless dishes and sauces, from our barbecued shrimp to Bloody Marys.

1 tablespoon olive oil	2 cups water
6 ounces fresh horseradish, peeled and chopped	4 cups white vinegar
	1 cup dark molasses
2 medium onions, diced	2 cups dark corn syrup
2 jalapeño peppers, seeded and finely diced	1 ounce anchovy fillets (8 to 12), chopped
	12 whole cloves
6 cloves garlic, peeled and chopped	1 tablespoon salt
3/4 teaspoon coarsely ground fresh black pepper	1 lemon, peeled and chopped
	1 tablespoon tamarind (optional)

PLACE the oil, horseradish, onions, jalapeños, and garlic in a large pot, and sauté over medium heat until the onions are translucent. Add the black pepper, water, vinegar, molasses, corn syrup, anchovy, cloves, salt, lemon, and tamarind. Mix thoroughly, and bring to a boil. Simmer over low to medium heat for 1 hour, or until the mixture coats the back of a spoon.

STRAIN through a fine sieve into a medium saucepan. Reduce by half over low to medium heat. The sauce should have a slightly syrupy consistency. As it cools, it will thicken. Use in any recipe, in this book or elsewhere, that calls for Worcestershire. When covered, it can be refrigerated up to two months.

If you want to improve any recipe calling for Worcestershire, use this instead of the bottled version.

 CHEF JAMIE'S TIPS

Roasted Bell Peppers

MAKES APPROXIMATELY 1 QUART

*G*ood roasted peppers are available commercially, but whether you buy them or make your own, they are a staple in the Creole cook's repertoire. We use them in sauces, as a condiment, on sandwiches, in salads, and on and on.

8 large ripe bell peppers, any color
½ cup olive oil
2 teaspoons kosher salt, or to taste

2 teaspoons freshly ground black pepper, or to taste

PREHEAT the oven to 450°F.

PLACE the peppers in a large bowl, add the olive oil, and mix. Season with salt and pepper, and mix again, coating all sides with oil and seasoning. Place the peppers in a large roasting pan, and pour any excess oil and seasoning in the bowl on top of the peppers. Set the bowl aside.

ROAST the peppers until their skins start to blister, then turn them over. When the peppers are dark and blistered on all sides (about 25 to 30 minutes, depending on how thick the peppers are), remove them from the oven.

RETURN the peppers to the bowl, along with any liquid in the roasting pan. Cover the bowl tightly with plastic wrap and place in a cool area. While they cool, the peppers will shrink and, if the seal is airtight, the plastic will pull into the center of the bowl like a tight drum. This will help pull skin away from the wall of the pepper. Let cool for about 45 to 60 minutes, and the peppers will be ready to peel.

WORKING over the bowl, gently remove and discard the stem of 1 pepper, taking as many seeds as possible with it. Pour any liquid inside the pepper back into the bowl. Peel and discard the skin, and return the pepper to the bowl. Repeat with remaining peppers. When the peppers are completely peeled, shake off any seeds or remaining skin. When peppers have cooled, place them in a glass or plastic storage container, and strain all liquid into the container. Cover and refrigerate with the peppers whole. Use as specified in recipes throughout this book, or as a condiment. They will keep for a couple of weeks.

CHEF JAMIE'S TIPS Roasted peppers are very flavorful. Most of the flavor comes from the oil, which is why I discourage frying the peppers or washing them after frying. There are other ways to skin peppers, but I like the method in this recipe best. Frying produces a greasy, messy product. And burning off the skin gives the pepper too much of a charcoal flavor, besides making the peppers so hard to peel that you never seem to get all the skin off. And I don't like rinsing the peppers under water and peeling because you lose too much flavor.

The liquid from the peppers also contains a lot of flavor, so I use the liquid, which includes oil, for a dressing or marinade, and, sometimes, in cold foods.

Crème Fraîche

Crème fraîche is so easy to make and so versatile. You can boil it in a sauce and it won't curdle. You can serve it over fruit, on a cobbler, with caviar, or as a sauce. It's much better homemade than any version you can buy. The French eat crème fraîche the way we eat Creole Cream Cheese in New Orleans. Is it better sweetened and served over fresh fruit, or served with caviar, hard-boiled egg, and green onion on a toast point? Wonderful question!

2 cups heavy whipping cream	1 cup buttermilk

COMBINE the cream and buttermilk in a large stainless or glass bowl, stir thoroughly, cover, and let stand at room temperature for about 24 hours or until very thick. Stir, place in a clean container, cover, and refrigerate up to a week.

CHEF JAMIE'S TIPS Use a clean glass or stainless container to make and hold the crème fraîche to prevent unwanted bacteria from forming. The final consistency can range from loose, almost runny, to stiff, like room-temperature butter. Consistency also depends on how long the mixture was left standing and at what temperature.

Creole Cream Cheese

MAKES APPROXIMATELY 2 CUPS

*M*ake your own cheese? Absolutely. Why? (1) This cheese is difficult to find, even in New Orleans. (2) There is no perfect substitute for this particular cheese. (3) It's easy! (4) Won't it be cool to tell your friends you made cheese? You'll need this to make the Creole Cream Cheese Cheesecake (page 268 and to die for), the Creole Cream Cheese Ice Cream (page 215 and also to die for), and the Granola Parfait (page 124 and you'll love us for this one).

7 cups skim milk	6 drops liquid rennet (see Note)
¼ cup buttermilk	

COMBINE the skim milk and buttermilk in a large saucepan over medium heat. Heat to 110°F (use a clip-on thermometer), whisking occasionally. Pour into a large mixing bowl, add the rennet, stir, and cover with cheesecloth. Let stand at room temperature for about 24 hours. The milk will separate into curds and whey. Line a colander with cheesecloth and gently spoon the cheese into the colander without breaking it apart. Let the cheese drain for 30 to 60 minutes until it's in one solid mass. Gently place the cheese in a container, cover, and refrigerate.

SERVE over fruit, on toast with sugar, on cakes and biscuits with nuts, eat as is, and use in recipes as called for throughout this book. It's best if consumed within 5 days.

NOTE: Whey is the watery liquid that separates from the milk solids or curds. Rennet is a coagulating enzyme from a young animal's stomach or is made from vegetables used in cheesemaking. It's found in most supermarkets in liquid, powder, or tablet form; in this recipe, 2 tablets could be used instead of the liquid.

CHEF JAMIE'S TIPS

Be sure all utensils are clean. Be very careful when straining and transferring cheese. In particular, don't stir it or you risk destroying its consistency. The cheese will thicken as it sits. Different rennets will give different results, so experiment.

Commander's Kitchen Pantry

Onion
Marmalade

MAKES 2 CUPS

armalade" suggests sweetness, and it's true in this recipe, where the sugar just seems to pull the natural sweetness out of the onions. It's a perfect complement to our lively Skillet-Grilled Tuna (page 146), but it also goes well with roasted pork, steak, or on sandwiches.

4 medium onions, cut in small dice

2 tablespoons butter

Kosher salt and freshly ground pepper to
    taste

3 tablespoons sugar

$^1/_3$ cup cane or cider vinegar

PLACE a medium-size heavy pot over high heat for $2^1/_2$ to 3 minutes, add the onions, stir in the butter, and season with salt and pepper. Stir until the butter is melted. Let cook for about 5 minutes, without stirring, letting the onions brown. Continue cooking for about 15 minutes, stirring occasionally to brown the onions evenly. Add the sugar and cook about 5 more minutes, or until the onions are dark brown, stirring occasionally. Add the vinegar, and cook for 1 minute or until the mixture comes to a full boil. Stir and adjust seasoning. Remove from the pot and let cool. This stores well in the refrigerator for up to two weeks.

CHEF JAMIE'S TIPS

I like to make this with Vidalia or Texas sweet onions when they are in season. The marmalade goes beautifully on any meat and on most fish, and it's great on sandwiches. Be sure the pot you use is heavy-gauge. Keep a close eye on the onions to make sure they don't burn. More frequent stirring will prevent burning.

*T*his is not your grandma's cornbread. What makes this one so much lighter than most is that we make it like a soufflé. We lightly fold in the ingredients instead of stirring them in. We whip the egg whites to a peak so that we fold in lots of air. Then we fold in the sour cream, too. We bake it in a cast-iron skillet and when it comes out steaming and golden brown on top, well, suffice it to say that there are too many of us doing "quality checks."

2¼ cups yellow cornmeal

1½ cups all-purpose flour

1¼ teaspoons kosher salt

1 tablespoon baking powder

⅔ cup sugar

3 medium eggs, separated

2½ cups buttermilk

¾ cup sour cream

4 jalapeño peppers, cores, membranes, and seeds removed, in small dice

1 red bell pepper, diced

8 tablespoons (1 stick) unsalted butter, in small dice

PREHEAT a seasoned, 10-inch cast-iron skillet in a 400°F oven.

SIFT the cornmeal, flour, salt, baking powder, and sugar in a large bowl. In another bowl, mix together yolks, buttermilk, and sour cream. Form a well in the middle of the dry ingredients and add the egg mixture and the diced peppers; stir without overmixing. Whip the egg whites to a stiff peak, then fold them and the butter pieces into the mixture.

POUR the mixture into the skillet, and place the skillet in the preheated oven. Bake for 40 minutes, or until golden brown and a toothpick inserted in the center comes out clean.

Crispy Bread

MAKES THREE 8-OUNCE
ROUND LOAVES

*M*ost people are so afraid to make bread that they miss out on the pleasure of freshly baked bread at home. Chef Jamie was determined to remedy this, so he came up with this unintimidating recipe for versatile bread. Use it as a focaccia, a pizza dough, a baguette, or even breadsticks. This is not as light as New Orleans French bread, but it is crispy and, most of all, easy to make. All you need is a few common ingredients and the desire for the smell of freshly baked bread wafting through your house.

1 package active dry yeast	1 tablespoon salt
1⅓ cups warm water (about 110°F)	1 tablespoon olive oil
3½ cups bread flour, or as needed	2 tablespoons cornmeal

IN A small bowl, combine the yeast and warm water, and set aside for about 5 minutes or until creamy.

SIFT the flour and salt in a large bowl, form a well in the center, and gently drizzle the yeast water into the well while mixing with your hands or a wooden spoon until all the water is absorbed. Work the dough into a ball, turn out onto a lightly floured surface, and knead for 8 to 10 minutes, or until the dough is smooth and elastic. If the dough is too sticky, add a small amount of flour during the kneading process.

SHAPE the dough into a ball. Wipe away any excess flour that has stuck to the sides of the bowl, leaving a clean, dry surface. Lightly coat the surface of the dough with half the oil. Return the dough to the bowl, and rub it with the remaining oil. Flip the dough to make sure it will not stick.

COVER the bowl with a damp towel that is not touching the dough. Place in a draft-free area at about 75°F and let it rest for 2 to 3 hours, or until the dough has more than doubled in size.

PUNCH down the dough gently with your fist, turn it out onto a clean work surface lightly dusted with flour, and cut it into three equal portions. Shape each portion into a smooth ball, and arrange the balls several inches apart on a large paddle sprinkled with cornmeal or on a cutting board. Cover the loaves with a floured towel, and place in a cool area until doubled in size.

ABOUT ½ hour before baking, place a baking stone or flat, heavy pan on the bottom of the oven or on the bottom rack (depending on where the oven's heating element is located), and preheat the oven to 450°F.

SCORE each loaf with a sharp knife. Gently slide the loaves onto the heated baking stone or pan. Place an ovenproof vessel with about half a cup of water near the bread (that puts steam in the oven and gives the bread a crisper crust), and close the oven door. Sprinkle the dough twice with water during baking.

BAKE about 25 to 30 minutes, or until the crust is browned and the bread is done, or until it reaches an internal temperature of 205°F on an instant-read thermometer. Remove and let cool on racks.

Be sure to use the freshest yeast you can find by checking the expiration date. Experiment with the flour if you wish, replacing some of the bread flour with rye or whole wheat, for example. And the bread can take any shape—flat bread, loaves, rolls, twisted, or sticks. When you place the bread in the oven, be careful not to disturb the dough when you slide it onto the cooking surface. I like to mist the bread with a sprayer.

CHEF JAMIE'S TIPS

Rosemary Garlic Focaccia

MAKES 10 TO 12 SERVINGS, OR ABOUT
50 HORS D'OEUVRES

ocaccia, our most versatile bread, is served with hors d'oeuvres, osso buco, salads, and as a snack food. We do a seafood version and another version with lamb sausage and feta cheese. It's easy to make and it reheats well. Try your own version. The possibilities are endless.

1 medium russet potato

1 cup warm water (110°F to 115°F)

1 package (¼ ounce) rapid-rise yeast

2 tablespoons honey

3½ cups all-purpose flour

3 tablespoons olive oil

1 tablespoon kosher salt, or to taste

1½ teaspoons freshly cracked black
    pepper, or to taste

2 tablespoons chopped fresh rosemary

1 medium head garlic, cloves peeled and
    minced

COOK the potato, covered with cold water, in a small pot for about 30 minutes, or until it's tender when poked with a fork or knife. Strain, and refrigerate the potato.

PLACE the warm water, yeast, and honey in a large bowl, stir, and let sit in a warm spot for about 5 minutes.

WHEN the potato is cool enough to handle, peel and grate it on the large holes of a box grater. You'll have about 2 cups of grated potato. Place 1 cup of the flour, 1½ teaspoons of the olive oil, and half the salt in a large mixing bowl, and combine with a wooden spoon until the mixture becomes well incorporated. Add the grated potato, and mix until well incorporated. Add 2 more cups of flour and mix for about 3 minutes, or until the dough comes together. Transfer the dough to a well-floured work surface and knead it for about 10 minutes, working in the remaining half-cup of flour. If the dough seems a little sticky, work in a little more flour.

SWIRL 1½ teaspoons of the olive oil in a large bowl, add the dough, and turn it so that it is coated with oil. Cover the bowl with plastic wrap, and let rise in a draft-free, warm area (75°F to 80°F) for about 1 hour or more, until doubled in size.

USE another 1½ teaspoons of olive oil to coat a 10½ × 15½-inch sheet pan. Place the dough on the pan and flatten it evenly with your hands so that it fills the pan. Place a clean, damp towel on top of the dough and let it rest for 10 minutes.

PRESS down gently on the towel and even out the dough, pushing it into the corners of the pan. Gently remove the towel, and cover the dough with oiled plastic wrap. Let rise a second time, again in a warm, draft-free area, until it doubles in size, about 1 hour.

PREHEAT the oven to 425°F.

REMOVE the plastic and drizzle the dough with the remaining 1½ tablespoons of olive oil, using your fingers or a pastry brush to create a light, even coat. Sprinkle with the remaining salt and the cracked pepper. Sprinkle the rosemary and garlic evenly over the bread. Bake in the preheated oven for 20 to 25 minutes or until brown and crisp. Transfer to a rack and serve warm.

 CHEF JAMIE'S TIPS

You can use regular active dry yeast, but increase both risings to about 1½ hours. You can bake on a stone, but the crust will be thicker and chewier.

Don't overcook or peel the potato before boiling or you'll add unwanted moisture.

Commander's has several ways of serving and cutting focaccia. It might be served with salads or stews or cut in rectangles or triangles.

Commander's Garlic Bread

MAKES 2 DOZEN 1-INCH PIECES

*Y*ears ago, a sudden rash of complaints from Commander's customers went like this: "Put the garlic bread back on the menu. I'm not coming back until you do." Needless to say, the garlic bread came back fast. It's another example of a food that's simple, inexpensive, and just plain good.

1 loaf (15 inches long) French bread
6 tablespoons butter, melted
2 heads garlic, cloves peeled and minced
½ cup grated Pecorino Romano cheese

½ cup chopped fresh dill (dried dill can be substituted, but cut amount to 2 to 3 tablespoons)

PREHEAT the oven to 325°F.

CUT off the ends of the bread and slice the loaf in half horizontally. Brush the interior generously with the melted butter. Spread the minced garlic, then the grated cheese, and then the dill evenly over the butter. Cut the bread into 1-inch slices before baking, which will make the sides of the bread brown and crispy. Place on a baking sheet, separating pieces slightly. Bake for 10 minutes, until crisp and browned (or broil for 2 to 3 minutes).

*M*ost of what you need to know about ingredients can be found in each recipe in this book. There are, however, a few things that occur so frequently that they ought to be stressed here.

ANDOUILLE (ahn-DWEE). A spicy sausage, often used in gumbo and jambalaya.

BOUDIN (boo-DAHN). A peppery link of pork sausage, onions, and rice in a casing; pig's blood is used in boudin rouge.

BUTTER. We use only unsalted butter and suggest that you do the same. Salting varies so much from brand to brand that you're better off using unsalted butter and controlling saltiness elsewhere in your recipes.

COURTBOUILLON (KOOR-boo-yahn). Whole poached fish (often redfish) cooked with tomatoes, bell peppers, and onions; in Cajun country, it is more of a stew in a reduced broth.

CREOLE MUSTARD. A coarse ground mustard, close in style to German mustard.

EGGS. We use medium eggs, which are the right size for our recipes.

ÉTOUFFÉE (ay-too-FAY). Means "smothered," or cooked in a covered pot over a long, slow period. Method most often used for cooking crawfish.

FILÉ (fee-LAY). Stew or gumbo thickener made of dried sassafras leaves, first used by Native Americans.

GARLIC. A member of the onion family and one of our favorite flavorings for many recipes. Garlic changes substantially as it cooks. Raw garlic can be harsh and bitter. But the longer you cook it, the mellower it becomes. Roasted garlic is often used as a spread in place of butter. With even more cooking, garlic caramelizes and acquires a toasted, almost sweet flavor.

GREEN ONIONS. Another member of the onion family, widely known as scallions elsewhere, although we, like most New Orleanians, refer to them only as green onions. They are frequently used to finish a dish. When we slice them, we generally use only the green portion, saving the white parts for stocks.

HERBS. New Orleans has a very long growing season and that allows us to use a lot of fresh herbs, which we prefer to dried.

HOT SAUCE. Markets sell literally hundreds of hot sauces made from the hot peppers grown in Louisiana. Brands vary in hotness, so try several before deciding on your house favorite. We prefer Crystal Hot Sauce.

MAQUE CHOUX (mock-SHOO). A dish made predominantly of corn cooked down with tomatoes, okra, onions, and bell peppers, often served with rice. Originated by Native Americans.

ROUX (ROO). Flour and fat mixed slowly over low heat, used as a thickener and flavor element in soups, stews, and gumbos; ranges in color from dark to blond, depending on the thickening required.

SALT. In most cases, we prefer kosher salt because it's coarser and has a cleaner taste, compared to common table salt. Except for the seasoning mixes, we use kosher salt almost exclusively.

TASSO (TASS-o). A seasoning meat, usually pork shoulder, dry-cured for days, almost to the point of resembling jerky. Outside of New Orleans, you may have trouble finding it, so mail-order is probably easiest. If you wish to make a substitute, cut a small amount of ham (1 ounce is probably sufficient for most recipes) in 1-inch strips and toss with a mixture of 1 part cayenne pepper and 3 parts paprika.

MAIL-ORDER INFORMATION

*A*lthough most of the ingredients used in *Commander's Kitchen* recipes are readily available in supermarkets around the country, a few are indigenous to New Orleans. Where substitutes will come close, instructions to that effect appear in each recipe. But for the most authentic results, the genuine article will always be best, and a number of mail-order sources are prepared to meet your needs.

Head-on shrimp and turtle meat, for example, cannot be found in most markets, but several mail-order sources can take care of that, along with virtually all seafood products you might want.

Some products can be ordered through distributors rather than the products' manufacturers. For example, Richard's Cajun Style Roux can be ordered through a distributor at the Web address: www.atlprem.com/richards_cajun_foods_corporation.htm or the toll-free phone number 800-826-8346. And Savoie's Old Fashioned Roux can be ordered from the Web address: www.realcajun.com/sav0090.htm, where other products can also be found. Or, it can be ordered by calling 318-942-7241.

Here is information on other products' sources:

Baumer Foods, Inc.
4301 Tulane Ave.
New Orleans, LA 70119
504-482-5761 or 800-618-8667
Sells Crystal Hot Sauce,
Worcestershire, mustards, jams

Big Fisherman Seafood
3301 Magazine Street
New Orleans, LA 70115
504-897-9907 or 888-567-9907
Web address:
www.bigfishermanseafood.com
Good source for Louisiana seafood

Bruce Foods Corporation
P.O. Drawer 1030
New Iberia, LA 70562
800-299-9082 or 337-365-8101
Good source of hot sauces

Chef John Folse & Co.
2517 South Philippe Ave.
Gonzales, LA 70737
800-256-2433
Web address: www.jfolse.com
A full assortment of entrées, soups,
sauces, etc.

Konriko Company Store
P.O. Box 10640
New Iberia, LA 70562-0640
800-551-3245
Web address: www.conradricemill.com
Sells assorted rices and filé

Little Fisherman Seafood
70420 W. Judge Perez Dr.
Arabi, LA 70032
888-271-9907

Louisiana Seafood Exchange, Inc.
428 Jefferson Highway
Jefferson, LA 70121
800-969-9394
Good source for Louisiana seafood

Magic Seasoning Blends Mail Order
824 Distributors Row
New Orleans, LA 70123
800-457-2858
Web address: www.chefpaul.com
Sells herbs and spices as well as
andouille sausages, tasso, and pure
dried and ground individual chiles

New Orleans Fish House
921 S. Dupre St.
New Orleans, LA 70125
800-839-3474
Web address: www.nofh.com
A full assortment of seafood, andouille,
and tasso

New Orleans School of Cooking and
Louisiana General Store
524 St. Louis Street
New Orleans, LA 70130
Web address:
www.neworleanscooking.com
800-237-4841
Good source for many indigenous
products, such as Zatarain's products,
Creole mustard, crab and shrimp boils,
cane syrup, coffees, rices, spice blends,
pickled peppers

Richard's Cajun Foods Corporation
P.O. Drawer 414
Churchpoint, LA 70525
800-826-8346
Sells andouille sausage and tasso

Riviana Foods
P.O. Box 2636
Houston, TX 77252
800-226-9522
Sells assorted rices

Savoie's Sausage & Food Products
1742 Highway 742
Opelousas, LA 70570
318-942-7241
Web address: http://www.realcajun.com
Sells andouille sausage and tasso

The C.S. Steen Syrup Mill, Inc.
P.O. Box 339
Abbeville, LA 70511
800-725-1654 or 337-893-1654
Web address: www.steensyrup.com
Manufacturer of cane syrup

Tabasco Country Store Catalogue
McIlhenny Company
Avery Island, LA 70513-5002
800-634-9599
Web address: www.tabasco.com
All Tabasco products

INDEX